# Mod Pop

## Ballad of a Young Offender

## Garry Johnson

NEW HAVEN PUBLISHING LTD

Published 2024
First Edition
New Haven Publishing Ltd
www.newhavenpublishingltd.com
newhavenpublishing@gmail.com

All Rights Reserved
The rights of Garry Johnson, as the author of this work, have been asserted in accordance with the Copyrights, Designs and Patents Act 1988.
No part of this book may be re-printed or reproduced or utilized in any form or by any electronic, mechanical or other means, now unknown or hereafter invented, including photocopying, and recording, or in any information storage or retrieval system, without the written permission of the
Authors and Publisher.

Cover design© Pete Cunliffe

Copyright © 2024 Garry Johnson
All rights reserved
ISBN: 978-1-915975-07-2

# Content

Introduction     5

Chapter One – Born In A House In Hackney     9
Chapter Two – I Could Have Been A Contender     29
Chapter Three – East End Boy     40
Chapter Four – Mad For It     61
Chapter Five – Every Day Was Like A Film     82
Chapter Six – This Is A Modern World     99
Chapter Seven – This Is No Soap Opera     110
Chapter Eight – Boy About Town     128
Chapter Nine – Growing Up And I`m Fine     154
Chapter Ten – Standing In The Dock     171
Chapter Eleven – They Broke the Mould     188
Chapter Twelve – Poetic Justice     204
Chapter Thirteen – Buzz Kid Adult Mod     212
Chapter Fourteen – Happy Ending     225

# Introduction

"Garry discovered The Stone Roses and took it upon himself to be our manager. He was fascinated by the band's cross-section of influences.

Like him we loved David Bowie, The Clash, The Sex Pistols, 'All The Young Dudes' by Mott The Hoople and Mod Fashion. I think that was the clincher.

The guy never stopped talking and was like Arthur Daley on speed. After just 2 London gigs he got us a full-page spread in Sounds music magazine.

We were staggered. From then on we thought top bloke, let's dig deep into this guy and see what he has got for us. We stayed at his flat, me and Andy, a trio of head cases on little-blue pills. He was a like-minded soul, a speed freak who always wanted to be in a band.

That was his whole thing, he'd put on The Small Faces 'Lazy Sunday', The Pistols 'Anarchy In The UK' and sing along to it. We were unknown and on the dole but he predicted we'd be the biggest band in the world. He was five years ahead of everyone else in the music business". - **Stone Roses singer Ian Brown**

"Garry Johnson's poems were truly the beat of the street and at a time when words really mattered. His snapshots of inner-city Britain now stand with the lyrics of Paul Weller as an essential record of the early 1980's.

The performance poet Garry Johnson embodied the punk spirit. Instinctively suspicious of authority in any form, he was nevertheless committed to the DIY ethos. His poems provided first-hand accounts from London's dead-end streets.

Best of all were the character portraits, 'The Buzz Kids' and 'Ballad Of The Young Offenders' getting caught up in a corrupt system. 'The Young Conservatives', all Daily Mail and bottle-fed, the 'Boy About Town', head turned by fascist lies, venting his personal insecurities through pointless racism, the 'Suburban Rebels' playing at leftie politics when in University before following their parents into the elitist establishment. The urban backstreets became sites of rage, frustration, but also cultural aspiration, where 'deadend yobs' looked to football, boxing or rock and roll as a way out from the dole.

Garry told the truth about power and false patriotism of self-serving elites in a Tory Party of unemployment and poverty, a 'them and us society'. He was an integral part of the Punk Scene that evolved into the 1980's, a distilled version of punk's early claims to be street level rock and roll. Against the class prejudice of a mainstream media that too easily conflated working-class youth culture with violence. Garry always presented Punk as an expression of urban protest.

"The white working-class got more in common with the black West Indian working-class than they have with the rich white champagne socialist middle-class". He personified one of Joe Strummer's better insights, 'the truth is only known by guttersnipes'. **- Professor Matthew Worley**


"Garry was the first Street-Punk Poet and more.

Part Johnny Rotten, part George Orwell. Gal's words painted vivid pictures of rebel youth growing up in a world betrayed by scumbag politicians and media whores.

His poems and song lyrics were a window to a teenage underworld of unemployment, violence and fast drugs populated by teenage tearaways in stolen wheels. But he balanced that nihilism with a passion for life and a raging social conscience.

Garry hated bigotry as much as he despised what passed for authority. His book of poems 'Boys Of The Empire' was a classic piece of writing.

Critically acclaimed by teenage punks, middle-class journalists and leading academics. He was a Cockney Dylan and lifelong rebel who always sided with the underdog.

The Robert Zimmerman of the Punk Generation. Garry Johnson was the original Cockney Rebel, the real voice of the streets. He's also the funniest bloke I've ever met.

Accept no substitute". **Author and Journalist Garry Bushell**


"Garry Johnson is one of Punk Rock's most enduring characters. He first appeared as a poet in the 1980s and has since been a singer, a rock and roll manager, a showbiz tabloid journalist and professional scammer. More recently he has found a new level of fame and admiration as songwriter for Swedish rocker Soren Sulo Karlsson and for surviving five heart attacks and two life-saving triple heart bypass operations.

His has been a life on the edge. A real-life X-rated soap opera lived in the glare of publicity. This book Mod Pop traces his journey from the back streets of East London, to West End night clubs and The Houses Of Parliament. This is the fascinating and true story of a genuine Cockney Rebel who infiltrated Fleet Street and the world of Showbiz. A man described by music writer Dominic Warwick as "Charles Dickens for the Punk Generation", Gal's words painted vivid pictures of rebel youth growing up in a world populated by low-life politicians.

He was more than a punk poet and proud of becoming Tabloid Terrorist Number One. Garry is a one-off who lived his dream without having nightmares or getting caught."

**-Journalist Jerry Harris**

# Chapter 1
# Born in a House in Hackney

In 1996 Senegalese conman Ali Dia posed as a footballer and tricked his way into the Premier League. He lasted twenty minutes in his first and last game for Southampton against Leeds United.

American politician George Santos miss-led voters about his background in 2022 and became a Republican Congressman.

In the 1970s Frank Abagnale conned his way across America pretending to be an airline pilot, Assistant Attorney and a doctor. He was wanted by the FBI and sent to prison. In 2002 Steven Spielberg made a movie of his life.

In a way, my story has a Frank Abagnale feel about it and Hollywood turned his autobiography into the movie `Catch Me If You Can` starring Leonardo di Caprio. So what odds on Mod Pop becoming a film starring Tom Hardy or Danny Dyer?

I know Fleet Street is going to crucify me for turning them over. But so what? There is no such thing as bad publicity. "You live by the sword and you die by the sword". At the end of the day and, unlike the Leverson Inquiry, I believe in a free press. The tabloids can write what they like about me as long as they spell my name correctly and don't make anything up! For those who know me that`s a joke.

We all know journalists never make stories up.

First, a confession, I am not a celebrity. I have never been an A-List celebrity but did enough to qualify as a Z-list celeb. Celebrity, as a concept, is nothing new. In biblical times Jesus Christ was a celebrity. He was the Sir Cliff Richard of his generation with Judas Iscariot in the Prince Harry role.

I tried to become a celebrity in the wrong era. There was no reality TV with shows like Big Brother or Love Island for talentless teenagers hungry for fame. I wasn't bad enough to become a celebrity gangster like Dave Courtney or a godlike genius to follow in the footsteps of David Bowie. There was no Tik Tok, Twitter, YouTube or Facebook for working-class youngsters to fake a talent or build a brand.

It`s 2024 I`m back in the public eye and starring, oh alright appearing in this year`s big ITV documentary Gary Glitter: The Popstar Paedophile. The programme explores the double life of the iconic performer and predatory abuser. Proud to say I 'slaughtered' the self-confessed and convicted child abuser. I was only paid a few hundred quid but the buzz of being back in a TV studio was worth a million pounds. I enjoyed being picked up in a car, taken for lunch, hanging out with talented young people then driven home in style. It was just like the good old days and for 8 hours felt like the 1990s

Hard to believe, I know, but it's not all about hanging out in Stringfellows and backstage VIP passes. For every reception at The Playboy Club, there's a night watching unknown bands in backstreet pubs. Not all the girls you meet are going to be page-three girls and some of the celebrities have bigger ego's than the moon. But posing as a showbiz journo is better than working for a living.

I left school without qualifications, not even a swimming certificate, but my imagination was endless. With no journalistic training I wrote showbiz columns for two national newspapers, front-page stories and world exclusives for all the British tabloids.

I mixed in showbiz circles and met celebrities including David Bowie, Sade, Michael Jackson, George Michael, George Best, Ozzy Osbourne and gangster Charlie Kray. I even had a pint with Sir Bob Gelfof and look forward to telling my story on TV chat shows and sharing the This Morning sofa with Amanda Holden.

My story might read like a novel, but believe me it's a one hundred per cent factual account of my life and not a figment of my fertile imagination. I'll willingly be connected to a Lie Detector machine and observed by a panel of body language experts while interrogated by Piers Morgan.

Read on and you'll discover why that's a brave choice of interviewer.

This is the true story about me, Garry Johnson, the Punk poet, the only man in England to take on and defeat the combined forces of Social Services and The Family Courts. The system was against me. I was arrested for a crime I didn't commit which isn't unusual in the UK, but this was sinister as there was no crime. It never happened. There was no guilty party on planet earth and the combined forces of the FBI, Scotland Yard and Interpol couldn't find a victim because there was no corpse.

The accusations came from the plot of a crime novel full of fictional characters living in a fictional town. The murder took place between the covers of a book and not on a street in Essex. I became a target on an establishment 'hit list' described as mad, bad and dangerous. I was Public Enemy Number One. They tried to silence me. They tried to intimidate me. They tried to destroy me. They tried to kill me.

I was arrested 5 times, twice sent to prison and spent 29 days in a coma on a life support machine. To quote the Chumbawumba song "I get knocked down but I get back up again, you ain't ever gonna keep me down".

Being able to cope with life's setbacks is key to living a long life, there is always light at the end of the tunnel. I am living proof of those beliefs.

Always fight back never curl up in the corner like a wilted lettuce.

I went to The High Court where Lord Justice Munby ruled in my favour. When the barrister for Essex Social Services stood up to object he was told:

"Whatever you say I will not change my mind"

Adding:

"There are no longer any restrictions on Mr Johnson"

It had taken me longer than it took Sir Winston Churchill to defeat Adolf Hitler and like our great wartime leader I shed blood, sweat and tears. To continue with the war theme "the enemy threw down their weapons".

Judge Moloney at Southend Family Court ordered Essex Social Services to hand over all their documents. Judge Roderick Newton at Chelmsford Crown Court ruled I could legally tell my story. In 2022 at Southend Magistrates Court another Judge whose name I can't recall lifted the final restriction on my Freedom of Speech, the final piece in the jigsaw. I finally had the redemption I'd been seeking since 2005. I went to court and represented myself as I had right on my side, and this time the Police were in my corner. They'd advised me to seek justice.

This is my story. "The truth the whole truth and nothing but the truth so help me God.

I'm not giving away any secrets by revealing I ended up on the winning side because there's enough twists and turns along the way to keep you hooked.

I lost many battles but won the war because as I said from day one "I was telling the truth". My barrister told the court in 2009 "Mr Johnson will not go away" adding "He is like a dog with a bone".

For good or bad that has always been my character. If I wanted something however much the odds were against me I'd always play to win. More importantly I always believed I could win. That of course was a combination of 'bollocks', 'bravado' and 'wishful thinking' but preferable to throwing in the towel. As I tell my kids we are nothing without hope, you've got to be in it to win it and never too old to stop dreaming. Three personal beliefs that trump anything my dad told me. He fed me a diet of rubbish from an early age with the main ingredient being "do as I say and not as I do".

He was one flash bastard with a selfish streak all down his back. I lived in his shadow but never walked in his shoes. I was/am a one off and never a chip off the old block. He broke my heart but never saw me cry.

I wasn't born with matinee idol looks but always wanted and often got the prettiest girl in the room. I didn't inherit my mum's cheekbones but my DNA contained my dad's gift of the gab. I inherited his funny bones so could always laugh women into bed. I was a former footballer, an ex-punk and life-long Mod who wrote lyrics like Paul Weller but couldn't sing or play guitar.

I was a sofa surfer in my 20's getting older by the day but still having teenage daydreams. At one point could easily have drifted into the shallow world of non-stop parties or even worse, gotten a proper job. Then I met The Stone Roses. I received a demo tape in the post and instantly hooked. Once again, the Gods were looking down on The Punk Poet. I'm not religious but always believed something or someone was looking out for me.

I started off as someone 'ordinary', someone any of us could know, someone who could live next door to you, but ended up living a charmed life. In my late teens and early twenties, I was a working-class boy living in an uptown world. I was like a kid in a candy shop. I was the ultimate consumer and gobbled up the good life. I appeared in a Canadian TV documentary and lived my fantasy life in a reality drama without a director pulling the strings.

I was born in 1957 (but could pass for Fifty) around the same time Elvis invented rock and roll and Sir Cliff Richard was a virgin (some say he still is).

The old Victorian house in Hackney where I grew up had no central heating and an outside loo and never forgot my working-class roots. I got my Cockney humour from my dad, Charles Alfred, a semi-pro footballer and professional bird bandit. He was a typical East End bloke who loved gambling, women and football. His dad was a bookies runner for an illegal Betting shop. Mum Mary from Dublin who had a strict Irish nationalist Father and eight siblings.

All three men were massive influences on my early life. My pre-teen heroes along with football star George Best. Apart from me the only thing they had in common was a mutual love of fashion. I got my love of brogue shoes and Abercrombie overcoats from my Irish granddad. The three of them were always suited and booted every day of the week. Each had a selfish character weakness which harmed those who got close to them.

My dad was a Ladies man. His father a compulsive gambler and my Irish granddad had a love affair with alcohol. When it came to vices, I only followed in one of their footsteps. Can you guess which one? The East End of London I was born in was nothing like the BBC soap opera and grew up singing along to my dad's Elvis and Al Jolson records.

I listened to my Cockney granddad animated and excited talking about the Second World War and famous Battle of Cable Street. Looking back he was a clean shaven Uncle Albert from Only Fools and Horses and I was born to be a `Del Boy`.

He was proud of the time Cockneys defeated Adolf Hitler and stood shoulder to shoulder with their Jewish neighbours to defeat Sir Oswald Mosley and his army of black shirts.

Between leaving school and joining the workforce I was, and at the same time wasn't just like any other teenager. For a start I had no intention of getting a job, I knew from an early age I wasn't cut out for a 9 to 5 lifestyle. I wanted a taste of the good life but had no idea how to get it. Determined to have the best time I could without having any talent. I was the man who could play guitar but only if it wasn't plugged in. When it came to work, I was a consciences objector but not a lazy sod, there were never enough hours in a day. No fan of spending all day in bed or lounging about on a deckchair.

After school I went from one drama to another living in institutions and surviving on the street. I slept on railway stations, friend's sofas and spent more time on the floor than a carpet layer. I lived on a diet of marmite on toast and amphetamine. A teacher predicted I'd end up in prison and chalked a picture of me on the blackboard but I knew without sounding Mills and Boon my story would have a happy ending. At 15 I was into all the usual things football, girls and fashion. Then I saw Ziggy Stardust on Top of The Pops and had what can only be described as a religious experience. I saw a vision of beauty on TV.

There was an alien rock star in the corner of the room. He/she/it was singing a song that changed the world. That night God came into my life but wasn't wearing white flowing robes or sporting a Jeremy Corbyn beard. Bowie was wafer-thin, with red spiky hair and more beautiful than most women. Next day in school playgrounds all over the UK teenage boys wanted to be Ziggy Stardust and girls wanted to fuck him (so did some boys).

The 6$^{th}$ of July 1972 was the day a singer/songwriter from Brixton or an alien from another planet changed the world and direction of my life. I'd started the day as a 15-year-old football fanatic obsessed with George Best and went to bed dreaming of Ziggy Stardust.

It was the start of my musical education and life-long obsession with Ziggy Stardust and all things David Bowie. It would be a life-long love affair and although never consummated the closest thing to intimacy without taking your clothes off.

I had no idea that one day we'd end up in the same room together and that I'd shake his hand. After this encounter the music press reported I didn't wash my hand for a month. I was floating, my mind was in a whirl and my hand felt hot and tingly. Very much like my penis after losing my virginity aged 13 at the back of Stanford Youth Club. After meeting Bowie I'd tell girlfriends, "You're being undressed by hands that touched Ziggy Stardust". A cheesy line I used for years. As with all things in my life it was unplanned and fate. Had I known we were attending the same party there's no way I'd gone along without ace snapper Tony Mottram. The man who photographed my meeting with Sade and encounter with pop pervert Gary Glitter. That picture now features in the 2024 ITV documentary where I talk about meeting the paedophile at various showbiz parties. I don't hold back and slaughter the child abuser in one of my proudest showbiz moments.

I can't imagine my life without the massive contribution of David Bowie. Just thinking about it scares me. My world would have been so grey and boring without Ziggy Stardust. Instead of scamming Fleet Street I could have been working on a building site or banged up in prison. Seeing Bowie on Top of The Pops was love at first sight. Was it a boy was it a girl? No, it was Ziggy Stardust. First impressions are always the most important.

The day he died was the saddest of my life and proudest the publication my book David Bowie Sings Again. It was right up there with the birth of my children and grandkids.

I cherish magic moments like the first time I saw Lyn in the school playground. She was a vision of beauty and my big schoolboy crush. If this was 2024 instead of 1970, she'd be a Tik Tok sensation. She was my first love but even then I was pretty smart when it came to `dating/networking` and deliberately didn't want to be her boyfriend because I genuinely liked her and never wanted us to `fall out` and become enemies. You know what teenage romances are like.

I only went out with girls I didn't like so it didn't matter if/when we `fell out` after 3 days or three weeks. Lyn was special and although we never consummated our relationship, we came close, but it didn't matter. I remember us going to the pictures in Grays and Southend on a Bank Holiday Monday, but never all the way. Her older sister lived in a tower block and we babysat, people who know me know I don't do lifts. I closed my eyes and gritted my teeth as we travelled up to the seventh floor. There's no greater proof to show how much I liked her so let me explain why she could never be my girlfriend. We were too young, and I was smart enough to know I wasn't boyfriend material.

At the time I was obsessed with playing football, hanging out with my mates and 'playing the field'. She was far too nice to be my girlfriend. This was the 70s when playground gossip was rife, but never heard a bad word about Lyn or stories of her getting up to anything with anyone. Not only the prettiest girl in the entire school but the nicest and best-looking teenager in the neighbourhood.

We met again after an 18-month interval, she was Seventeen and even more beautiful. It wasn't planned. She was working for a bank in Liverpool Street, and I was appearing at Guildhall Courts on a trumped-up robbery charge. We bumped into each other during her lunch hour while I was waiting for a "not guilty" verdict.

There was still a 'spark' and agreed to meet at 5pm outside Fenchurch Street Station. What happened next was a real-life 'Sliding Doors' moment the 1998 film starring Gwyneth Paltrow. That movie always reminds me of 'the one that got away'. I got a custodial sentence, three months at Kidlington Detention Centre in Oxfordshire, now known as Campsfield House, where they bang up illegal immigrants.

We never met again and often wonder how different life would have been if I'd been given probation. My partner in crime got off and I joked the judge was racist because he looked like Bob Marley and I was white.

Though probably because of my outburst in court when I shouted at the prosecutor, "you wouldn't talk to Reggie Kray like that".

A stupid act of teenage bravado which made my mate laugh but the judge was not amused. As you can see back in the day I was a mouthy little sod. I enjoyed being mischievous but always preferred being a loveable rogue to a villain. My memory which is legendary reminds me that Lyn was a combination of Britt Ekland (Get Cater) and Susan George (Straw Dogs). In adulthood I've always imagined her as a thirty-year-old Debbie Harry who today resembles Amanda Holden.

The phrase 'drop-dead gorgeous' is the perfect description and rose-coloured spectacles are not playing tricks with my memory. She started my life-long addiction to blondes. Bottle or natural, it didn't bother me as long as women were blonde. As well as having natural beauty she had two older brothers, both local tough guys with one being a 'proper face', but 'honest Guv' that didn't influence me in wanting a strictly plutonic and innocent relationship'.

I genuinely liked her as a mate and my character doesn't do 'falling out' and then 'kissing and making up', it's not in my nature. A friend is for life as is an enemy. As a dedicated life-long atheist the only words I believe from the bible are "an eye for an eye" and "they shall not commit adultery". I'm not gay and to my knowledge never have been but loved Ziggy Stardust all my life. I wanted to be The Thin White Duke more than I wanted to be me, that's why I stopped being Garry Johnson and invented an alter-ego. Apart from the ability to play football I wasn't blessed with any other gifts and like the majority of contestants on Britain's Got Talent didn't have any. I had no 'star quality' but wanted to be an entertainer.

I fell in love with all things David Bowie. The music, the look, attitude and sex, drugs and rock 'n' roll lifestyle. It would be a life-long love affair and although never consummated the closest thing you could have to a sexual encounter without taking your clothes off. When David Bowie died on January 10$^{th}$ 2016 I was still obsessed with and addicted to Ziggy Stardust the man who changed my world. I spent 24 hours in shock glued to the internet and swapping TV channels praying it wasn't true.

Apart from the births of my children and then grandchildren it's the only time I've cried as an adult. For many people, discovering and exploring his world was an integral part of growing up. I just took it further than most. There's a psychological name for this addiction. Erotomania. He shaped my life, morals and view of the world. If David Bowie believed in something and thought it was okay, then so did I. I no longer wanted my sporty physique and went on a crash diet. I became anorexic without even knowing what the word meant. The skinnier my waist, the more sunken my cheekbones the more girls I attracted. It was a 'win-win' situation. I was in awe of him and never stopped asking myself how so much genius could come from the mind of one man.

It was the same with George Best who at the time had the most talented feet in the history of football. I was a fanatical West Ham fan but admired him so much I even cheered when he scored against us. It's because of my Granddad and George Best I've always supported the Ireland football team and Irish boxers.

Years later I got to play football with George and shake hands with David Bowie. Who in 1972 could have predicted these encounters? I'm sure both Paddy Power and Ladbrokes would have given better odds on a blind three-legged horse winning the Grand National. Up until the age of 14, my life was going pretty good. I was the local football star (a 'fox in the box' goal machine), had plenty of mates and the 'naughty' girls liked me. I called myself 'the white Pele' or 'Cockney Georgie Best'.

Then BANG my dad fucked off with his latest bit of skirt without even saying "goodbye". My once happy life spiralled out of control and years later in adult life a doctor claimed that part of my brain froze in shock. Maybe that explains why today I've got the face and body of a forty-five-old and half my brain reacts like a teenager. I always see things in black and white and have massive problems when situations are grey.

Even as a 10-year-old I had 'brain problems' and thought 'outside the box' I went to a new school weeks before the 1967 FA Cup Final between Spurs and Chelsea. Anyone who knows me knows all about my life-long hatred of the club from White Hart Lane. Not because I'm a West Ham fan, but because of what that North London club did to my dad. Call the shrink as once again most things lead back to my dad. On the first day at my new school, I noticed the playground was split 50-50 between Spurs and Chelsea fans and the school tough guy was a Chelsea fanatic. So what did I do? Most 'new kids' to ingratiate themselves with the 'king of the kids' in the playground would pretend to support Chelsea. Not me. I claimed I supported Spurs and even wore a Spurs rosette, pretty much sacrilege for a West Ham fan, but it won me his respect and we became best of mates. So much so three years later he lost his virginity to a girl in my spare bedroom. The same year he fought at a National Boxing Tournament and won the title of English Schoolboy champion.

After my dad left I changed overnight from a cheeky chap into a 'full-blown' teenage tearaway which wasn't a career choice. I'd always enjoyed being a loveable rogue but didn't enjoy being a 'bad boy'. My heart wasn't in it but to survive on the street you have to put on a front. You have to shout, threaten and swear when all you really want to do is have a laugh. I've never been a low-life thief or stolen something not owned by a multi-national company. I was never a villain I was a rogue. I had to play the tough guy when all I wanted to be was the joker. But as I always say "every cloud" because most girls like a 'bad boy', and when you're a randy little teenager it's the 'naughty girls' you want to attract and it's a fact of life that most are attracted to 'bad boys'. My 'brain freeze' at fifteen was caused by so many life-changing shocks in quick succession. I never recovered from 'losing' my dad, my home, my schooldays and football career.

What can I say about school? I hated the academic side. A fact I'm not proud of, but it's too late to change now. I loved the comradeship of school, the gossip, chatting-up girls, bunking off school (with the girls you've chatted up), the playground politics, the school disco and of course the football team. I was into everything at school except the culture of abusing targeted girls, even as a teenager I didn't believe in sexual violence against females of the species.

I never recovered from not participating in a school tradition that took place at the end of every year. On the last day of term the best players from the 4th and 5th year played football against teachers in front of the entire school (even after all these years I still get choked-up remembering). I was forced to leave school a few weeks before the match kicked-off, if only my dad had met his fancy woman a few months earlier in the year.

Before David Bowie football was my life, more important than anything else, including hanging out with Lyn. I loved playing for the school football team and representing them at Rugby, Athletics (twice winning the Victor Ludorum) and Cross-Country Running. I was selected for the District and one year the 5$^{th}$ best Long Distance Runner in Essex, but none of that gets you into Oxbridge or pays the bills. I'm ashamed to say I was expelled from three schools and left with no qualifications. I wasted the opportunity of a decent education and blame that partly on my dad. But when it comes to football I blame him entirely for ending my career as without being big-headed I could have been a contender. I was a born goal-scorer, a fox in the box and they are always in demand.

I represented the District at Football, Athletics and Cross Country running, had trials with West Ham, QPR, Leyton Orient, Southend United and destined for a life in sport. The odds are I would have made it or at least been a semi-professional footballer like my dad. That's no big-headed boast or looking back at my ability through rose-tinted spectacles. Two of the boys from my District Team went on to be top professional footballers. Geoff Pike played 150-plus games for West Ham and won a FA Cup Winners Medal. Martin Robinson made 300 appearances for Charlton Athletic. The truth is Pike was slightly better than me but I was a much better player than Robinson. It was a well above average District Team selected from the Twenty-odd schools in the area. Two other team mates also had pretty good semi-pro football careers. Glen Case played about 250 games for East Thurrock United and Nicky Smith signed for Tilbury. As a teenager Smithy was all over the newspapers and appeared on Match of The Day when Tilbury played Southend United in the 2$^{nd}$ Round of the FA Cup. In my opinion it's safe to say had my dad not walked out I would have been a footballer and music lovers would not have heard me singing 'If Looks Could kill' with Frankie Flame. Some say (very few) that football's loss was a gain for the world of showbiz and tabloid journalism. And for-the-record and worth pointing out whenever I played against Pike or Robinson I was always on the winning side and scored in every game. One year we won the League and Cup double (and I've got the pictures to prove it), though to be fair that doesn't compare to winning the FA Cup at Wembley.

My greatest football memory was without doubt playing in a Cup Final at Grays Athletic Football Stadium. My one and only game under the magic of floodlights and for 90 minutes I was 'George Best'. I would spend my life savings for a DVD or video of that game. I'd watch it every day and so would my kids and grandchildren. (they would have no choice). We won 2-1 with me scoring in each half, including the last-minute winner. I was also voted Man of the Match and got a glowing write-up with my picture in the local paper. That was my personal World Cup Final and peak of my brief football career. Up there with my Sam scoring a brilliant 30-yard volley in a trial game for West Ham Under 14's and Adam scoring the winner for Essex in an inter-county Cup Final.

The truth is my boys achieved more than me at football with both signing schoolboy forms for Southend United. Back in the day before English football became a magnet for players from all over the world both would have played professional football. They also played in bigger matches and at better grounds with games at Chelsea, Southend United, Leyton Orient and Dagenham and Redbridge. Each had trials with West Ham, Arsenal and Chelsea. The icing on the cake was both playing in Cup Winning sides at Roots Hall.

My greatest performance was a semi-final away to Cup favourites Rainham. Their ground wasn't situated in leafy suburbia but on the Essex/East London borders. They had 100s of supporters from the local working men's club, grown men, bully boys shouting and screaming from the touchline at 14-year-old boys. Some of these plastic football thugs were also drinking pints of beer.

I was more fired up than ever before and scored 5 goals in a 6-1 thrashing of the shell-shocked opposition. It was one of those days, like I was wearing magic boots. For ninety minutes I dribbled like Georgie Best, tackled like Bobby Moore and scored like Jimmy Greaves. If I had that game on DVD I'd watch it every day.

I once scored fifteen goals in a one-sided game on a muddy pitch over Blackshots Park, we won 16-0 but that memory doesn't mean quite so much as in the second half the other team only had eight players. At 16 I hung up my boots and regretted it every day since. There was a method in my madness which I'll try to explain later. I wear my heart on my sleeve, for better or worse I am what I am.

I don't know if I've already said this but I don't do 'grey', I always see things in black and white. It was the biggest gamble of my life, and I got it wrong.

The Garry Johnson Story is a roller-coaster ride (Margate, not Vegas) through the coke-fuelled world of rock stars, soap actors, gangsters, Glam Models, family entertainers, blue comics, football hooligans, strippers, dippers and tabloid journalists. My showbiz career is unique and taken me from backstreet pubs in East London to West End clubs and the Houses of Parliament.

I was once told by someone, can't remember who 'If you do something you like you will never work a day in your life'. The best advice I was ever given and which I followed for fifty years. I turned my hobbies into a career. In life you've got to make the most of what you're given and I wasn't given a lot. But I used it wisely. Like the day I met superstar Michael Jackson.

This funny little tale will set the tone and give you an idea of my life as a tabloid terrorist and Showbiz Journo. Crowds gathered at 9am, and by the time the paparazzi arrived at mid-day had grown to 10,000. With the roads sealed off, Wacko Jacko did a private tour of Madame Tussauds followed by a photo-call in front of over 100 photographers from Fleet Street to the smallest local paper, swelled by hard-bitten hacks from the USA and British TV.

But yours truly was the only British reporter to get close. Thanks to my friend Pat Stead, who at the time was UK Head of Press for Wacko Jacko.

Pat was married to my friend and Jam guitarist Bruce Foxton. We both did fast drugs at each other's wedding receptions. I sneaked in an hour before kick-off. Jackson was dressed in rhinestone socks, with matching gloves, and a gold Sergeant Pepper style jacket. I managed a 25-minute private chat with the Peter Pan of Pop. Or did I? It was more like a 30-second conversation. As Michael admired his fibreglass dummy I asked: "What do you think of it Michael?"

Jacko: "It's so beautiful. I would love to take it home with me".

Me: "Are you looking forward to performing in the UK?" Jacko: "Yes.

Adding: "I love my fans". That was it, the interview was over but when I wrote my article I 'sexed it up' like Alistair Campbell's 'weapons of mass destruction' document. It was just a bit of fun which didn't kill millions of innocent people. Me: "What are your plans?"

He replied: "I want to meet the Queen". Adding: "I'd love to have afternoon tea in Buckingham Palace and want to appear on Top of The Pops".

My article claimed the Prince of Pop was visiting the set of Eastenders, had the Cockney delicacy Pie and Mash delivered to his hotel suite where he worked out wearing a West Ham football shirt. This was picked-up by the BBC and read out on Radio One. It gets more amusing as there's almost a 'diplomatic incident' between the UK and America as a result of our brief conversation. I tipped off The Sun that Jacko was planning to record a pop video with Diana, the Princess of Wales. Unlike my 'sexed-up' encounter with Michael Jackson this was 100% kosher but got me into trouble with The Royal Family. A source close to the superstar told me the bizarre pop idol had acquired telly footage of Princess Diana playing the piano during her recent trip to Australia.

And that he planned to superimpose his own image onto the film to make it look like they were performing a duet. I sold the story to The Sun and they printed it on the front page as a World Exclusive. Officials at Buckingham Palace were furious at what they saw as a cheap publicity stunt, especially as the future King and Princess Diana had agreed to attend one of his sell-out Wembley concerts. A Royal aide was quoted: "We hope Mr Jackson can be prevailed upon to drop this absurd idea. Americans often make the mistake of treating the Royal Family like showbiz personalities. They are not".

Maybe Prince ginger and Princess porky pies should be reminded of that fact. The self-centred couple have done more damage to the Royal Family than Michael Jackson and yours truly. Today, the Royal Family is more like a posh version of the East End soap. I replied at the time: "My source told me Jackson had a fixation about Diana and thinks of her as a perfect fairytale character". Luckily for me the fuss died down and I didn't end up in The Tower of London.

I was born lucky with good-looks, gift of the gab, a tiny amount of star quality but no talent or the ability to sing and dance. But by standing in the right place at the right time had a Number One hit record. How many talentless people apart from The Wombles can say that? The working-class boy from a house in Hackney with an outside loo had a million-selling single with Sir Paul McCartney. Even Noel and Liam can't claim that.

In 1987, the ZeeBrugge Ferry sank and 193 passengers drowned. The Sun's showbiz column had the inspired idea of forming an ad-hoc group called Ferry Aid and recording a charity single. A version of The Beatles classic 'Let It Be' for families affected by the disaster. Members of the star-studded band included former Beatle Sir Paul McCartney, Kate Bush, Boy George, Holly Johnson, Mark Knopfler and Rick Astley. I was present (hanging around) at the recording session and sneaked into the top secret filming of the video though sadly didn't make it on stage at TV's Top Of The Pops.

But as they say 'every cloud has a silver lining'. The truth is my involvement with the chart-topping record produced by Pete Waterman did win me my one and only Gold Disc.

I carried it around with me for weeks like a badge of honour and used it as a novel chat-up device. In those days I'd do or say anything to chat up a girl. Luckily most didn't pick-up on the fact I was a fake pop star who didn't sing on the record or appear in the video. I'd just blag it and say "I was standing at the back". Hard to believe now but back in the day I was quite popular with the opposite sex. I got by on good looks, gift of the gab and a sense of humour. The truth is I always had genuine affection for the female of the species, and having more front than Blackpool also helped.

Talking of that seaside town reminds me of my last great hurrah in the summer of 2016. Not talking about my Rebellion appearance but meeting a girl with long legs, short skirt and stud in her nose. Her name was Carly and five years away from her 30$^{th}$ Birthday. This brief encounter made a big impact and recently reunited on Facebook.

As a teenager I leaned so far to the left it's a wonder I never fell over but becoming middle-aged changed all that. I'm still anti-Royal Family and want to abolish The House of Lords but hate the modern-day Labour Party. It's the enemy of the working-class. I saw through the chimera of state power and lies of champagne socialist politicians. Middle-class suburban rebels who'd hate Jack Ford from TV drama 'When the Boat Comes In' and don't want people liberated from council estates. I am a mod but old-fashioned when it comes to politics. I believe in manners, politeness and respect. All good old-school working-class values.

My dad was light-fingered but never stole from his own. He told me 'if you're going to steal do it from supermarkets and not corner shops".

He believed in never doing anything 'bad' on your own doorstep, pity moral code didn't apply to adultery or betraying his own flesh and blood. I'm proud of working-class culture, but as it was and not how it is today, it's been stolen and manipulated by champagne socialists.

Nowadays posh Labour MPs are only in politics to get knighthoods, appear on TV shows and sign book deals. Everybody knows Sir champagne socialist Starmer and Angela Rayner will end up in The House of Lords. It's all about self-service and nothing to do with public service.

They don't care about kids on council estates condemned to 'slave' their lives away on the hamster wheel of human existence. That life wasn't for me. I just wanted to be rich and famous without working for a living. I was ahead of my time thinking like an influencer years before the invention of the internet. I've never had a proper job but that doesn't mean I was lazy. There were never enough hours in the day for me to make a few bob.

Most of my life I worked seven days a week as a self-employed entrepreneur on the fringes of showbiz. I did everything from making-up reviews to riffling through celebrity dustbins. I don't know why but always fancied doing a TV commercial. Good money and no talent required so I'd be ideal. I'd promote everything from Viagra to hair clippers. I'd happily shave off my beloved hair for a £50,000 pay packet. I'd do most things for money apart from a 9 to 5 job.

Even as a veteran veggie I`d have no qualms about promoting meat if the price was right. Unlike Morrissey I can`t afford to stick to my principles.

My dream commercial would be a shower scene with Love Island star Maura Higgins and I`d do that for free, any bathroom companies out there give me a call. Like most Z-List celebs I`d promote any old rubbish for money, as like Stormy Daniels I`m a bit of a whore. Most people born poor will do anything legal or illegal for money. This book sets out to prove I deserve a place (however small) in the story of popular culture. I was much more than a wind-up merchant and professional scammer. Lecturers could use my story in Media Studies. Not as daft as it sounds. My poetry book `The Cockney Bard` is available in both libraries at Oxford and Cambridge University.

I became a DIY journalist on a punk fanzine before blagging a job on Sounds magazine. Along with football music was my first love. As a kid I had a massive record collection because my mum managed a local pub and every Friday, she`d bring home records from the Juke Box.

Out of date hits but still top tunes. Songs like `Something In The Air` by Thunderclap Newman grabbed my attention but the 12-year-old skinhead became obsessed by a song called `Space Oddity` having no idea David Bowie would return as Ziggy Stardust. Music has always played an important part in my life. I still play the first record I bought from a stall in Hackney market The Small Faces `Lazy Sunday`. It cost five shillings (that`s 25p in today`s money folks).

I was 10 years old when I became a life-long Mod and started wearing Fred Perry T-shirts and Levi Jeans. When I was bought my first Crombie overcoat that was it, I was hooked. It`s a special look, that never dates. I dabbled with skinhead, glam rock, soul boy and punk but always reverted to being a Mod. There`s something special and addictive about wearing a Crombie, monkey boots and Ben Sherman shirts. As my grandkids sing today "He`s a Mod".

Without wishing to be controversial I don`t think you can be a fat or a bald Mod, it just doesn't work. The clothes don`t hang right and you need good hair to look like Paul Weller, Steve Marriott or Liam Gallagher. Before talking my way into my dream job I hadn't learnt shorthand, I just scrawled my own version or made up the quotes. I stopped using a tape recorder after interviewing The Partisans, a Welsh punk band with a pretty girl singer. They were all very young and excitable. teenagers with heavy accents. I understood them face to face but the resulting tape proved as hard to decipher as alien hieroglyphics. If sheep could talk they`d sound like the singer in this band, but I made up friendly quotes and gave them a great review.

I became legendary for writing friendly reviews. As legendary gangster Dave Courtney, one of the funniest blokes I've ever met said "It's nice to be important but more important to be nice". I reviewed the David Bowie album `Let's Dance` and gave it such a gushing review my Editor moaned it read like a `love letter`. When I started working at Sounds I was doing three or 4 interviews and reviews every week. I was also attending every party and record launch in London.

I was hanging out in all the right clubs and infamous pubs picking-up girls and looking for stories. I was never off duty. It's true to say `Billy Whiz` did help me to survive (and stay awake). Wherever I lay my hat was my home and rarely slept (or ate). The early years at Sounds were a non-stop party and a million miles from life on an East End council estate. It was long hours but going to work was a pleasure. I saw new bands and different girls night after night.

My first superstar interview was with Sade. She was the best-looking and coolest soul singer of her generation. It was `love at first sight` on my part.

I've never forgotten the five times we met (bet she has) but hope she remembers my five star of review of `Diamond Life`. For me it was up there with meeting David Bowie, Paul Weller, George Best, Charlie Kray, Buster Edwards, Dave Courtney, The Stone Roses and Joe Strummer. All these are magic moments in my life. I became a `talent spotter` and started championing new bands. The Babysitters, Ring of Roses, The Immaculate Fools all `died a death` but as the world knows The Stone Roses became massive.

I rated The Immaculate Fools and not just because of the music. I loved the bad boy image, which included sex, drugs and rock and roll parties in various hotel rooms. They were party animals into everything from fast drugs to pretty girls and Polaroid cameras I was on their side from day one and biased beyond belief. The skinny singer sounded like David Bowie and one of their dad's taught Ziggy to play the saxophone so no wonder I was a massive fan. What happens on the road stays on the road which is a shame as I have a great story about the band involving vast amounts of cocaine, groupies and a video camera. Nowadays those clips would be a sensation on Only Fans.

The interviews I wrote were over-the-top as were my 5-star reviews of their records and gigs. Their debut album has dated but still sounds better than Phil Collin. Throughout my time at Sounds I was always hungry and enthusiastic, had to be, as I had no journalistic qualifications. I went a long way for a bloke without any formal education so imagine how far I could have gone if I'd listened to my teachers. I'd probably be a millionaire now like punk pundit turned best-selling author Tony Parsons or a cheeky chat show host like Jonathan Ross. I'm no fan of war criminal Tony Blair but his mantra of "education, education, education" unlike most political slogans was spot on. I digress and this will upset a lot of people (posh champagne socialists) but honestly believe Maggie Thatcher carried out the greatest political act of my lifetime.

Maggie made it possible for working-class people to buy their own council houses. It was a offer sensible people couldn't refuse. The parents of my mates 'bit her hand off'. Why shouldn't the working-class be homeowners?

We all buy food, clothes, cars, and pay taxes, so why do champagne socialist politicians (who own mansions) hate us plebs owning houses? Things were going well at Sounds but I still had ambitions about singing and performing. I wrote 'Suburban Rebels' for punk band The Business which got top 5 in the Indie Chart and 'If Looks Could Kill' with Frankie Flame.

I insisted on singing my own song and it 'died a death'. A great song but because of my out-of-tune singing didn't stand a chance. I loved that song and my performance because in my drug-induced state I'd convinced myself I sounded like David Bowie. The truth is I didn't and numerous music critics have voted it one of the worst records of all-time. Luckily, I wasn't so deluded about my singing ability when it came to 'Suburban Rebels'. My version was crap and I found myself in the recording studio with London punk band The Business. I hummed the tune and they played it. Singer Mickey Fitz performed a vocal performance I could only dream of. In 2025 I'll be appearing in a documentary about The Business and talking about the recording of "Suburban Rebels'. A song that's been covered by bands from around the world.

As is my character I never gave up on 'If Looks Could Kill' and years later a real singer recorded a half decent version far superior to mine.

I also formed a short-lived double-act with Cock Sparrer guitarist Garrie Lammin, who like me loved Colombian marching powder. He was a funny bloke with a Rod Stewart haircut obsessed with The Rolling Stones. The first thing I liked about him was his access to fast drugs and in the pub together we were brilliant. At the time Garry Bushell was our biggest fan though some would say our only fan. We both talked a great song and plotted a walk to fame but never put our master plan into action. Garrie quit rock and roll, lost his Rod Stewart haircut and became an actor. His first role was playing a drug dealer in ITV's The Bill. I know what you're thinking 'playing himself'.

Chris Fulford another old mate also became an actor and starred in an episode of Minder. It was great watching him interact with Arthur Daley. I don't do 'jealous' but was so envious my face turned green. Love me or hate me, people sometimes have the wrong perception. I am nothing like the Cockney tearaway of my teenage years. That was just a front. I was a far better actor then my old mate Garrie Lammin and unlike him I do a great Ray Winstone. I survived for many years of my life pretending to be his character from the classic movie Scum. You need a big front to survive when you grow up in Children's Homes, Detention Centre and Borstal. No places for a Mister Nice Guy.

I like to think the adult me became thoughtful, self-effacing, funny, friendly, mischievous, humble and dare I say even charming. But some people won't let you change. Loyalty, daydreaming and optimism are the only character traits linking the teenage me to the adult I am today. I was then and still am today an eternal optimist. As Del boy Trotter said: "one day I will be a millionaire".

The young Gal Johnson wanted to be a footballer, the adult me a rock star, now the old me just wants to carry on breathing to be with my kids and grandchildren. I failed when it came to appearing on Match of The Day and Top of The Pops but touch wood I'm putting off a guest appearance in the local graveyard.

After my two big triple-heart operations I was given a fresh chance at life but and another shot at stardom. I made another comeback then decided it was time to to put pen to paper or sit at a laptop for 8 hours a day. I wanted everything on-the-record in case my recovery was only temporary.

What took me so long? Previously I wasn't sure the time was right but now the goalposts had moved. My children were older, a Gagging Order had been removed plus I had another shot at stardom. It was a bit of a long shot and against the odds. I was older, a voice from the past, but even at my lowest I never gave up. Maybe delusional, no very delusional, I never stopped dreaming. Even at my age I still fantasise about playing for West Ham or spending the night with Kate Moss. Since rising phoenix-like from what many called my 'death bed' I decided to re-launch my career and re-build my private life. I wrote songs most days and fell in love most weeks. Being in a coma messed up my short-term memory and destroyed part of my brain.

For the first time in my life (apart from Sade) I fancied women who were not blonde. They still have to be slim with small bums and long legs but no longer have to look like Kate Moss or Debbie Harry (circa 1979). I'm still the old me but in many ways I've changed. Dare I say finally grown-up? All my adult life I've loved Ziggy Stardust, fast drugs, skinny blondes, music, alcohol and football.

Today only my David Bowie and music addictions remain. I no longer snort cocaine, drink alcohol, watch football, or only sleep with blondes.

Well at my age beggars can't be choosers, only joking, that's just a throwaway line for the militant feminists at the BBC. Nowadays I genuinely find dark-haired women in size 12 dresses attractive and realise what I was missing for so many years.

How could any red-blooded sane bloke not fancy Love Island star Maura Higgins? I'm sure it has something to do with my 'first love' being blonde, my dad leaving and some of my character stuck in a time warp. I was told by a therapist that part of my brain will always remain aged 15. I was genuinely told that by my therapist.

I didn't have a 'middle-class moment' and betray my class as I got my counselling on the NHS. It had nothing to do with me being 'mentally ill' or trying to behave like a snobby celebrity. I'm not ashamed to admit I sought medical help because at the time I was living in fear. The MSM was full of stories about child abuse and perverted kid killers.

Scum like Ian Huntley and Roy Whiting were all over the news. Any form of child abuse has always affected me badly and is linked to my own childhood. Since becoming a Dad I had always been terrified that something or someone would harm my children and it affected my health. I was the most over-protective dad in the world.

In 2000 my anxiety started to get out of control when schoolgirl Sarah Payne was kidnapped and murdered by Roy Whiting. The double murder in 2002 of Holly and Jessica the 8-year-old girls killed by Ian Huntley freaked me out.

These tragic events sent me over the edge and I became a nervous wreck and sick with worry. My GP, Doctor Simms put me on medication and arranged for me to see a counsellor. These terrible crimes happened hundreds of miles away so why was I suffering from extreme anxiety? My sons were now of an age where they wanted to visit the park with their mates and without me.

I was mortified and feared there'd be a monster hiding in the bushes. I was on medication and had twenty-six weeks of counselling and ended up at Basildon Hospital where I was diagnosed with 'extreme anxiety'. My only mission in life was protecting Sam and Adam and years later this would come back to bite me on the bottom. My ex-wife told social services I was 'mentally ill' and implied I was 'mad, bad and dangerous'. She convinced social worker Peter Brown that I was a danger to my children and repeated a remark I made back in 2000.

People who've known me all my life and who know my character would confirm it was just 'me being me'. Hours after my daughter was born I joked "She'll have a shaved head and braces on her teeth until she's sixteen". I said it partly because I know what teenage boys are like and as a joke, at the time everyone including my ex-wife laughed.

In 2007 my ex-wife told The Family Court "Please don't let Mr Johnson see Lucy because he's threatened to shave her head". It got worse. She told Social Services "The children are terrified of Mr Johnson and I believe he's going to kill them".

This is why I've not seen, kissed or cuddled my daughter since 2007. I enjoyed losing my virginity but have never recovered from losing my dad and my daughter. I was extremely lucky to have the dad I have. I only had him for thirteen years but he made such an impact that he both influenced and destroyed me.

My daughter was only with me for five years but losing her came close to destroying me. What the authorities failed to understand is that my anxiety was brought on by the very special link I had with my children.

Sam was an emergency caesarean and almost died. The first week of his life was spent in intensive care and I stayed with him night and day. I was the only person apart from medical staff to see him for seven days. I was terrified when he nurse told me to put my hands inside the incubator and change his nappy. My hands were shaking, and I was drenched in sweat from head to toe. I was so wet it was as if I'd just got out the shower.

My ex-wife knew I'd been treated for stress but told anyone who'd listen I was mentally ill. I was transformed in her tissue of lies from an 'overprotective Dad' into a 'dangerous head case' who was mad, bad and dangerous. They say mud sticks and it stuck to me for years. I had to fight, fight and fight again to clear my name. I've never understood why as a blonde obsessive that my second sexiest pin-up of all-time is Sade. We met just before the release of her debut album 'Diamond Life' and for me it was lust and love at first sight.

She was drop-dead-gorgeous, beautiful and charming with the velvety voice of an angel. I gave her a 5-star review in Sounds music magazine, and she invited me to her Royal Festival Hall gig. The invite included VIP backstage passes so took along a couple of mates, who like me were seduced by her charm.

There are some things I can't give up. David Bowie, Debbie Harry, George Best, Paul Weller, Mod and TV shows 'Minder' and 'Only Fools and Horses, but things I have given up include 'fast drugs', alcohol, watching football, meat, dairy, young skinny blondes (or did the give me up? but the hardest addiction to kick is ambition. I never stopped believing that one day I'll crack it. Such is my character I have to have something to aim for.

# Chapter Two
# I Could Have Been a Contender

My current obsession is the Lottery. I do various versions six days a week and truly believe that one day my numbers will come up and I'll be interviewed on TV as the UK's biggest 'lottery winner'.

Always wanted to live like a rock star but never had the funds or the talent to be rich and famous, so my last hope is winning the Lottery. The only talent I ever had (apart from chatting-up girls) was for playing football. I was a genuine contender to make it as a professional footballer but for a number of reasons (beyond my control) it never happened. I would like to thank my dad and my f*****g stepmother for ending my dream. To use a football analogy my writing ability was Conference level and my singing ability Sunday morning kick-a-bout but never gave up on becoming a Fleet Street legend or a rock star. Fast drugs are good for that.

Having stared death in the face I grabbed what seemed my 20$^{th}$ chance of stardom with both hands. I was going to enjoy my second lease of life and grab it with both hands. When my comeback started I had no idea where it would lead. I shared a stage with TV star Phil Jupitus and was signed-up by Hollywood director/producer Sandie West. She promised to make a movie of my crime novel Serial Killer. I thought I'd cracked it but Sandie was more Walter Mitty then Quentin Tarantino so six years on I'm still waiting for the film to be made and unless Terry Stone comes to the rescue don't see myself ever walking the red carpet with Kate Moss on my arm.

Sandie blames the delay on Covid but not convinced. She took Garry Bushell to Hollywood promising to make him a movie star but it all went wrong. There was no luxury hotel or stretch limo and GB ended up sleeping on her floor, driving about in a bashed-up van and returned to the UK with a bad back and sore throat.

The film was more like an Ealing Comedy and Carry On caper than a 2020 version of Spinal Tap. Ever the optimist I still believe there will be a movie but not directed by Sandie West. She has put a 90-second trailer on YouTube but as yet nothing to see on Netflix. My comeback started with me talking about the past like a guest on Radio 4's Desert Island Discs. Then Swedish rock star Sulo Soren Karlsson got in touch and we recorded an album for Cargo Records. I found myself on the same Record Label as John Lydon. Punk Rock Stories And Tabloid Tales got a five star review in StreetSounds Magazine. Once again, I was dreaming of a world tour and buying a mansion in the Essex countryside.

After so many years of trying I was going to live my dream. So how do I tell my story? The answer to that question is in my own way. I want to tell you a story from 'schooldays to old age' in my own style. These are the memoirs of a Tabloid Terrorist told in a conversational style and not written like a chronological A to Z shopping List. It's drawing on the DIY attitude of Punk Rock and quoting Frank Sinatra/Sid Vicious I really want to do it 'My Way'.

First, a statement of fact, I'm not and never been a genuine mainstream celebrity. I've performed in front of 100s but never to an audience of thousands. I was known to readers of the NME, Sounds, Melody Maker, Front Magazine and StreetSounds but not a household name to those who read The Sun, Mirror and News of The World. On occasions I became the 'story' and made it onto the front page of The Daily Mail. I also got a full-page write-up in Private Eye magazine which I loved. Nowadays because of Tik Tok and Twitter people have a very low attention threshold. Boredom is like rigger-mortis in a rotting corpse and kicks in pretty quick.

Welcome to the modern world of Soundbites and clickbait. I only deal in facts, the events might not be in the correct order, but unlike Harry and Megan my truth is the real truth. Unlike the adult fairytale 'Spare', my story has not been cobbled together by a ghost writer. Loyalty, honesty and good manners are the most important things in the world, which is why I could never be a politician or a policeman.

I'm not a Little Englander (I'm half Irish), and as Morrissey said ("English blood Irish heart") I've always disliked champagne socialists and English people who fawn all over the Royal Family. I say England because I never refer to myself as 'British' or coming from the United Kingdom. I'm a old-school Londoner and Cockney Rebel, not a British citizen. I might not make sense to the upper class elite who control the British Establishment and destroyed this country but I would not fight for the United Kingdom.

The only person I'd follow into battle is me. I'd defend my family, friends and neighbours, but wouldn't fight for the Royal Family, posh politicians or people like arrogant Owen Jones or compulsive liar Sir Champagne Socialist Starmer.

There's a theme here as I hate the Prime Minister almost as much as I love Ziggy Stardust. It's true to say that from my background and without discovering David Bowie I could have ended up dying in poverty on a concrete jungle council estate.

I left school with no qualifications but knew I didn't want to live on the dole, as I can't handle boredom. You've got two choices in life either choose to be a survivor or a victim. When my dad left I was broken-hearted and in pieces. I could have wallowed in self-pity but 'thank God' it didn't grab hold of me.

I went very quickly from shock to anger and soon discovered being 'down' and in a depressed 'state of mind' wasn't for me. I self-medicated myself out of the doom and gloom with the help of amphetamine sulphate. For the rest of my life I convinced everyone I was a 'happy bunny' without a care in the world. I was always the 'joker in the pack'. There were never any tears from this clown.

The authorities say drugs kill you, The Verve sung "Drugs don't work" but I disagree they saved my life. I'm only talking about 'uppers', 'fast drugs', 'speed', 'cocaine'. They are the only drugs I took and must have worked because I'm here to tell the tale. I was never a drug addict, I was a drug user. I never related to fat, sexist, homophobic beer drinking heavy metal fans with beer guts into geezer birds with big boobs and WWF wrestling who smoke weed.

Although I'm a self-confessed rebel I'm no fan of modern-day criminals as I have very high standards. As a Mod I'm very particular about what I like and don't like when it comes to clothes, music, women, comedians and criminals. My two favourite criminals, if that's the right description are Celebrity gangster Dave Courtney, who I met and Great Train Robber Ronnie Biggs who sadly I didn't.

Both had showbiz connections, appeared in films and made records. Those are my kind of fun loving criminals. They had all the glory without doing a lot of time behind the door. In their own way, although they never worked, both were working-class boys done well.

Although a teenage tearaway I wasn't cut out for a life of crime. I did brief spells in Bellmarsh and Chelmsford Prisons and for someone with my imagination the boredom is almost unbearable. Luckily, I found Ziggy Stardust, Colombian marching powder and spent a lifetime being a rebel with a cause. I genuinely believe that living by his rules, checking out the bands, writers, films he recommended made me a better person. I loved Bowie's anorexic look, love of fast drugs and exotic friends like Iggy Pop, Lou Reed and Andy Warhol. It was Bowie and not teachers that gave me my morals and education. I would not have had such an exciting life if I'd not discovered David Bowie and cocaine and then The Sex Pistols and speed.

I have few regrets in life and enjoyed almost every moment. I always needed a new obsession as I got bored very easily. I'd be madly in love with a girl at 10pm and then out of love by 8am the next morning. Like

David Bowie and Paul Weller, I constantly changed my appearance. My hairstyles, clothes, diet, but never my beliefs or taste in music. Mod and Bowie have been a constant in my life.

It didn't make sense, but I liked being an individual even when I was a member of a cult, a tribe or a gang. I was never a sheep. That's why I could never join the army, or an organised religion and follow the rules. For me religion begins and ends with Father Christmas and maybe Easter eggs, all the rest is bollocks.

I'm an outsider and a loner who at the same time loves to be surrounded by people, I like to be loved but not in 'love'. I don't trust sexual love as it always ends in tears. (or divorce). But loving one's family is a different life-long kind of love. The only people I've genuinely 100% loved from day one are my children and grandchildren. It's a different kind of love then I had for my parents, can't explain, but it's different. I'm not a new romantic (or even an old one) but am a bit of 1960s hippy in Mod clothes. I am I admit a mass of contradictions. Wow, that was a bit of a rant, or baring of my soul, but what's the point in writing an autobiography if you don't tell the truth? Just trying to paint a picture of who I am and explain what makes me tick. Telling my story because no matter who you are, famous, infamous or unknown after you're dead the best of friends and worse of enemies always re-write history.

This is me baring my soul and putting everything on-the-record. I've come to terms with the good and bad things in my life, always bounced back like a rubber ball from my darkest moments. But when it comes to getting old there's only one winner and that's old Father Time. You can fight the ageing process but you're always going to lose. Give up drugs, booze, cigarettes, dairy, go to the gym but whatever you do there's only going to be one winner. Even Madonna with all her millions failed to turn back the clock and now looks like the Bride of Frankenstein in her high heels and leggings. The best you can hope for is having a young mind and a healthy old body. Whatever you do, or however much you spend, it's not going to get any better than that.

I was born on January 21$^{st}$ 1957, hard to believe when you look at me but true. Around the same time Elvis Presley invented rock and roll, and Sir Cliff Richard was a virgin (he still is). I got my Cockney humour from my dad, Charles Alfred, who was a semi-pro footballer and professional bird bandit. My mum was from Dublin and had no mother but a strict Irish Republican for a father. Both those men were massive characters and along with my Cockney Pop influenced my early life. Growing up in East London they were along with footballer George Best my earliest heroes. They had nothing in common apart from me and a mutual love of fashion.

They would religiously wear their Sunday best every day of the week. Each of them had a personal weakness which in one way or another wreck theirs and other people's lives. My dad was a Ladies man and compulsive gambler who rarely backed a winner.

My Irish Pop had a love affair with Guinness. Cockney Pop, a bookies runner for an illegal bookie was a life-long ducker and diver who never held down a 9 to 5 job.

I have inherited a bit of all three in my DNA. My 'weakness' was a 16-year love affair with fast drugs, I took it to party but also to self-medicate. When my dad left I was down and depressed and didn't like the way it made me feel. I survived on 'little blue happy pills' before discovering the benefits of white powder. I was at war with myself, the world and anything or anyone who came into my orbit. Some-one recommended 'pep pills' and they helped. I self-medicated for the rest of my life and never suffered a single day of depression. When it came to vices, bad habits, character traits I only inherited one of their weaknesses. Can you guess which one? It was girls, women, Females of the species. I've always loved women but not in a sexist way. Three women had the biggest effect on my life and I only slept with one of them.

Elle, a sassy smart Jewish girl who doubled up as a rock photographer and Press Officer predicted I'd move from music magazines to Fleet Street. Her prediction would eventually come true but I still had unfinished business as a performer. The Buzz Kids were over, but I hadn't thrown in the towel.

I decided to become a poet, a Cockney Bob Dylan with a better haircut. I visited a bookshop in Kingsland Road Hackney that specialised in poetry. A lovely gay guy more theatrical than Alan Carr suggested I send some of my 'punk anthems' to a publisher named John Muir. John, a wheeler-dealer hippie ran a Manchester company called Babylon Books who specialised in punk. I sent him fifty of my finest poems and within days John got in touch saying how much he loved my work. Result.

Before I knew it my poetry collection 'Boys of The Empire' was published and as well as my character now had something else to flog. John sent me fifty copies of the book, which I set about selling and sending out to people I wanted to take notice of me. Time Out gave me a rave review. Janet Street-Porter presenter of LWT's London Show sent a letter saying she liked them, and the music press were generous with their comments. I did a few benefit gigs and appeared on various 'spoken word' albums, and with my reputation growing was approached to write lyrics by various punk bands.

Babylon Books also approached me to write a Punk Book which sold well and led to book deals with Proteus Books and Omnibus Press. The boy who left school with no qualifications was hired to write biographies about David Bowie, Paul Young, Queen, Gary Glitter and Ozzy Osbourne. I decided the time was right to quit the world of Street Punk. I wasn't deserting my roots but such is my character I get bored very easily. New Punk was going nowhere and no new band would emulate The Sex Pistols, The Clash, The Jam or The Buzzcocks.

I'd outgrown the revolution and was returning to MOD culture. My real love was always the glamour side of popular music. The David Bowie School of Rock and Roll with a bit of Art School Roxy Music. I wanted to swap backstreet pubs for West End Clubs. When I started at Sounds I decided the best approach was not to reinvent the wheel. I already owned old copies of Record Mirror and the NME so now set about buying up as many back issues I could get my hands on.

I went to Jumble Sales, second-hand shops and replied to adverts in various newspapers. If they were out there I found them. I bought them up and collated piles of magazines and began recycling reviews. They proved to be a goldmine and a nice little earner. I'd stockpiled thousands of interviews and reviews which by changing names and venues enabled me to look good in print. It taught me all about structure and I learned on the job. I self-educated and within a year I had the confidence to publish my own original copy. To be honest, when it was `all my own work`, the by-line looked even better and the buzz was off the scale. I never needed all that hippie re-birthing bollocks or champagne socialist regression rubbish to confirm I was a happy kid. I was always over-confident, happy-go-lucky, extremely popular with all ages and both sexes. I wouldn't change a thing about the first 13 years of my life. I was the kind of annoying kid who bounced out of bed every morning (I still do). I'd drive my ex-wife bonkers by starting to talk before my feet touched the carpet. Even as a teenager in a brutal institution I still jumped out of bed with a smile on my face. The glass is always half full, never half empty is my philosophy of life. Things will only get worse if you allow yourself to be beaten into submission.

I was born in a house in Hackney with an outside loo, massive record collection and a famous relative. My Pop's cousin was Music Hall legend Marie Lloyd, the Taylor Swift of her day. Crowds would gather in the street when she visited 25 Overbury Street in Hackney before WW2. My pop told me how she woud hand out food and give money to hungry kids. Eastenders star Barbara Windsor played my famous relative in a movie of her life.

I grew up singing along to Pop's Al Jolson albums and my Dad's Elvis records. However, by 1967 other music began infiltrating my ears.

At the age of Ten, I became a Mod and fell in love with the music of The Kinks and The Small Faces.

The best Cockney pop group in history really got into my head. I saw them on TV and was hooked. I also saw Marianne Faithful and got my first `hard on`. She was slim, blonde, with short skirts and long legs. She also had a really sexy voice (though at Ten I didn't know what sex was), it was the first time I felt movement in the trouser department. I had no idea she was the girlfriend of Mick Jagger or that years later she'd record a version of `I Got You Babe` with Ziggy Stardust. In the 1970`s she shared a stage and a bed with David Bowie.

Seeing The Small Faces singing on TV with Cockney voices wearing cool clothes with great hair was the day I decided to become a Mod. The next day I went shopping in Hackney market with my Nan and bought me a copy of `Lazy Sunday` I soon had the other hits `Itchycoo Park` and `All or Nothing`. Around the same time, I became a massive fan of American pop band The Monkees who had a zany TV show. In 1976 The Sex Pistols would record a cover of their classic hit `Stepping Stone`.

My teenage years were all about hair. In 1969 to be one of the boys I had a dramatic haircut. I became a Skinhead. I shed my Stevie Marriott mop top for a Number One crop. Within months I was a Suedehead and as my hair got longer the beat got stronger and replaced Reggae with rock and roll. It kept on growing and eventually became a Mick Ronson/Rod Stewart Glam Rock `work of art`. At first, I was just copying Slade, the skinhead group who grew their hair and became the biggest band since The Beatles. Then I saw Ziggy Stardust and discovered eyeliner and nail varnish looked good on teenage boys. Skinheads all over the UK were swapping bovver boots and braces for velvet trousers and satin jackets. Hairbrushes replaced knuckle dusters as must have accessories. It`s a funny old world as years later I would hang-out with Slade singer/songwriter Noddy Holder. Imagine that for a minute. Today it would be like a 15-year-old Oasis fan growing-up and going on pub crawls with Liam Gallagher.

The Slade singer wrote the multi-million selling festive classic `Merry Xmas` and I was half responsible at the same time 100% innocent for him being exposed as a `love rat` on the front page of The Sun. At the time I was hanging-out and living on and off with singer/model Cindy Jackson in trendy Fulham. She went onto become world famous as a `real-life Barbie`. One night she accompanied me on a Soho pub crawl with two members of Slade and my mate Dan Higson (soon to be front-page news himself) in The Sunday People. Cindy was hilarious with long blonde hair and long legs, has anyone noticed a theme in this book? She was a very bright, loud American girl who was left a fortune by her dad and decided to spend it on what back in the day was called 'plastic surgery'. Cindy had a new nose and drove a white sports car, and I can best describe our relationship as 'friends with benefits'.

There was a little bit of sex and a lot of drugs. I found her very funny and in small doses loved her Texan accent. She was a part-time model, wannabe singer and five-star scammer. Nowadays she's always in the papers and appearing on TV discussing plastic surgery. She's done really well and become a media expert on the subject. She calls herself a "real-life Barbie" and is rumoured to be a millionaire. Cindy had her picture taken with Noddy Holder and ended up on the front page of The Sun.

It was all innocent, but she made it out to be the 'love affair of the century'. We were all having a few drinks (and snorting stimulants) around Soho and ended up at The Rise Bar in Covent Garden. What started as gang of 5 had by now grown to a group of ten or 12. Cindy was pictured sitting on Noddy's lap and having a friendly, harmless kiss. The next day she was famous all over the UK for being 'Noddy's girlfriend' and being a 'smart girl' with a business head like Lord Sugar she went along with the headline. She 'milked it' for all it was worth and made a nice few quid. Pop star Noddy an innocent married man blamed me and we never spoke again.

A few weeks after I started seeing Elle there was a awkward situation in her office, I turned-up and Noddy was sitting in the corner of the room.

I'd forgotten she was his PR. He gave me dirty looks, but no punches were exchanged, though her boss banned me from visiting the office. I stuck to the rules during the day but at night (she had the keys) we'd pop in to snort drugs and use the sofa (if you get my drift) because her office was just a few minutes from The Marquee Club. Cindy's antics inspired my mate Dan Higson to became a 'love rat', only difference he was telling the truth. He was having a 'fling' with Bicks Fizz singer and Eurovision winner Jay Aston. He sold his story and pictures to the Sunday People. It was front-page news because at the time Jay was a household name. Dan made £10,000 but paid a price for his 5 minutes of fame, lost his job as a press officer and fled to Australia, where he became a very rich and successful businessman. His brother is comedy writer Charlie Higson from The Fast Show.

After Slade it was all about David Bowie, Roxy Music, Marc Bolan, Rod Stewart, Cockney Rebel and Mott The Hoople who turned skinheads into Glam Rockers.

Teenage culture was now all about new exciting modern music, fashion and make-up (for boys and girls). Shaven heads had been replaced by feather cuts, mullets and corkscrew hair. In 1976 I would cut my longhair, shed my precious locks and became a short spiky-haired punk, but whatever my appearance I was always a Mod at heart. That's why I eventually followed The Jam after being drawn in by The Sex Pistols, The Clash and The Buzzcocks. Johnny Rotten was a rebel, Joe Strummer a politician, Steve Diggle a pop punk, but Paul Weller was a Mod. Weller was the bloke I wanted to be. He looked like a member of The Small Faces and eventually wrote the best songs. The first four Sex Pistols singles were brilliant and two 'Anarchy In The UK' and 'God Save The Queen' will still be classics 100 years from now. The Clash gave us brilliant albums and The Buzzcocks great singles but only Weller kept on getting better. The Jam to The Style Council and then as a solo performer

In 1980 because of Weller mohair suits and Small Faces haircuts were back in fashion worn by 2-tone bands like Madness and The Specials, and for a while Mod revivalists like Secret Affair and The Purple Hearts. I saw all those bands wearing a Crombie overcoat, monkey boots, and Levi 501's in various venues all over London. I worshipped Bowie and loved punk but once a Mod always a Mod. People forget that David Bowie was an 'ace face' who wrote the Mod classic 'The London Boys'.

That is why as a 30-plus married man with kids and a mortgage I became a massive fan of Brit Pop. I was according to my birth certificate an 'old man' but the quality of the songs and attitude of Noel and Liam Gallagher made me feel young again. Back in the day people couldn't choose their favourite Beatle. Was it John or Paul? I'm the same with Oasis, in different ways on different days I love Liam more than Noel. I was never a Beatles fan, only got into them in the 90s because of the Gallagher brothers always name-checking them. The same way Bowie got me into Lou Reed, The Velvet Underground and Iggy Pop.

Even in my weird and wonderful drug-free mind I genuinely (from a distance) felt part of Brit Pop culture. A musical revolution and fashion movement that would not have happened without Paul Weller and Ian Brown of The Stone Roses.

Had Liam and Noel read my Sounds article on The Stone Roses, probably not, but definitely maybe? It was pretty obvious the song-writing of Weller inspired Noel and the Ian Brown 'walk' and dress sense was a massive influence on Liam. The Gallagher brothers have confirmed this in various TV, Radio and magazine interviews. Oasis and Brit Pop rivals Blur made genuinely great records high on 'fast drugs' dressing like new-age Mods with classic 1960 haircuts. They also associated themselves with legendary Mod icons. Noel collaborated with Weller and Blur worked with Quadrophenia star Phil Daniels.

Brit Pop was also great because both Pulp and Suede had a bit of David Bowie about them, which was another reason to be a fan. Oasis,

Blur, Pulp, Suede, throughout pop history, every new youth movement has always had 4 great bands. There were never five.

The Swinging 60's had The Beatles, The Rolling Stones, The Kinks and of course The Small Faces. Glam Rock was led by David Bowie, Marc Bolan, Roxy Music and Mott The Hoople. Punk Rock exploded with The Sex Pistols, The Clash, The Buzzcocks and The Jam. Two-Tone had The Specials, Madness, The Selector and The Beat. I was for 25 years the undisputed genuine working-class hero of tabloid journalism. I was a one-off who built a career and got to the top of the tree with no recognised qualifications. All I could do was talk and was luckily blessed with more front than the seaside town of Blackpool.

I wasn't a phone hacker or a Cockney version of disgraced PR guru Max Clifford (who I met) but more like the Leonardo di Caprio character in the movie classic 'Catch Me If You Can'. I wasn't a political pundit pontificating in the MSM who earn fortunes telling lies for a living. When I moved from Sounds music magazine to work on national newspapers people just assumed I was a Kosher journalist, and who was I to spoil the illusion? No-one asked to see my A-levels or University Degree, which was lucky for me as I had neither. Only once did I come close to being rumbled.

I was on a press junket to Birmingham, travelling first class with a load of journalists from various newspapers and magazines. The very funny and highly educated Julia Kutner from the New Musical Express reached into her bag and pulled out a Scrabble Board. She asked "Who wants to play?"

I thought 'no way', not in front of a dozen journalists, not even a Oscar winning actor' could bluff his way through a game of Scrabble. So made my excuses and faked a migraine. It's strange how things work out as years later (2001) I worked for her dad Stuart, a high-up at News International. It was he and Rebekah Wade who were first to phone after my release from top security Bellmarsh Prison. As football legend Jimmy Greaves would say and turn into a national catchphrase "It's a funny old game". My story does read like a Rocky-style romp from the slums of East London to the wonderful world of Fleet Street. I was there, I witnessed it all first hand, but even I find some of my stories and various anecdotes hard to believe. But believe me every word of this book is the 100% Gospel truth. As a kid the first Cockney journalist I saw on TV was the late great Derek Jamieson who from memory worked for the Mirror, Sun and News of The World. Legend has it he introduced Sun Bingo and Page 3 to the masses. Before 1976 working-class kids rarely got jobs in the media. That's why I remember Jamieson who was like a 1970's Jonathan Ross who in the 1980's had his own chat show on TV. Back in the day Fleet Street was a magical place full of big names and massive characters. By hook or by crook I wanted to be part of it. Tabloid Journalists get a bad name, but I'd rather be a showbiz hack than a corrupt politician, biased barrister or bent copper.

My football dream died, but I never stopped dreaming about some kind of life connected to showbiz. I failed when it came to following in the footsteps of George Best but succeeded in becoming what many would call a 'Poundland' version of Piers Morgan, who for 12 years was my brilliant and loyal boss. I don't care what others say about him I always found him a great bloke. He was the same genuine guy when in charge of the NOTW and the Daily Mirror.

Using a football analogy he was a world class Premiership player and I was Conference League level but always enjoyed myself. My job was working as a 24-hour party person and getting paid for pursuing my hobbies. Piers did me many favours and always looked after me so never gave him or Rebekah Wade made-up stories. I had too much respect for them both. When Piers left News International he invited me and my wife to his leaving party at Planet Hollywood. We shared a taxi to the venue with future TV and Radio star Matthew Wright who was also a guest at my Sam's $3^{rd}$ Birthday Party. It was a top night attended by celebs and every top journo in Fleet Street. As a football fan it was great hanging out with England and Arsenal football star Ian Wright. Piers told Andy Coulson to look after me in his absence describing me as his "number one tipster". He was soon paying me a retainer to go with the dosh I was earning from other outlets.

Andy became Prime Minister David Cameron's Press Officer before being sent to jail for phone-hacking. We both attended Piers Morgan's leaving party and ended up in Bellmarsh maximum security prison.

## Chapter Three
## East End Boy

So, who was tabloid imposter Garry Johnson? In 2013 I was given five years to live. I now want to tell my story before it's too late. Dead men can't talk but they can be slandered and smeared. I don't intend to be a silent victim of written or verbal abuse. I'm a East End boy who looks like Ray Winstone (when I'm pumped full of heart medication), talks like Danny Dyer and dresses like Paul Weller (when I'm on a diet). I've always wanted everything in my life to be stylish, be it music, fashion, football, films or women.

I think that's why I never liked Elton John as a kid, why would anyone want a picture of pop's Mr Blobby on their bedroom wall? All my male heroes from Bowie to Best to Weller to Liam Gallagher have always dressed like 'Dandies' and of all the women I've wanted to sleep with or slept with the majority have been slim and blonde. I know beauty is in the eye of the beholder, but when it comes to beauty, I only look at it through my eyes, and I don't see anything attractive in beer guts, fat legs or bald heads. Am I shallow?

You could say that, definitely maybe.

I've always judged people by their appearance, sorry, but it's the life-long Mod in me. I was a singer in a rock and roll band called The Buzz Kids (who I wanted to call The Dandies but was outvoted). We looked the part, I looked great but couldn't sing and the band couldn't really play a note.

Punk legend Garry Bushell ended our brief career. The year was 1980. I'd spent the last 6 months of 1979 writing songs and performing in various bedrooms, garages and rehearsal rooms. I bumped into Garry Bushell for the first time in November 1979 at The Bridge House pub in Canning Town and told him about my band. He promised to come to our first gig. He grew more interested by the day because for the next 3 months I bombarded him with more and more stories about The Buzz Kids and how good we were. I promised and boasted that he would love us. I was wrong. Unfortunately he kept his promise and turned up. He liked me (still does) but hated the band. Garry's response after the gig "Garry you're a good writer and a great publicist but a F***ing shit vocalist". He said it from a good place. It wasn't just him being the hard-hitting controversial pundit for effect. As history proved he was right.

Within a year he was my boss and my best mate, but always honest when it came to my singing ability.

He said of my single `If Looks Could Kill` "That has got to be one of the worst records I've ever heard". Adding "You still can't sing". I disagreed and still think it's the best thing I've ever done. What does that say about my other records? After attacking my vocal ability and destroying my band in a backstreet Hackney pub he added:

"Make use of your other talents, stick to what you're good at". At that time in my life I didn't need or want career advice like that so took it quite hard. I was down for what seemed like minutes before bouncing back fuelled by amphetamine and helped by a personality that don't give a toss about criticism. It was like water off a ducks back. I didn't cry because East End Boys don't cry. Within ten minutes I was looking for another girl to cheer me up and spent the next 6 months refining my writing ability. I bought copies of every weekly and monthly music paper and got into plagiarism in a big way. Garry Bushell's harsh (but honest) criticism was a bitter pill to swallow but as is my character took it on board and used to my advantage. I'm blessed with a skin thicker than an elephant's backside an accepted his criticism it in the spirit it was given.

Despite a savage face-to-face verbal kicking followed by a printed tirade we became best of mates. He was best man on that tragic day I got married and then Godfather to my two sons. I'll return to our historic meeting and The Buzz Kids debut gig later on. My first performance as a Punk Poet was also a nightmare as I suffered both stage-fright and eyesight problems.

I was out of my head on speed, wearing Ray-Ban glasses and because the stage was so dark I couldn't read the words. Fronting The Buzz Kids was a piece of cake compared to standing alone centre-stage and having what can only be described as a confidence meltdown. Like Rishi Sunak I had a plan, and like his it didn't work. I took to the stage looking cool, well in my eyes I did. I was speeding out of my head, wearing Lou Reed ray-bands, a Crombie overcoat and a trilby hat. The venue was so dark I couldn't read my book of poems and managed to perform a 30-minute set in under 5 minutes. I know what you're thinking `I wish I was there` but believe me you don't.

Afterwards in the dressing room the penny finally dropped that the Punk Poet was not a live performer. Although years later in 2016 and without the dark glasses, Crombie overcoat or Trilby hat I made a showbiz comeback.

I was also drug-free (if you don't count various heart tablets) and performed all over London and in Blackpool. And unbelievably I was pretty good and got rave reviews. I shared a stage with TV star Phil

Jupitus (Never Mind The Buzzcocks), Reggae poet Linton Kwesi Johnson and London's finest Tim Wells. The highlight was appearing at The Roundhouse because in the 70s David Bowie performed on that stage. The punk poet got to use the same dressing room as Ziggy Stardust.

After the nightmare gig of 1980 it was back to the drawing board for the eternal optimist. I decided to become a pop pundit and tabloid journalist. It's a funny old world when a person with minimal talent in the performing Arts can make a living writing about singers, actors, comedians who all have a genuine talent. I knew the secret of getting away with it was to always write positive reviews as no one ever complains about praise.

And to make-up fun stories that made people laugh. Amusing tales like pop superstar Rod Stewart buying a Sinclair 5 car to get around the fifty rooms of his massive mansion. Madonna has written a West End musical about Maggie Thatcher. Pop superstar Prince putting on weight to play Mohammed Ali in Hollywood movie and Michael Jackson filming pop video with the Princess of Wales. I believed my job was to make people smile over the breakfast table or on the train journey to work. I was performing a valuable service by raising the mood of the nation. I didn't just hang out with and create stories about the rich and famous that Arthur Daley would be proud of. Sounds once sent me on an all-expenses trip down memory lane.

As a kid I stayed at most of Billy Butlin's holiday camps and have nothing but happy memories. That's why I loved the BBC sit-com 'Hi De Hi', starring Teddy Boy comic Ted Bovis. It reminded me of life as it was before my dad walked out. Mind you, Clacton was a khazi, very much the runt of the litter, and not a patch on the old Barry Island camp in South Wales.

I went twice as a kid but my return as an adult is the one that stands out. It was without doubt the best of the three visits. Just thinking about their Festival of The Sixties leaves me in more stitches than an episode of Casualty on a busy night. They called it the Festival of The Sixties but most of the acts were from the '50s or the 70s. Wishful thinking always had more to do with it than historical accuracy, as the cries of middle-aged mums struggling to shoehorn 1980 figures into their authentic Swinging Sixties outfits testified.

By ridiculous planning it was possible to drink legally from 11am to 5am the next morning. So we did, it was the only way to appreciate acts like Screaming Lord Sutch and Mungo Jerry. Who had their first hit in 1970. They opened the set with a 15-minute sound check behind the curtains in the Pig and Whistle. After that, it was downhill all the way. Wayne Fontana was so instantly forgettable, I can't remember a thing. On the first night the non-musical moments was the best laugh. The mini-skirt competition had to be seen to be believed, I am a life-long legs man, but this almost cured my addiction. It wasn't clear if the lady with the `25` card was talking about her contest number, the size of her feet or her weight. If you think fat Heather from Eastenders, you`lll get the picture I'm painting. When man-mountain did a twirl to reveal no knickers, I made a dash for the exit.

Braver men than me stood their ground, but I bottled it and bolted. Some old stars were worth seeing: Mud first hit, 1973 were superb, and Marty Wilde, four smash hits in the Fifties, was a real pro. He got away with performing `Teenager In Love`, despite looking 65. But it didn't matter how good or bad the bands were. Being there was the crack. People came for a good time and no lousy act could ruin that. My finest moment of the long weekend came with the Elvis Presley lookalike contest. I was talked into entering despite looking `anorexic chic`, years before the phrase was invented and having blonde spiky hair. I did a punk rock version of Hound Dog and came $3^{rd}$ out of 12. The highlights for me took place off stage and included having a beer with wannabee MP Screaming Lord Sutch, a chat with member of The Angelic Upstarts and a quickie with a middle-aged divorcee from Weston-Super-Mare. This Festival took place in either `82 or `83 which means this woman if still alive would now be in her Eighties, that genuinely turns my stomach and feel sick at the very thought. One of the funniest moments involved Business guitarist Steve Kent who was losing his hair but trying to hide it with an Arthur Scargill comb-over. The morning after the night before and still `half-cut` I went to the reception and reported that my mate had lost his wig. They put out an announcement over the loudspeaker tannoy, "if anyone finds a toupee please can they hand it in at reception or take it to Chalet 132" and they named the owner as Steve Kent.

The rest of us thought it was hilarious, but he went ballistic. Punk fans will be aware that Steve was also my former song-writing partner and that together we wrote the classic anthem `Suburban Rebels`. We could have been the Lennon and McCartney of the 80s, but after this joke he refused to work with me. As is my character I did have the last laugh. Months later I reviewed his new band and `slaughtered` them. I wasn't critical of their musical ability but wrote 700 words mentioning his disappearing locks. We laugh about it now, though it took him years to see the funny side.

Butlins ruined my song-writing career, but it will always have a special place in my heart. One day I will return and win the Elvis Presley lookalike competition. I will now tell how the man who ended my pop career launched me as a music writer. He got me into journalism and changed my life. I met Garry in a Covent Garden boozer armed with a copy of my poetry book 'Boys of The Empire', a tatty notepad, a Bic biro and a packet of Billy Wizz. I was a speedfreak, a failed singer and flop as a performing poet. I wanted to be Ziggy Stardust and he was the Godfather of Punk. Gal Bushell was the number one writer at Sounds Music magazine, and soon to be promoted to post of Features Editor. I listened because this guy knew what he was talking about. He'd met Joe Strummer and Paul Weller.

He also knew Debbie Harry, who at the time was the most beautiful woman in the world. She'd sat on his lap in the back of a New York cab and I was well impressed and dead jealous. I still genuinely believe that from 1977 to 1982 the Blondie singer was the best-looking woman in the history of the world. Debbie Harry was perfection. Over a few pints and a couple of lines and much banter, a genuine friendship was formed. We discovered we shared many interests and beliefs, though we disagreed about the Royal Family, he was a supporter, and I was not. He also liked old-school stand-up comics whereas I believe great stand-up started with Frank Skinner, Jimmy Carr, Ricky Gervais and Sean Lock.

He lived on the Ferrier Estate a rusty old dustbin of a council estate in Southeast London. It was a concrete jungle warzone back then, so God only knows how bad it is now. I met and hung-out with punk legend Frankie Flame, Mr Fixit/wannabe gangster Lol Prior, Dodgy Dave Long and Micky Fitz. As always, I ended up staying at their houses and flats. Throughout my life I'd meet people and end up sleeping on their sofas. If people couldn't afford a cat or a dog they'd have a Garry Johnson.

I must have been the only homeless person in London between 1975 and 1988 who didn't sell copies of The Big Issue. That's the main reason I took so many drugs and was drawn to girls/women who had their own place. I didn't just want sex but a place to sleep. The only perk of being homeless meant I didn't exist so never paid tax. The 'gang' hang-out in The Watt Tyler on the Ferrier Estate, The Bridge House Canning Town and in various Soho and Covent Garden boozers. The Bridge House was East London's premier music venue and frequented by all leading members of West Ham's ICF, from Carlton Leach to Cass Pennant. East End boxers, the infamous Geggus brothers, Mick and Jeff, the founding members of The Cockney Rejects launched their band at The Bridge House.

One of their roadies and my old mate was Andy Russell (Skully). He was born in Blackpool but made an honoury member of the ICF. Later he moved onto heavier circles and got banged-up for hijacking a helicopter and springing East End gangster John Kendall from Gartree Prison. It was all over TV news bulletins and his mugshot was on the front page of every newspaper.

He was given Ten years at The Old Bailey. The old bill wanted 20-plus and were furious. So outraged they stitched him up for the Archway security robbery, an armed robbery he swears he didn't do. The judge gave him 10 years for that, on top, not concurrent, so he ended up getting a full Twenty years behind bars.

He was in top security Whitemoor prison when the IRA broke out. At the time Skully was the only Cat A prisoner who wasn't a terrorist, so he went along for the ride. Of course, when they all got captured, the politicians made sure the Irish prisoners weren't touched by the screws, but the bully boys beat Skully to a pulp.

He served more than 15 years in total. We last met in 2016 at a Birthday Party in South London and had our picture taken while reminiscing about the good old days. I said "your story would make a great Hollywood movie" but he wasn't interested in re-living his criminal career on the silver screen. He`s had many offers and so far turned them all down. Skully was a nice bloke in the early 80s before he went inside and as far as I'm concerned still is. He`s currently serving a 9-year sentence for his involvement in the famous Hatton Garden heist of 2017.

British films always make doing time look easy but could Tom Hardy or Jason Statham cope with doing 24-hours a day as Cat A prisoners? Skully did time with genuine East End hardman Tony Argent and contract killer Kevin Lane both rated among the toughest Cat A prisoners to ever be banged-up in English prisons. We are talking harder than Ron and Reggie Kray. Nowadays so many plastic gangsters appear on Podcasts claiming to have been the hardest prisoner of all-time, but Tony Argent and Kevin Lane were the real deal.

I love most of the genuine gangsters and kosher hardmen who tell their stories on TV, and with all my experience of interviewing celebs it isn't` hard spotting all the bull shitters. One of the best and most authentic characters to turn up as a guest has been Essex boxer Dominic Negus who swaggered into the ring against giant Audley Harrison without a care in the world. So f***** fearless he was disqualified for head-butting the British champion. It takes real balls of steal to do something like that. There are hundreds of Podcasters on YouTube and the best of the UK bunch are Liam Tuffs, Shaun Attwood, James English, Dodge Woodall and Terry Stone. Former Sex Pistol Steve Jones also does a great one from America.

I don't know what I'd do without YouTube and Google. It gives me all my information and entertains and educates me at the same time. It also means I can re-live my past watching old films and TV favourites from my youth. The kosher gangsters, boxers and genuine hardmen I've met in my life from the legendary Dave Courtney to Charlie Kray all have one thing in common. They hate bullies, child abusers and sex offenders. Outside the ring most boxers are real gents. The Bridge House was run by Terry Murphy, a member of a proper East End family, former boxing champ and father of actor Glen Murphy. The Canning Town pub launched the careers of heavy metal superstars Iron Maiden, Depeche Mode and East End legends Cock Sparrer and The Cockney Rejects.

Months after appearing at The Bridge House both Basildon's Depeche Mode and The Cockney Rejects were appearing on Top of The Pops. Terry Murphy was a great Cockney character who always had time for everyone. I'm proud to say that years before I 'made it' and still a unknown journo I did a deal with the great man. He owned a record label and was planning to release recordings featuring interviews with pop stars. He'd heard I'd interviewed Sade and wanted to put it out on his label. I handed over the tape and he pulled out a big wad of notes. I didn't want a penny because of our link from the old days but he insisted I had a 'drink'. That was typical of Tel, a true Gent, lovely bloke and Old School.

Another buddy from the old days is Simon Spencer, the Bob Hoskins of the Punk Generation, better known as Si Spanner, who apart from losing his barnet hasn't changed a bit. Celeb gangster Dave Courtney had the best address book in London, but Si has the best photo album. Endless pictures of him posing with everyone from Paul Weller to Dame Karen Brady to ICF Legend Carlton Leach. Suggs from Madness, Cass Pennant, Sir Trevor Brooking and Dave Courtney.

The sex shop owner who still follows the Hammers all over Europe has pictures of himself with most East London faces, boxers and West Ham players (1980 to the present day). There's also a great picture of Si, Skully and me taken in 2016.

Back in the day Simon ran successful sex shops in Soho, and I was a regular customer. No, I wasn't a dirty old man or a punk rocker with a porn addiction. Please allow me to explain. This was before the Internet and online shopping. A lot of my female friends at various record companies and in PR companies would ask me to pick-up various sex toys and adult movies for the weekend.

They asked me because they were either too shy or classy to enter a sleazy Soho sex shop. They all knew me as a bit of a wheeler-dealer and to be honest I'd buy and sell anything to make a pound note. I was Arthur Daley with spiky hair, buying and supplying everything from concert tickets, records, sex toys, porn videos and of course drugs. They'd met or heard about Si and his shop so knew I could get my hands on whatever they wanted. My mate Tony Preston managed one of his shops and we had a great scam flogging blank tapes to tourists. We were on a nice little earner. Sometimes I'd hang out in his seedy sex shop frequented by local strippers and prostitutes who were great fun. It was just around the corner from The Marquee Club in the middle of Soho. When punters came in we'd listen for foreign accents and offer them 'special hardcore porn' from under the counter and they'd happily pay a fortune for a blank tape in a fake case.

It would be many hours and maybe travelling hundreds of miles before discovering they'd been conned, so no danger of violent reprisals from irate customers demanding their money back. Unlike Marks and Spencer we never gave refunds. Tony from the Sex Shop was my driver around Central London and when we went to see David Bowie at Milton Keynes with two barmaids from Stringfellows. It was a beautiful sunny day, Bowie was brilliant, the girls were beautiful, and I had pockets full of money and cocaine. Life couldn't get any better I really was living the dream. Si Spanner was a funny fella, bloody hilarious which is why we got on. Always up for a laugh and willing to do anyone a favour. When punk band The Blood required blow-up sex dolls for their stage-act Si supplied them free of charge. They filled them with tomato sauce, butchers' offal and God knows what else before chopping them up with a chainsaw. I can't understand why they were never asked to appear on The Jonathan Ross Show or Top of The Pops.

Simon is now a multi-millionaire with sex shops all over England.

Talking of Si reminds me of Dannielle Lux, another interesting character, who was also Jewish, but unlike Si she was very posh. Back in the day she was a mutual friend. We met at a gig and got talking. She was a very pretty girl but only 16 or 17, so it was strictly plutonic. Although I looked Eighteen, I was about 21 at the time.

A nice girl with a feather cut hairstyle from Golders Green and a big fan of punk rock and Skinhead/Mod fashion. Like Simon she was North London Jewish with a quick wit and a way with words. She was highly educated and in a nice way very posh, but we hung out and attended a lot of gigs together, they do say opposites attract. We travelled across London together on the tube watching punk bands and drinking in East End pubs and West End clubs. Danielle loved my punk poems and Cockney sense of humour, and I was attracted to her personality and intelligence. I never understood how we met or why we gelled, but we did. She went onto become a C4 Executive and the last I heard she was high up at the BBC.

Simon and Danielle were great people to hang about with because I've always been attracted to characters. The Bridge House pulled in youngsters from all walks of life and from every part of London. The clientele included future rock stars, boxers, actors, poets, football hooligans, villains, and various exciting but dangerous `Jack the Lad`s`. Such as `The Glory Boys` a notorious Dagenham Mod gang led by future bouncer Jamie o`Keefe. As well as being a self-protection expert Jamie was also a singer with the band `Untamed Youth`, like me Jamie was also verbally slaughtered by Sounds journo Garry Bushell. He recalls: "I took a demo to Terry Murphy and pestered Garry Bushell to listen to a few songs, but he was not impressed". He said: "Jamie, you`re a decent writer and a good fighter, but a rubbish vocalist".

So Gal Bushell destroyed two singing careers, but with hindsight maybe he was right and just being honest. I swapped Punk Rock for showbiz and worked for all the big beasts of Fleet Street.

It was Pat Stead, head of Press at Epic Records and wife of my mate Bruce Foxton who tipped me off about a vacancy at The Sun. She was a lovely lady, beautiful on the inside and out, the spitting image of Erika Hoffman, who at the time played Jacko`s girlfriend in the BBC comedy Brush Strokes.

The Bizarre pop column was on the lookout for a young gun with his finger on the pulse. I'd freelanced at The Sun, News of The World, Sunday People, Mirror, Mail, Evening Standard and Daily Star, but this was my big break but turned it down and recommended my best mate Garry Bushell. He got the job and became Showbiz and TV Editor at The Sun because unlike me he was a top of the range kosher journo.

My first big break got me my job at Sounds music magazine, but I wasn't going to push my luck and grab what on the surface looked like the offer of a second big break. I knew my limits and my ability to blag, pretty easy doing it as a freelance but pulling it off 8 hours a day and five days a week in an office environment is a different ball game. As luck would have it I ended up with the best of both worlds. I was put on a retainer which meant I could come and go as I pleased. I now had a VIP ticket into the world of showbiz and could hang-out with the rich and famous without any worries. I'd landed on my feet, it was like I'd died and gone to heaven.

My entry into the wonderful world of showbiz was a scam Arthur Daley would have been proud of. I was never going to be the hottest gunslinger in town up there with Tony Parsons, Julie Burchill and Danny Baker. I 'd was never in the same league as Piers Morgan or Ally Ross but enjoyed the ride.

I wasn't University standard when it came to spelling and the only grammar I knew was the School at the end of my street. Luckily, I had enough ammunition and a massive imagination to fulfil my journalistic ambition. A vast collection of old magazines, copies of NME, Sounds, Melody Maker, Record Mirror and Smash Hits. I re-wrote old articles, changing names and no-one ever suspected foul play. When it came to smoke and mirrors, I was right up there with David Blaine and Penn and Teller. I was no Clive James or Paul Morley but it has to be said I do deserve a tiny place in the history of British journalism. A teenage boy with no qualifications became a showbiz journalist. I conned Sounds Editor Eric Fuller, and Front boss Piers Hernu to give me a job so Fleet Street Editors assumed I was a kosher journo and who was I to argue? I did the job and always delivered the story because you don't need a degree or qualifications to watch a stage performance or chat to someone in a bar.

I never lied to anyone as there was no need. I was never asked any difficult questions as people just assumed I was what it said on my NUJ card. The evening I got my NUJ card was one of the proudest days of my life. The longer it went on the easier it was to impersonate. I ended up a better impressionist than Rory Bremner. I got away with it for so long because 95% of the time, I only wrote nice things about people. In the early days I wrote a nasty review of singer Becky Bondage saying, "Last night she reminded me of Marilyn Monroe...if you were to dig her up tomorrow". Her furious mum phoned up the office and complained. I learnt my lesson. What celebrity is going to complain about a reader friendly story, a positive interview or five-star review?

The likes of David Bowie, Michael Jackson, Rod Stewart, Sade, The Stone Roses and George Michael certainly didn't complain. The truth is various journalists for hundreds of years have made-up quotes or written biased reviews. Celebs don't complain as long as you say their latest record or film is the best thing since slice bread. To quote music writer Dominic Warwick from 2018 "Garry Johnson was a modern-day Charles Dickens for the Punk Generation". I never complained but would of been tempted if he'd compared me to William Shakespeare. Genuinely don't get all the fuss about The Bard, Opera or Ballet but always been a fan of Charles Dickens.

I found myself starring in my own reality soap opera which was much more fun than the depressive episodes of Eastenders. I wrote the plots and gave myself the best lines. I was starring in a fantasy, not participating in a fraud. I was a spin doctor before Peter Mandelson and war criminal Alistair Campbell made PR a dirty word. I never `sexed-up` dossiers which would lead to millions of innocent people dying in faraway lands. It wasn't always a fraudulent enterprise. I genuinely did discover The Stone Roses and set them on the road to world stardom. As with The Beatles they were turned down by every record label in London. One afternoon we were all sitting in the reception at Arista Records when in walked 70's heart-throb David Cassidy.

The former number one pin-up and biggest pop star in the world was making a comeback on the hottest day of the year. But for some reason he was wearing a massive overcoat that looked like it belonged to Meatloaf or Elvis Presley.

If only we all had mobile phones back in the 80's. Cassidy was on the verge of a comeback and The Stone Roses of making it. We all sat there staring at him and trying not to laugh. The new guard was looking down on the old regime.

The exciting future of rock and roll were about to replace the former teenybop idol from the past. I thought the 70's heartthrob was barking mad as he was also wearing a woolly hat with his massive overcoat on the hottest day of the year.

When I asked him why, he replied "I don't want to be mobbed". This encounter occurred in 1985 and pretty sure David Cassidy was last mobbed in 1975. That night it was another showbiz party where all the guests apart from The Stone Roses were rich and famous. The place was packed wall to wall with A-List celebrities. This included a couple of Rolling Stones, Duran Duran, Bananarama, Boy George, Spandau Ballet, Nik Kershaw, Paul Young, John Entwhistle of The Who, Wayne Sleep, various Eastenders, a bevy of Page 3 girls, Status Quo, Captain Sensible, The Cult, Gary Glitter (before he'd been exposed as a nonce), and David Cassidy minus his woolly hat and over-sized overcoat. Standing at the bar was Coronation Street star Chris Quentin and night club legend Peter Stringfellow with a scantily clad model on each arm. Ian Brown kept saying to me "I feel like an imposter", but not enough to leave, as every time The Roses came down to London, we'd go to another party.

For Pete Garner the highlight of the evening was meeting Captain Sensible because he'd always been a fan of The Damned. As the night wore on Ian Brown was loving the vibe and moving about like a rock star, the drugs had kicked-in and was swaggering about doing the 'walk' that a few years later Liam Gallagher would turn into a art form. Over the years there have been many claimants from people claiming to be the first person to 'discover' The Stone Roses. Well that 'soldier was me'. I discovered them and spent a year living the dream. John Robb their official biographer in his brilliant book published by Ebury Press quotes Ian Brown naming me as the man who discovered The Stone Roses.

I am mentioned many times and pictured with the band on page 253. I was also the first person in 1985 to predict superstardom. As unofficial manager (no contract was signed) I was on a one-man campaign to promote and bag them a record deal. I dragged every A and R man in London down to their gigs and dropped their name in all the right places. I got Rough Trade Records to see them at The Fulham Greyhound. Arista

Records at The Marquee and Epic, RCA, EMI and CBS at Dingwalls in Camden Town.

But not one so-called talent spotter saw what I saw. It was a sex divide that once again proved women are the smarter sex. The female press Officers loved them but not the blokes in the A andR department. Jump forward 18 months and every record label in London wanted to sign them Ian Brown has since told everyone "Garry Johnson was the first journo to big us up". The charismatic front-man had singled me out as the journalist most likely to get behind the band and he was spot on. Ian had read a lot of my features and reviews in Sounds and knew we had a lot in common. We were both ex-skinheads, who liked the spirit of punk and the look of Mod. Ian was also a former scooter boy and a football and boxing fan. Contacting me was an inspired move by Ian that without doubt changed the future of rock and roll. Let me explain. If it hadn't been for me putting The Stone Roses in the spotlight and Ian becoming the voice and look of a generation where would Liam Gallagher have got his haircut, walk and attitude? Liam Gallagher always admits he`s part Johnny Rotten and part Ian Brown.

After I joined Sounds Ian became a fan of my writing. He posted me a cassette of his demo tracks. If only I`d kept the letter and the tape. (God how I wish I`d kept it, would be worth a bloody fortune) The tape was brilliant, and I got it immediately. In the letter Ian invited me up to Manchester. The cassette cover had artwork by John Squire, if only I`d kept it as that really would be worth a fortune, sadly somehow I lost it.

I was so impressed I rung Ian that night and arranged a meet. Within 48 hours, my partner in crime and ace snapper Tony Mottram were on a train up to Manchester. We were met on the platform by Ian and the others, and we all spent the weekend hanging out in Manchester. Stone Roses guitarist Pete Garner confirmed this in an interview with Blitz magazine saying: "Garry rung us up because Ian had sent him one of our demo tapes. We all read Sounds and Ian knew he was the one writer who could be into us. He came up to interview us on November 30$^{th}$, and we met him off the train".

The fact is without the influence of The Stone Roses, Oasis would not have been the band that the world fell in love with. I was always a showbiz junkie and that`s why I quit Sounds (before I was sacked) and moved onto Fleet Street. Towards the end of my music magazine days, I was getting lazy and going to more parties than gigs. I was even attending mid-day bashes at places like Kettners in Soho and the Playboy Club in Mayfair, because it meant free booze, better drugs and naughty girls. Most modern women have the same morals as men and really do practise sexual equality in all it`s forms.

A few parties stand-out. A lunchtime meeting of the Elvis Presley Fan Club Convention at The Hippodrome night club double-up as a press launch for the Gary Glitter comeback single. The granddad of Glam Rock (this was years before the pop pervert was exposed and jailed as a vile child abuser and nonce) was promoting another crappy record 'Dance Me Up'. I'm currently appearing in a ITV documentary (May 2024) slagging off the convicted paedophile. What attracted me to this event was not his music, new toupee or re-holstered chest wig it was the scantily clad page 3 girls on his arm. As luck would have it I found myself sitting at a table with Glitter and veteran Carry On star Irene Handel. The pictures feature in the ITV documentary. For the avoidance of doubt this was ten years before he was exposed as a paedophile.

Irene Handel was lovely, a bit eccentric with a bit of the Joe Biden about her, though she could still walk and talk at the same time. She had worked with all the greats of British comedy from Sid James to Tony Hancock. Also present was a beautiful young girl soon to be a TV star, who years later would marry a millionaire pop star. On my life I pulled her, we left by taxi and went to a flat in Victoria. She was stunning with a posh accent and natural beauty. I followed her career, and she aged like a fine wine.

Out of respect I won't name her as she recently died but it was the best of brief encounters. If anyone has doubts I'll willingly take a Lie Detector Test. We never met again but always had pleasurable flashbacks whenever I saw her on TV. I did reveal years later how my old mate Jamie o'Keefe met Gary Glitter and set fire to his wig. But that's another story. I just thought of another funny incident involving West End bouncers.

London's Burning star Glen Murphy had a party at Soho's Wag Club to celebrate the premiere of his gangland movie Tank Mailing. It was a low budget English crime thriller but not as good as Dave Courtney's Hell To Pay. His famous friends, including Eastenders Nick Berry, Steve McFadden, Karl Howman of Brush Strokes, Barbara Windsor and former World Champion boxer Terry Marsh when bouncers turned them away from the private party and told them to "fuck off".

Glen was disgusted when his mates told him that the bouncers had snatched their invites and handed them to a bunch of Hooray Henrys. There was a much better party the following week at Faces in East London, just for family and friends. The guest list included the cast of London's Burning, the A-list actors from Eastenders, West Ham footballers, Page 3 girls and some heavy-duty Underworld aces, and not a Tory Toff within twenty miles of the place.

Another great night in the East End of London took place at The Phoenix Apollo in Stratford. I organised the launch party for ZIT magazine, a Southern version of Geordielands VIZ magazine. I'd blagged a job as its TV pundit and showbiz columnist. The place was full of Eastenders stars, West Ham footballers, boxers, page 3 girls and old mates like Hughie Gadson who's now the Manager of Madness. I loved attending these showbiz events as a tabloid terrorist and mixing with the rich and famous.

Not once in my entire 'career' did I regret posing as a showbiz journalist, it was better than working for a living. The truth is I never felt guilty about lifting reviews or re-writing old articles from my music magazine collection. I wasn't hurting anyone, just earning a living. It was 'happy days' as I blatantly changed the names of bands, songs titles and venues. It would take a few years before I felt confident enough to be 'me' and provide original copy to the Editor at Sounds.

Tony Mottram was my regular sidekick at Sounds and now regarded as one of the great rock and roll photographers of his generation. I'll be forever in his debt because he took the first Stone Roses pictures and photographed Sade sitting on my lap. He looked like Queen drummer Roger Taylor, so I'd wind him up by asking everyone from Ian Brown to Noddy Holder to ask him questions about Freddie Mercury.

After a while (many months) he was not amused and it would drive him nuts, so of course I did it even more. Mott was my 'loveable sidekick' and together we travelled the world (well the UK and Eire).

He was the Liam Gallagher of snappers who liked a 'free drink' and shared my fondness for fast drugs and loose women. The stories I could tell you about Mott, his camera and groupies, if he did today what he did back then he'd probably be locked-up. So would I after what happened at The Holiday Inn in Birmingham, but as they say "what happens on tour stays on tour". Another ace snapper I worked with was Steve Payne who had a very interesting sideline. His Sunday afternoons were spent in a Wapping studio taking test shots of amateur models wanting to become Page 3 girls. They came from all over England, and I volunteered to be his unpaid assistant, never earned a penny, but there were other benefits if you get my drift.

Most were nice girls and very friendly and nothing like the prejudiced image of topless models. Very few were thick or brassy bimbos. They were often quite sweet and, off camera even shy. Steve and I gave one girl a lift back to Euston Station and I was convinced she'd be the next Suzanne Mitzi (probably the best page 3 girl of all-time).

At the end of the session, I'd sometimes take one of the girls for a drink, and, as is my character, always behaved like a perfect English gent. I always was on my best behaviour around women and still am. Although I've always been attracted to the female of the species I've always treated them with respect. I always looked up and never down on women. If I wasn't a bloke, I could happily be a powerful and independent woman. That's why I was always friends with Press Office girls and got on with female journalists. The biggest influences on my career were all women. My mentor Rebekah, Erica and Nike

One of them the nicest, smartest, kindest and most educated person I've ever met my life. At one shoot I connected with a lovely girl from Birmingham, funny accent but nice hair. After a drink in The Prospect of Whitby where years later my stag night would kick-off before ending in a blur at Stringfellows, we went straight to the 5-star Tower Hotel next to London Bridge and to quote Frankie Valli and the Four Seasons "Oh what a night".

You've got to remember that back then I didn't look like I do now. I was ultra slim with long blonde hair. To quote Arista Records Press Officer Patsy Johnson I was "A bit of a tart". I wasn't showing off or being flash because it didn't cost me a penny. I was friends with a top PR and part of her job was to book hotels for important clients visiting London. When they didn't need them for extra-marital affairs or whatever they got up to she'd give me the room which was already paid for.

I often stayed there with her friend who shared my love of freebies and cocaine. She was a middle-class girl from Kent who spoke nice and looked like a young Carol Vorderman in her Countdown days.

I enjoyed being her bit of rough. I mean what young working-class bloke wouldn't enjoy it? I always took advantage of everything I was offered because I knew you don't stay young, free and single forever. I wasn't a typical man of the people and maybe I'm a bit of a hypocrite but don't apologise for enjoying the finer things in life. I always wanted the best food, drink, women, drugs, clothes. Isn't that why people do the Lottery? I am at heart a working-class bloke with middle-class manners, politeness doesn't cost a penny. Like Reggie Kray I never swear in front of women and children. One of the best qualities I inherited from my mum was 'good manners' and from my dad, for all his faults was never verbally disrespectful to women or hit children. How did he square that with walking out on my mum and me?

He was against corporal punishment, never hit me in his life but was happy to hurt me emotionally. I never disciplined my own children, I'm proud to say I don't even think I shouted at them growing up. As a teenager my dad gave me three bits of advice, all a bit hit and miss, and not traditional parenting. Never fall in love with a teenage crush, it's a waste of time because it doesn't last, put your mates first because they play football. Never talk to a fat girl in the street as I don't want you showing me up in front of my mates. Never give a girl your name and address.

My PR friend quit the wonderful and wacky world of showbiz and last I heard was working for a world-famous boxing promoter. Another night I stayed there with 28-year-old Lorraine from Dartford who looked like Susannah Hoffs from The Bangles. It didn't last more than a month because she was married and had dark hair. At the time I was more concerned about the colour of her locks than her husband.

Take it from me there are many perks and various treats in being in the world of showbiz. I can only imagine how great it must be for A-Listers. It must be like heaven on earth. Back in the day I honestly attracted a lot of female attention. I was two inches taller and three stone lighter. Now look at me the only thing I can pull is a muscle. I also had a 28-inch waist and well-pampered head of hair to go with my gift of the gab. I was a fast drugs and sex addict who didn't want to be cured. Believe me folks losing your looks doesn't compare with the magic of losing your virginity. There are no benefits to growing old and ugly and must be far worse for women.

I've witnessed many ex-stunners become totally invisible and get totally ignored by men who in the past would have been all over them like a rash. But that don't help me. I still see women through the eyes of a 25-year-old bloke, but they don't look back at me in the same way. Nowadays for me a younger woman is 45. It's a cruel world. But at least I've got treasured memories which I call my 'Golden years'. So many memories I could write a book. As with hanging out with Steve Payne at his page 3 auditions, another career highlight involved a number of stunning models.

I got another unpaid job, (no financial rewards, but many other perks) 'working' behind the scenes on Bushell On The Box, the number one show on the ITV Night Network, winning a audience share of 75%. A bevy of beauties appeared every week including Page 3 girls Joanne Guest, Angelique Houston, Christine Peake, Dee Ivens, Zoe Anderson, Fluer Madison and Theresa May (no, not that one).

It was a great show to be involved with and celebrity gangster Dave Courtney was in charge of security. We bonded over having mates in common, not least Steve Whale of The Business, who played guitar on my song 'Suburban Rebels'.

Over the next few years I kept bumping into 'Dodgy Dave' as he was fondly known at various showbiz bashes, launch parties, at Garry Bushell's house and legendary stag-do. It was held at Dave's pub and when one of the strippers recognised Gal Bushell she refused to perform. She was terrified of being pictured in The Sun and her husband finding out about her job. Dave spent ages convincing her it was a Private Function. While I was busy making coffee for page 3 girls and flirting with Zoe Anderson who was my favourite pin-up, Dave was providing security for Gal Bushell, his beard and star-studded guests.

In 2007 I was lucky enough, along with my sons, to visit Dave at his Camelot Castle home in Plumpsted. He is without doubt one of the funniest blokes I've ever met and would have been a great guest on the Jonathan Ross sofa.

Other famous faces who also appeared on the show included Carry On Legend Barbara Windsor, comics Jim Davidson, Bradley Walsh, Bobby Davro and Telly presenters Bob Monkhouse and Dale Winton. I'd meet Dale a few more times over the years and will never forget the day he rung me at home and had a funny conversation with my 9-year-old son.

I also got to meet legendary bare knuckle fighters Roy 'pretty boy' Shaw and Lenny McLean, who was promoting his comedy gangster movie 'Lock Stock and Two Smoking Barrels'. Actors Ray Winstone and Jamie Foreman also appeared on the show, as did presenter Lily Savage, Mad Frankie Fraser, Gladiator Rhino, comic Chubby Brown and Steve Harris of Iron Maiden. I also met model Antonia Moore, who became famous as the world's only black Marilyn Monroe impersonator.

She was a stunner who worked for Benny Hill as a 'Hill's Angel' and now a respected photographer. I bumped into her on my stag night in Stringfellows night club when she joked 'what about me, don't go through with it'. We last spoke in 2016 during a long 5-hour drive from Essex to Blackpool and broke the boredom with a string of funny stories during a 30-minute phone call.

I always got on well with models, very few were airheads or bimbos, and most were great company and a good laugh. I loved the way they oozed confidence.

Over the years I met a lot of attractive women and those who say men and women can't be just good friends are talking bollocks. Never forget that on a good day sex can last for 6 and a half minutes but friendship can last a lifetime.

May have mentioned this before and will probably mention it again but always wondered why all the women I put on a pedestal are the females I've never shagged. The famous one's like Sade, Debbie Harry, Kate Moss, Amanda Holden and Maura Higgins I can understand. As they all have millions of admirers.

I'm talking about 'plutonic relationships' that all had a massive impact on my life, the females I met from schooldays to the present that confuse me. It's the ones I've only kissed and cuddled and never shared a bed with that I've never stopped fancying or admiring. Are they more like sisters because we never had full-blown sexual intercourse? What would Sigmund Freud make of it? As a Toddler I was a captive audience for my Cockney Granddad who, just like Uncle Albert from Only Fools and Horses loved talking about the war. I enjoyed his stories and version of East End culture and working-class history. He was more entertaining than any schoolteacher. Before going to school, I liked education and enjoyed listening and learning because there were no distractions. Between being a toddler and starting work I'd been to more schools than an Ofsted inspector.

One Infant, Two Juniors and Four Senior Schools which means I can reveal `playground secrets` without revealing the identities of those involved. I can protect the guilty and the innocent from being named and shamed.

To be honest none of the posh middle-class teachers had a clue what was going on behind their backs. Outright naughtiness and genuine bad things went on behind the bike sheds and at the back of the out-buildings. Sometimes there would be consensual and non-consensual sex behind the wooden annexe building, the Sports Hall, in the Boys Changing Rooms and empty classrooms. More like Clockwork Orange than Grange Hill. Most of what went on is featured in graphic detail in my novel Serial Killer and is not suitable for a family friendly autobiography. Up until the age of Fifteen, I was into all the normal teenage boy stuff, things like Football, fashion, music, cinema and of course girls.

Apart from constantly skipping school and not passing any exams I swaggered through school without any problems. Blessed with good looks and football ability meant I was always popular. In or out of school I was always in minor bits of trouble, but always prided myself on being a loveable rogue rather than a bad boy. One of my old teachers said "you're a nightmare, but there's no malice in you". I was proud of that. The truth is if my dad hadn't of fucked off with his latest fancy woman I would of remained a cheeky chap and probably become a professional footballer. I was born to be a funny fella and prolific `fox in the box` goal-scorer not a f*****g full-blown teenage tearaway.

But thank to my selfish bastard of a dad and so-called stepmother (I never called her that, wouldn't give her that respect) I turned into a teenage tearaway. I became a method actor and my first part was playing a messed-up kid with chips on both shoulders. At fifteen I went off the rails and spent the next 15 years with my brain bitter, depressed and hating the world, but projected happiness, there was always a smile on my face. It never got the better of me. I would never succumb to depression as I despise `self-pity` and wouldn't give it time to `kick-in`. I can't cope with depression in others so certainly couldn't have it f*****g up my character. It has no place in my world. No-one knew because I hid it well and was always smiling. I self-medicated with every type of 'fast drug' and lived each day as if it was my last. I swore nobody would ever hurt me again so never fell in love. I had many moments but never allowed crushes to turn into romance.

I survived on a diet of 'fast drugs' and knowing when to walk away. Then something happened I wanted to be a dad. All my friends had kids and for the first time in my life I wanted one of my own. A few years earlier a girlfriend had an abortion and luckily for me I had no desire to father a child. I picked her up from the clinic but it took about 48 hours for the guilt to overwhelm me. She was older than me, it was her choice, her body but still felt a little guilty, maybe it was the Irish Catholic in me. I now wanted a bloody football team of kids.

It was a life-changing moment which would eventually lead to me giving up drugs overnight. There was no 'cold turkey' I just quit and it was easier than giving up three sugars in my cup of tea. The night my eldest son was born I just quit, I replaced 'Charlie' with my eldest son Sam. Although I'd had a passionate relationship with drugs I never dabbled with other so-called illegal substances and was always a moderate drinker. It was nothing to do with taste or morals, it was all about vanity, I could live on Guinness, but didn't want a beer gut or double chin.

I preferred starving myself if it meant attracting more women. To this day I have never smoked a cigarette or a joint in my life, some find that hard to believe and roll their eyes, but it's true. Aged 12 at the back of Stanford Park I once had 3 draws on a fag, turned green and threw up everywhere, and I never tried again.

It was one of the best things that ever happened to me because knowing my compulsive character I'd have ended up smoking 60 fags a day like David Bowie and dying of cancer. I like the smell of weed, (my Sam and Adam can vouch for that) and the aroma of freshly cut grass but as with dope I don't want to smoke it.

My only incurable addiction has been David Bowie. Fast Drugs I eventually gave up through personal choice but had no choice when it came to giving up skinny young blondes as they gave me up first. Father Time is a bastard.

In my day working-class kids had football, boxing or rock and roll to save 'em from the dole. I became a Punk Poet when John Muir of Babylon Books from Manchester published my anti-establishment book 'Boys of The Empire' which received rave reviews. That book really did change my life as first Garry Bushell in Sounds and then Time Out magazine gave it rave reviews. I was well happy that teenage punks liked it, but such was my working-class ethos couldn't get my head around `posh people` liking it.

I was still a Class Warrior and they were the enemy to me. I didn't appreciate rave reviews in trendy Time Out magazine or the champagne socialist Guardian. It was re-released in 2016 and received rave reviews in the communist Morning Star newspaper and various punk magazines. Although I looked like Johnny Rotten at the time I didn't have his brains to go with the attitude. My poems attacked the posh middle-class bastards who control our lives so why were they praising me? The world was a different place back then and I didn't know any posh people.

I thought the sons and daughters of well off bankers were all the same who lived with Mother and Father on country estates or in safe and leafy suburban neighbourhoods. At that time the only posh people I'd met had either been schoolteachers, solicitors, probation officers or social workers. Authority figures like police and prison officers. Bully boys and mindless thugs in uniforms who I hated and slaughtered in `Boys of The Empire`.

Why would they like me? I should have kept my mouth shut and soaked up the plaudits but was too honest for my own good (and egged on by Gal Bush) and in interviews slagged off the champagne socialists who'd praised me.

My argument with myself was, I knew by birth, background and DNA that I was genuine working-class and didn't appreciate posh people preaching to me about working-class culture. They had no idea about living on a council estate and had never lived on the top floor of a tower block (neither had I) but that's not the point, I knew plenty of people who had. All those people knew about poverty was learnt from reading books or going to Oxford University, whereas I'd been to a Detention Centre in Oxford. I came from a background of genuine rebellion where the police, politicians and posh people were considered the enemy. I thought I was writing about things and situations they knew nothing about.

I was the typical angry young man who shot from the hip, spoke without thinking and took no prisoners. Twenty years on, older and wiser I admit I got most of it wrong, not everything but how I said it. Back in the day I wasn't intelligent enough to explain myself to a wider audience. I still consider myself an expert on the working-class and far more knowledgeable than some trendy Notting Hill barrister or Hampstead lawyer. I was wrong about posh girls and upper-class women they make the best lovers. Sex as with most things in life is all about confidence and intelligent women are the best between the sheets. I've not abandoned my beliefs, I still dislike The Royal Family, want The House of Lords abolished and public schools like Eton shutdown. I'm left-wing in an old-fashioned traditional way but never been the tabloid definition of a Leftie.

I've never been a middle-class suburban rebel like arrogant ego maniac like Owen Jones and hate snobby Sir Keir Starmer with a passion. I admired genuine working-class hero and left-wing firebrand Derek Hatton. He was the `Arthur Daley of politics`. Today he's a millionaire but still anti-establishment with genuine working-class DNA. The best thing about the Labour Party was setting up the NHS but what sort people make human beings live in tower blocks like Grenfall Tower?

It was Labour politicians who knocked down the terraced houses and their friends who made fortunes putting up the skyscrapers. I refused to do any gigs for Red Wedge because it was fronted by posh kids from public schools and Oxbridge universities. I agreed with the message but not those delivering it. Paul Weller said the same years later, so as with many things I'm very often on the right side of history. The Mod-father admitted the Punk Movement and The Jam were used by Neil Kinnock and the Labour Party. The Welsh windbag is now Lord Kinnock swaggering around the House of Lords and claiming £350 a day. His son is also a Labour MP. Like all self-serving Labour politicians Kinnock was a fraud and never a man of the people. I was also disappointed when Noel Gallagher attended the Tony Blair party at Number 10, but like the rumour he snorted cocaine in the loo.

# Chapter Four
# Mad for It

Back to the glory days of the Bridge House where many who drank there went on to became household names like Ray Winstone, Carlton Leach and Cass Pennant. Many others formed bands, became actors or wrote books.

Frankie Flame my great mate from the Ferrier Estate, who read peoples palms at my wedding, went onto perform with The Stone Roses. Back in the 80's the Ferrier Estate was like Al Catraz without the rocks, a warzone, full of unfortunate people but Frankie was one of the good guys. For some reason the boys at the Bridge House and the ICF really took him to their hearts. To this day still not sure who invented the light-hearted chant of "Who's that pratt in the Granddad hat?". I think it was me, but both Gal Bushell and Cockney Reject guitarist Micky Geggus have claimed credit.

Frankie was like a Dickensian character and close pal for many years. He was a man of many talents. Singer, artist, football hooligan, psychic and fortune teller which is why he read people's palms at my wedding. He could see the future and told my Aunt she was going to die and thirty years later she did. This guy was better than Mystic Meg. Frankie was a hard bloke but I'll never forget the day he broke down in tears. I was there when an OAP Gypsy Rose Lee floored him.

The life-changing encounter took place in stockbroker belt Surrey. Our crowd always attended the Derby when the world-famous horse race was held on a Wednesday. We'd meet up at Blackheath in George's cafe for breakfast, then straight into the Newbridge Working Men's Club for a livener in the bar, then snort some marching powder in the Gents. We'd then all climb aboard the coach where Frankie would lead the singing all the way to Epsom. We'd arrive around 10.30 which was a good 4 hours before the race.

The place to visit was the Fairground and all its attractions. Being one himself Frankie decided to visit a clairvoyant. She really touched a nerve as he emerged from her tent in tears. She'd told him he had a daughter he'd never seen or known about. We all laughed and took the piss but it turned out she was telling the truth. They were reunited within a year and their story had a happy ending when she made Frankie a Granddad.

Frankie really hit the beer after his encounter with the Crystal Ball and on the pub crawl home was banned from one of our favourite boozers. He crashed out in the Ladies loo of a posh village pub and scared the locals.

The Derby was a great British tradition where half a million Londoners would invade the Epsom Downs. One year I pulled some tipsy office girl who'd left her work colleagues looking for fun. There were hundreds of coaches, buses and cars parked on the Downs but luckily for me she came my way. We got talking and were seen by everyone disappearing onto our double-decker bus. We emerged ten minutes later to a chorus of cheers and jeers. I was mocked for the rest of the day and called "30-second Gal". I found it funny because I knew the truth and it was more like 90 seconds. I also got a result on the track by backing the winner in the big race. I think from memory it was ridden by Lester Piggot and called Teenisso. Frankie went onto become a cult figure all over Europe, recorded a duet with me and shared a stage with The Stone Roses. No, not Wembley Arena, The O2 or Hollywood Bowl.

The historic performance took place at The Cockney Pride boozer in Leicester Square. It was a great night because at the time Frankie had a residency in the West End pub. The drinks flowed (as did the speed) and Ian Brown, Reni and myself joined Frankie on stage for a rowdy version of Ian Dury's "Sex and Drugs and Rock and Roll". Frankie Flame was so impressed by The Roses he wanted to produce them as did Bruce Foxton of The Jam. Both had heard The Stone Roses demo tape and wanted to be involved, like me they knew they were special.

I'll tell you later how Hughie Gadson, one of my best mates, declined my request (plea) to sign them. His reason was bizarre saying: "I've just signed a band called Ring of Roses' and can't sign another band called the Roses". Just imagine if Hughie had signed them, and Frankie produced, Oasis and Brit Pop might never have happened. So scary it's not worth thinking about. How depressing is that thought?

Back to the Bridge House in Canning Town which launched more people to success than any other East End pub. In the early days it was such an exciting place to be, full of mad, hectic teenagers. It was a lively mix of characters and a great place to hang out. Owner Terry Murphy, father of London's Burning star Glen and musician Darren of Mod/Punk band Wasted Youth also ran a record label which helped local bands. He had the knack of spotting new talent which is why he declined my offer to sign The Buzz Kids, as like Gal Bushell he wasn't impressed. Other regulars included Grant Flemming who became an award-winning photographer and documentary filmmaker. Andy Swallow bought Grays Athletic football Club, then formed a dance record label and became a successful mover and shaker in the Rave Scene. Several of his acts went onto sell millions of records. He now owns a successful radio station with millions of listeners. Terry Hayes, a founding member of the Jolly Prankers, is now a top club DJ and performing with his band East End Badoes.  Lol Prior managed The Business who recorded my song `Suburban Rebels` and set up Moon Ska Records and managed SKA band Bad Manners who sold millions of records. Mod DJ Eddie Pillar and Cockney comic Mickey Pugh both went on to long careers and better things. Mickey played a hitman in the Dave Courtney gangster film `Hell To Pay` which stopped him getting a part in Eastenders.

I can`t stand liars and a lot of lies are told about 1980 and the second coming of Punk. I know the truth because I was there. I`d like to dispel the myth that the NME was the punk paper, the truth is at first they hated it. Sounds covered the scene first. The NME had the best writers in Tony Parsons, Julie Burchill and Danny Baker but Sounds fought back with Garry Bushell,, Jerry Harris and some bloke called Gal Johnson. The office was next door to the best pub in Covent Garden. Everyone from Sex Pistols Steve Jones and Paul Cook, Bono, Paul Weller, Bruce Foxton, Iron Maiden, Chrissie Hynde, Jimmy Pursey, Def Leppard, Ozzy Osbourne and Heavy Metal Heather hung out and drunk in The White Lion. Heather was a great character. She was not a professional groupie, more an enthusiastic amateur. She claimed once she had worn out her fanny from over-use and got more feeling and enjoyment from anal sex, it was a long time ago, but you don't forget when such an innocent looking girl tells you something like that, although sadly, I never put her to the test. The last time I saw her was at a recording of Telly Addicts. She freaked me out during the day in my hotel room, when she revealed she has séances and had managed to conjure up the spirit of Adolf Hitler on an Ouija Board.

As with Garry Bushell, the first time I met Frank Marshall (Frankie Flame) I knew I'd made a friend for life. He was a crazy combination of Ian Dury, Chas and Dave and Russell Grant. Frankie was a one-off with a heart of gold and a brain full of madness. A football hooligan, a white witch and a druid who once played the piano for Woody Woodmansey`s U-Boat.

Another Bowie connection, as Woody was the drummer in The Spiders from Mars. He`s not the best musician in the world but was, and still is, the number one Punk astrologer. Frankie would read palms, Tarot Cards and the Runes. But wasn't a paid up member of the Magic Circle. We had a scam. He would ask me to find out people`s birth signs and feed him their background information before they had what they thought was a `cold reading`. The girls at the record companies loved him, but the scam had to stop when Frankie lost the plot. He didn't just go off script, he re-wrote it. He started ad-libbing like an out-of-control actor in a Mike Leigh play. Frankie's party piece changed dramatically as he stopped behaving like a loveable daytime TV psychic and transformed into a late-night horror act.

He started telling people "I'm not Mystic Meg and always say what I really see". Adding "if I see bad news or even death I'll tell you". He told one girl "You only have months to live" and was banned from the office. I lost count of how many girls were impressed by his 'readings', but the 'death' prediction went too far, word went round, and he was barred from every Record Company in London.

Another classic performance from my Wedding Day, no, not the goings-on in the Honeymoon suite, I'm talking about the reception where Frank mistook my future mother-in-law for an 80-year-old OAP, straight-faced and deadly serious he said: "your granddaughter looks beautiful today". It was a genuine case of mistaken identity, but the 'Mrs Brown lookalike' was not amused. He also reduced my aunt to tears after revealing she was going to die. Thirty years later she did, so in a way Frankie was telling the truth.

I also formed a long-standing friendship with Pat Stead and boyfriend Bruce Foxton, The Jam guitarist and her future husband. I was a massive fan of The Jam from day one, in those days (1977) you could see them for a fiver. I first saw them on the same bill as The Buzzcocks and The Clash. What a night. Weller was always his own man. He outraged hard-line punks by ripping up a copy of Sniffin Glue fanzine on stage. I saw them throughout 1978-81 and they kept on getting better and better. I loved The Jam and Bruce Foxton as a bloke and ended up staying at his massive house in Bramley, Surrey. A lovely fella who liked a beer and Colombian marching powder. As a boozer he was right up there with George Best, and Ozzy Osbourne.

I first met Pat in The White Lion when she started out at Epic Records and remained friends as she rose through the ranks to become Head Of Press and Michael Jackson's mouthpiece in the UK. She also looked after pop superstar George Michael who I met at her Birthday Party. My ex-wife idolised the former Wham singer so I asked George for a favour. He was a lovely bloke and wrote a signed message for my wife, not just a scribbled autograph but a genuine message. He was a multi-millionaire but hadn't forgotten his roots. Pat and I both had our picture taken with him and George couldn't have been friendlier. When I got home I placed the note next to her pillow. Julie was gutted she missed out on meeting him but treasured her memento which as far as I know she still possesses.

I attended Pat's wedding to Bruce and both were present at mine. The stag night was a riot' and Bruce ended up with a right shiner. He painted the town red and ended up concussed. He came up with a great line at the reception held in the sleepy Essex village of Ingatestone saying: "There's more people here than I get at my gigs". A funny reference to his faltering solo career not going to plan, after he left The Jam we became good friends and although he had a few hits, never became a major star like Paul Weller. Sadly Pat died of cancer in 2007.

My last two great nights out with Bruce were a Soho pub crawl and a drug binge that ended at The Video Cafe. We were birds of a feather and the last two standing at his wild Birthday Party held in stockbroker belt Surrey. When I started at Sounds I was bottom of the Food Chain and at first given mostly unknown bands to review and interview. I soon got bored with that and used my treasured NUJ card to gain access to all the top West End venues and night clubs.

It's much more fun meeting the likes of David Bowie, Sade, Whitney Houston, Ozzy Osbourne, Bob Geldoff and famous faces from the world of TV then hanging out in grotty clubs. It was only a matter of time before I fancied a crack at Fleet Street. I'd already supplied stories to national newspapers but got my big break thanks to Pat Stead. She told me of a vacancy on the Bizarre pop column at The Sun and said I should go for it. This would be like a Semi-professional footballer signing for West Ham United. And the rest as they say is history. I bottled it at the last minute and told best mate Garry Bushell to go for it.

He jumped at the opportunity and went onto become their number one writer. It was 1985 when I decided to remain freelance but would a few years later accept the offer of a retainer. For the next 25 years I hung out with rock stars, pop singers, soap actors, footballers, football hooligans, page 3 girls, gangsters, strippers, blue comics and family entertainers. From East End Pubs to West End clubs, I ducked and dived and had a bloody good time.

This is the story about my roller-coaster ride to Z-List stardom. I didn't get to play for West Ham or have a hit video on MTV but so what? I met some great people on the journey and had lots of laughs along the way. I haven't got millions in the bank but do have memories no amount of money can buy. Would I change anything? Yes.

I'd like to have been good at something, had sex with Kate Moss and won the Lottery. But without a few losers in life there wouldn't be any winners. The sad truth is we can't all be David Bowie or George Best. I'm living proof of that statement, but such is my character I've still not ruled out having my five minutes fame completely. This ain't no ordinary autobiography. It isn't really an autobiography.

There isn't a beginning, middle, and an end. It's more like a stream of consciousness, an extended poem, a series of scattergun memories spray-painted on a wall like a Banksy painting. A story which starts on the wrong side of town, with many twists and turns in the middle which against all the odds somehow ends in a happy place. So here goes. The early days at Sounds were like a non-stop party but as my fondness of fast drugs grew, I moved away from attending Punk gigs and hanging out at swish showbiz parties. And I liked it, I liked it a lot.

At first combining Punk ethics with a hedonistic lifestyle was confusing and played tricks with my mind, but not my morals. I enjoyed the 'anything goes' lifestyle which meant long hours but going to 'work' wasn't really a job, more of a hobby and a real pleasure.

I saw different bands, better-looking girls and went to classier night clubs night after night. The more I got into writing about mainstream showbiz the more I liked what it had to offer. I remember seeing David Bowie, Rod Stewart, George Michael, Paul Young, Tears For Fears, Boy George, Michael Jackson, Nik Kershaw, Frankie Goes To Hollywood and even Shakin Stevens. So, like all great writers I suffered for my art. Shaky, the Welsh Elvis was a nightmare to interview. The former West End performer was more wooden than the green door he sung about. He was plastic pop. Nothing more than a two-bob Elvis impersonator but was so big-headed truly believed he was the King of Rock and Roll. As you can imagine I gave him a terrible review, to this day, still one of my best hatchet jobs.

But going mainstream had massive advantages as I got to meet and interview superstars like Sade. As with meeting David Bowie I was in awe and Sounds snapper Tony Mottram and my partner in crime on many escapades took the picture of her sitting on my lap. Sade wasn't blonde but believe me it was on my part love at first sight, she was stunning. She had inner and outer beauty, personality and charisma. She had the voice of an angel and the looks of a supermodel. Sade was pure class and I gave her a five star review comparing her to legends like Diana Ross and Billie Holiday. We got on really well, unfortunately in a plutonic way, but she invited me for drinks and after show party when she performed at The Royal Festival Hall.

I still believe her debut album Diamond Life is a modern-day classic. She was classier, more talented and sexier than Adele, Amy Winehouse and Whitney Houston but doesn't get the credit she deserves. I remember one magic moment more than most from my childhood. It was the summer of 1966 watching England (and West Ham) on TV winning the World Cup. That afternoon I felt closer to my dad than ever before. A memory that rates alongside singing 'Football's Coming Home' with my

2 sons in 1998. It's still hard to believe that just five years later the selfish bastard would walk out of my life.

In that time, he'd transformed me from an average footballer into the star player in my school team and Sunday football side. I was also banging in goals for my District Team. I had trials for West Ham, QPR, Leyton Orient and Southend United. I'd been asked to train with Ipswich Town but then it all ended. My dream was over. My dad walking out took the edge off my game. I couldn't concentrate and never recovered. I was traumatised even before I knew what the word meant.

I also never forgave him. I spent the next 15 years self-medicating with fast drugs to cope with my loss. I don't do depression or self-pity so made sure that on the surface I was always up and happy. People who met me would think I never had a care in the world. That's the way I liked it and amphetamine and cocaine gave me the ability to survive and deceive. Girls were my first drug of choice, but it was 'fast drugs' that saved my life and stopped depression becoming part of my life.

Back in 1972 a whole generation saw David Bowie on Top of The Pops and immediately knew their lives changed forever.

Some of those millions watching included Boy George, Gary Kemp, Jarvis Cocker, Morrissey, Steve Strange and Holly Johnson who would all go onto become the pop stars of tomorrow. Also glued to the screen and mesmerised by Ziggy Stardust was a teenage tearaway wearing Mod clothes and sporting a Suedehead haircut. Like those future pop stars my life would never be the same again.

This is the true story of a wannabe working-class hero, the only man in England who one day would take on the combined corrupt forces of the police, Social Services and Family Courts. I don't care who you are or how much power you have you don't talk down to kids or this Cockney Rebel. I don't respect bully boys in suits or social workers in sandals. I was up against a fascist British establishment, posh biased judges and a corrupt CPS run by champagne socialist Sir Keir Starmer. The state declared war on a working-class Irish Cockney rebel and it was a conflict I dare not lose.

Defeat was not an option I had to win at all costs, even if it killed me, which it almost did. I had to stop history repeating itself. My dad destroyed my childhood by walking out on his family. Every kid wants and deserves mum and dad and the fallout of his selfish act affected the rest of my life

Almost overnight I went from being a nice little kid, cheekier than naughty into a full-blown teenage tearaway. From the day my dad walked out I found it hard to love or trust as I feared being hurt. I believed those you love will always let you down. I was emotionally scarred by losing my dad which is why as a teenager I went 'with' but never 'out with' plenty of girls. I was scared of being hurt and wouldn't risk being hurt again. I'm lucky that my dad was a bloke, so never took my anger out on women. Never had a 'problem' with the females of the species. The only woman I hated was his f*****g wife.

Social workers were nothing new to me as I'd experienced all their lies and dirty tricks as a kid. They do more harm to kids with their emotional abuse then a prison full of evil child abusers and vile perverts. So I was ready for a fight.

In court it's both a personality and beauty contest and has nothing to do with the truth, facts or justice. If you look pretty, have a posh accent or excel as a liar then your odds on favourite to win in a British Court. There is no such thing as fair play or justice anywhere in the United Kingdom. If you don't believe me I give you the Royal Mail scandal, NHS cover-ups, Lockdown and Grenfall Tower Inquiry plus the innocent people found guilty in UK courts every day of the week. The establishment have unlimited access to money and use every trick in the book to stitch you up, destroy and convict you.

If you're a working-class bloke with a Cockney accent there is no such thing as a fair trial. The corrupt champagne socialists have a licence to lie, abuse, intimidate, bully, to shut you up, and then lock you up. They tried to silence me. They tried to intimidate me. They tried to destroy me for telling the truth. On one occasion the mask slipped, and they admitted they wanted to kill me. I was told to my face by a frustrated social worker, who we'll call Peter Brown,

"Mr Johnson if you were dead all our problems would be solved."

They didn't run me over with a police car, burn down my house or hire a hitman but they tried to kill me. I was arrested six times, had 5 heart attacks and twice sent to prison. I ended up on a life support machine and spent 29 days in a coma. Every time they knocked me down I got straight back up again. As my barrister said in court "Mr Johnson has fought them with every fibre of his being".

I went to the High Court and Lord Justice Munby ruled in my favour.

When the posh public-school barrister for Essex Social Services stood up to object he was told by the Judge:

"Whatever you say I, will not change my mind".

Adding:

"There are no longer any restrictions on Mr Johnson".

He also ruled that I had to be handed every single document from 2005 to 2010. This included internal reports. The cat was out of the bag which is why I went onto win.

After 5 years of being bullied and called "Mr Johnson" now they all wanted to call me "Garry".

At Southend County Court Judge Moloney ordered Essex Social Services to handover all their private documents. After years of secret corrupt kangaroo court Hearings behind closed doors at Chelmsford Family Court Judge Roderick Newton was forced by the highest court in the land to rule I could legally tell my story. My statement to the court was a combination of Arthur Daley meets Sir Winston Churchill. It was a classic use of the English language which flowed like a Boris Johnson speech.

So theatrical it could have been written by Oscar Wilde. On the day in question the spoken word really was far mightier than the sword. My impassioned speech spoke louder than 100,000 rowdy English football fans singing the national anthem at Wembley Football Stadium. I suggested in my elegantly crafted statement "Writing my autobiography without mentioning every detail of my life would be like Sir Geoff Hurst penning his memoirs and not mention his World Cup winning hat-trick".

Adding:

"How could Sir Paul McCartney write his and not mention The Beatles or David Bowie without mentioning Ziggy Stardust".

Judge Newton had no power to object as The High Court in London outranks a tiny court in Essex.

The truth is in football terms Lord Justice Munby was Manchester United and Judge Roderick Newton was AFC Wimbledon. Newton was a pigmy with a massive ego to go with his massive baldhead. He was fuming when he realised I'd have the last word, but there was nothing he could do about it. I could now legally write a hard-hitting, thought provoking 'kiss and tell' featuring everything from bedroom secrets to home-made movies. I could expose the dark dealings of Essex social services and the cover-ups of Basildon police. It had been a long-time coming but now I had the final piece of the jigsaw. I now possessed a smoking gun with more firepower than a KGB hit squad.

So this is it.

"The truth, the whole truth, and nothing but the truth so help me God".

I heard a top author on TV say, "Always write about what you know".

So here goes.

This is my story told in my trademark style. It doesn't start with A and end with Z.

It isn't a chronological account, as I want you to read about my adult adventures (good and bad) and then decide if my school days and teenage years were responsible for the life I led.

It begins in Working-class East London.

Most you will like, some you won't.

There are parts of my life some people will wish I'd forgotten or hadn't mentioned.

I know that and to some I apologise in advance.

But whatever I say and however it's explained or revealed the fact is the content of this book is 100% kosher. It's the gospel truth. I would pass the strictest of Lie Detector tests and all the controversial revelations are lifted straight from official documents (Police, Court and Essex Social Services).

If it's facts you're after, you'll find them here.

My memories are never dull or in black and white, they are always graphic Technicolor. I close my eyes and remember handshakes with David Bowie and gangster Charlie Kray. The first time I met the East End villain was in a West End nightclub; the second time was at The Hippodrome when he was managing various rock bands but was more Arthur Daley than Malcolm McClaren.

I'm convinced he bathed in expensive aftershave as he always smelled like the perfume counter in a posh department store. I found him charming and couldn't believe I was meeting a member of the legendary Kray gang. As always, I was outshined by best mate Garry Bushell who met both Reg and Ronnie Kray behind bars.

He visited the twins in various maximum-security prisons and Broadmoor high security hospital. Meeting Charlie Kray impressed my dad and all his mates more than me meeting Sade or David Bowie. Like most Eastenders my old man had a soft spot for The Twins as did most of the people I grew up with in East London and the Essex borders. Most believed they were political prisoners and kept behind bars far too long.

During their time in jail all governments (Labour and Tory) released child killers, rapists, paedophiles and terrorists. The Twins were persecuted because of their friendships with Lord Boothby and other politicians. What they knew about the corrupt elite terrified the establishment. Had they committed their crimes in the 90's or now they'd be released after 15 years.

The truth is, were they around today the streets of East London would be a far safer place. During their reign OAPs never got mugged and child abusers were punished without the need of a police investigation. There was a Robin Hood element to The Twins. They handed over thousands of pounds to local boxing clubs and community centres starved of cash. Without The Krays patronage those places would not have survived. I know it's not fashionable to say in today's woke PC world but the Kray Twins were political prisoners

I see myself drinking with 2 MPs on the terrace at The House of Commons, chatting up a Miss World contestant in The Video Cafe, next to The London Palladium. The Video Cafe was not a greasy spoon establishment, but an upmarket restaurant and wine bar frequented by the rich and famous.

I went along on the opening night and talked myself into the VIP bar full of pop singers, soap stars, footballers and models. The event was hosted by TV star Gaz Top and filmed by MTV. It's a long story which I'll return to later, but by the end of the night 'coked out of my head' and firing on all cylinders I'd blagged a 'sort of job' which came with a free bar tab. My 'brief' was to bring celebs along to the West End eaterie.

I not only impressed the owner but his stunning blonde girlfriend, about 25 years his junior and even though I looked quite good in the 80s I thought she was out of my league. 'Fast drugs' mess with your mind and sabotage you're antenna.

It was months before I found out this classy woman fancied me on the night in question, she'd split up with the millionaire owner and phoned me, but even on a daily diet of cocaine I had my ego under control. I knew classy Chelsea girl would be punching above my weight. And to be honest although she had long blonde hair, cheekbones to die for and great legs her accent was more annoying than Queen Camilla's. As you can imagine I immediately became a Video Cafe regular and took advantage of everything that was on offer, except the stunning blonde with the supermodel looks.

Back in 1970 who would have predicted such a massive change in my fortunes?

Then as a Skinhead I was running up and down Southend seafront as a skinhead and then again as a Mod in 1980. The homeless sofa surfer had gone from taking little blue pills at the Youth Club, to sniffing speed in The Marquee to snorting coke in West End clubs.

From living in a council house to residing in a Kensington flat two blocks from Harrods. This was the icing on the cake I now had a West End nightspot where I could hang out, entertain friends and chat-up girls. My first guest was Jenny Tee, the high-profile PR and Debbie Harry lookalike who I'd fancied since blagging my job on Sounds music magazine. Not only was she drop dead gorgeous but also supplied the best cocaine in London. She was a great character who had more stories than JK Rowling. She dated a guitarist friend of mine and one night he was too pissed to perform. Jenny got the right hump. She didn't put on sexy black stockings and all the gear to get him going. Instead, she pulled out a gun.

It was a case of either shoot up or get shot up! I don't recommend it, but Jenny said it did the trick. It's hard to believe but their relationship didn't last. And sadly, our sexual relationship never got started. We were always the best of plutonic friends and never fuck buddies but shared many adventures with our clothes on.

Between leaving school and joining Sounds music magazine I was and at the same time wasn't like every other teenager. There were girls, youth clubs, football, cinema, discos, clubs and run-ins with the law. I wasn't a massive drinker and always preferred `fast drugs` to alcohol. Speed, E's and cocaine were always my drugs of choice. Ever since seeing Ziggy Stardust I wanted to be skinny and high.

I was christened Church of England but my taste in music was always Catholic. Before discovering David Bowie I was into Motown, Ska, Reggae and then Glam Rock. Not the plastic crap of Gary Glitter, Mud and The Sweet. Before seeing Bowie on Top of The Pops I was into Marc Bolan and T Rex.

Bowie introduced me to Lou Reed, The Velvet Underground and Iggy Pop.

Years later The Sex Pistols made me aware of The Clash, The Jam and The Buzzcocks. I must mention the under-rated and almost unknown all-girl band The Slits because of guitarist Viv Albertine.

She was/is a genuine working-class hero who at the same time was ultra cool, sexy, sharp and smart. The ex-girlfriend of Clash guitarist Mick Jones won`t like me for saying it but had `legs to die for`.

She was almost as stunning as Transvision Vamp singer Wendy James but refused to use her sex appeal to sell records. Years later she'd write the brilliant autobiography `Clothes, Clothes, Clothes, Music, Music, Music, Boys, Boys, Boys. She'd probably hate me on sight but the truth is found her attitude very attractive. She is the female working-class voice of her generation.

Punk Rock took me to places like The Marquee, The Bridge House, Dingwalls and The 100 Club. As admitted earlier I wasn't a typical or well-behaved teenager, which is why I got expelled from 3 different schools and ended up in care.

But believe it or not I wasn't a bad boy, or a thug, always preferred being a cheeky chappie to a teenage tearaway. I was born a rebel, but circumstances turned me into a feral youth suffering with a mental illness. No, I didn't need a straightjacket and wasn`t waiting to be admitted to Broadmoor but was suffering with a form of mental illness. Nowadays I'd be diagnosed with PSD as I never got over my dad walking out on me.

In those days people didn't talk about such things or know PSD existed. Years later medical experts said part of my brain froze and still stuck in 1972. Maybe that explains why I still dress like a Mod and marmite and peanut butter sandwiches are still my favourite food. I left the world of education with no qualifications, which is something to this day I'm still ashamed of. I wish to God I'd listened to my teachers and taken advantage of the education I was offered. But as with the police and social workers, I saw schoolteachers as the enemy and did everything to wind them up. I'm genuinely ashamed and take no pride in admitting I have no A-Levels, let alone a degree. I won't apologize for becoming a teenage tearaway because it genuinely wasn't my fault. I was messed up and crying behind closed doors but in public there were no tears from this clown. I was an innocent child betrayed by two selfish adults. I was (still am) a rebel by nature, it's in my DNA, but I'm not a low-life criminal.

I love old school East End gangsters, the Great Train Robbers and faces like Dave Courtney but have no time or admiration for petty criminals. The truth is between the ages of 12 and Sixteen I did time in various prisons for teenage tearaways and mixed-up kids. Boyles Court Essex, Little Heath East London, Kidlington Detention Centre Oxfordshire, Redhill Unit Surrey, Herts Borstal Hertfordshire.

The worst place was Kidlington Detention Centre, now called Campsfield House, currently used as a prison for illegal immigrants awaiting deportation.

It was a horrible and brutal place where on a arrival you were beaten-up by bully boy screws. Most were ex-soldiers or coppers, who bullied kids because they themselves were bullied at school. They were all cowards and absolute scumbags. The place was surrounded by 12-foot-high walls and barbed wire. After I'd been there a few days and done my introduction, they decided to introduce me to the world of work. I was sent to slave in the prison factory. It took less than 5 minutes to realise it wasn't for me. No way could I spend 8 hours a day assembling and packaging what looked like burglar alarms. I refused to participate and decided to take whatever punishment was handed out. The bully boy screws screamed and shouted insults, gave me a few digs, but nothing like the extreme violence handed out to Ray Winstone in Scum.

I was sent to join an outside Work Party and there was no sex, drugs or rock and roll involved. This was a punishment squad. It meant digging a massive hole in the ground from 9am to mid-day, like a grave for giants. Then after a crap dinner of cold food you'd fill it in and start again the next day. I did that every day (except Sunday) for 3 months. As always 'every cloud has a silver lining', which is one of my favourite sayings, and also true. If it weren't for those days, I would not have written my critically acclaimed poem 'Ballad of The Young Offenders'. If it weren't for those days locked-up in teenage prisons I would not have written my first poetry book 'Boys of The Empire'.

At the start of 1976, very few people had heard of The Sex Pistols, The Clash or The Jam. A full-scale youth movement would soon explode in London and spread out beyond the suburbs. Soon The Buzzcocks from Manchester would join big Fab Four of Punk Rock. I deliberately ignore The Damned because of the vile remarks guitarist Captain Sensible made about David Bowie. Though they did make one great record and 'New Rose' was also the first punk single.

A year before Punk I hated most of the acts on Top of The Pops and was going to more live gigs. I was without knowing watching bands that are now known as Pub Rock. Doctor Feelgood, Eddie and The Hot Rods, Kilburn and The High Roads were the best bands I saw live. They were filling a void because Slade and Marc Bolan had faded. Rod Stewart had broken up The Faces and moved to America and David Bowie was no longer appearing on Top of The Pops. He was now a World star and living in Hollywood so all we had before Punk was Roxy Music, Cockney Rebel and Mott The Hoople. I remember seeing the New York Dolls on the Old Grey Whistle Test and feeling excited. Not quite a Ziggy Stardust on TOTP moment or Sex Pstols on Bill Grundy Show, but very memorable and life changing.

As with the Bowie and Sex Pistols TV appearance it would become an historic moment in the history of rock and roll. Inspired by The Sex Pistols I formed The Buzz Kids and although it didn't take off it launched m into the world of showbiz. It was my first step on the ladder. The Punk Poet didn't make it onto Top of The Pops but did find his way onto Fleet Street. I was proud to work for The Sun and get by-lines in every tabloid newspaper.

The Sun, Daily Mirror, Daily Star, Daily Mail, News of The World, Sunday People, Daily Express and Evening Standard. I'm proud to say I was a tabloid terrorist. I moved in high places but never stopped being a working-class liberal or an anti-establishment character. I wasn't betraying my background by entering the world of tabloid journalism. The only snobs I encountered were the champagne socialists who worked for The Guardian. People have described me as the Artful Dodger of Punk and Arthur Daley of tabloid journalism. How fucking great is that? My story is like life itself full of ups and down, with a few dark moments but lots of laughs. Apart from the custody battle with my ex-wife and war with Social Services, I have never taken life seriously. Do I regret anything? Yes and no. Unlike a politician I don't find it hard giving straight and honest answers. My way of life wasn't planned. I just blagged a job on Sounds music magazine and, without a masterplan ended up in Fleet Street.

I could pretend I had a big scheme, that it was a grand subversive act on my part and build up my role as a scammer, but, the truth is, it was all a fluke.

Tabloid terrorism was like a dug. I became addicted and couldn't give up. It was well paid and great fun, so no regrets on that score. The truth is, I didn't write stories about the man or women in the street and never wrote anything nasty about the rich and famous. I got away with it for so long because I always flattered egos. As in life, if you can't say something nice about someone say nothing at all. That's why I'm not writing a revealing kiss and tell story about my 15-year marriage or mentioning any adult antics. What happened in the bedroom stays in the bedroom. Having mixed with so many educated people I regret not going to school and getting a proper education.

I was never a proper journo, or a talking head showbiz pundit on TV. I had the gift of the gab and a genuine love of showbiz and all things celebrity, but didn't have the qualifications to go legit. The fact is, I didn't wear a t-shirt saying 'kosher' or have it tattooed on my forehead, people just assumed I was a bona-fide journalist, and I was more than happy to play the part.

I must have been a good a good actor because my career lasted longer than that of most soap stars. I was given by-lines in The Sun, then selling 6 million copies a day and my own column in The Sunday People. I also had my TV Column in Front magazine where celebrity gangster Dave Courtney was a columnist. In those days I a bit of a 'gambler' with the Midas touch, I went for a drink with Editor Piers Hernu who offered me a job. I was lucky like that.

The same thing happened when Rebekah Wade, a heroine of mine (my daughter has her middle-name), joined News International. Piers Morgan, who'd been my boss on The Sun's bizarre pop column, suggested we meet.

Meeting Rebekah for me was like seeing David Bowie on Top of The Pops. She was stunning and ultra-charming, and it was another genuine life-changing moment.

We went for a drink, and I came away with a job that would last fifteen years and a friendship that never ended. She took me to a posh Wine Bar in Canary Wharf, and we got on like a house on fire.

Rebekah a dead ringer for Aussie actress Nicole Kidman and had the charm and personality of Princess Diana. I had never met such a classy and well-educated woman in my life. It's no wonder she became best friends with Prime Ministers and married a TV heartthrob. The next eighteen years saw her rise from Sun Editor to the boss of News International.

I fell for Rebekah in a massive way, but our relationship was always strictly plutonic. I respected her more than any woman I'd met before or since. She was super smart and destined for the top.

I have since that day been a massive fan and supporter. Years later she would appear at The Old Bailey on trumped up charges and I wrote a character reference for her legal team. It was an honour to support her. Don't know if it helped but she was quite rightly found "not guilty" of all charges.

We were in contact most days after that Wapping lunch and I enjoyed watching her rise to the top. She never changed, was always a class act and 100% loyal.

She sent a Fortnum and Mason hamper after my heart op and was first to phone when I came out of Bellmarsh Prison.

It had always been my ambition to play centre-forward for West Ham, appear on Top of The Pops and to have sex with a page 3 girl. But lacked the dedication (talent) to pull on the famous claret and blue shirt and couldn't sing.

I didn't shag a genuine page 3 girl but came close as I did get off with an amateur wanabee in a London hotel. As with most things from football to pop stardom I gave it a go and had plenty of fun trying. I was always the 'nearly' man.

After hanging-up my football boots, dumping my boxing gloves and ditching my guitar I replaced them with Bic biro and a notepad. I wanted to write, had plenty to say, but nowhere to say it. Before Punk Rock there were no vacancies in the media unless you'd been to university or had the right connections. 1976 would change all that.

Music had always been a massive part of my life, before and after Bowie on Top of The Pops, but always as a fan and bedroom singer. Punk offered you a chance in the spotlight. As a 10-year-old kid it was The Small Faces and The Kinks, as a 12-year-old skinhead it was SKA and Trojan Reggae. I spent my early teenage years into Glam Rock then David Bowie but I wanted to be part of a Youth Movement.

Then came Punk and it happened. Teenagers could stop listening to a music scene dominated by people over the age of 23. The cavalry came marching over the hill led by Johnny Rotten and Joe Strummer. The baton would then be handed to Paul Weller and once again Mods were back in fashion. I was the original 24-hour party person enjoying all that this brave new world offered.

Everything was up for grabs, and I grabbed it with both hands. The anything goes generation was my dream come true. I embraced the lifestyle of one-night-stands, hangovers and comedowns. I lived fast and was tipped to die young, but didn't care because I had no family.

An old mate from those days recently told my eldest son "back in the day your dad took more drugs than anyone". I was over the moon as it vindicated all the stories I`d been trotting out for years". I didn't take drugs because I was stupid, but because I was looking for something, but didn't know what.

Perhaps I was looking for love, stardom, fame, wealth, the ultimate high or a bit of both. I convinced myself I could sing like David Bowie, looked like Johnny Rotten with the attitude of Joe Strummer. I thought I looked the part, but a wasted looking Rod Stewart in a Crombie overcoat was not what the world was looking for. I was skinny, almost anorexic had the body of Iggy Pop and care stare like Johnny Rotten but wasn't welcome at the party, as all seats had been taken.

Generation X, Siouxsie and The Banshees, X Ray Spex and Sham 69 were all following in the footsteps of the Big Four and there weren't any room at the inn for The Buzz Kids. It would be another 4 years before we played our first and last gig on the same night.

I wrote the best lyrics since Paul Weller but without the tunes of The Jam but still couldn't sing or hold a note. We`d spent months rehearsing in bedrooms and playing in garages and thought we were ready. We had seven song, one bad tune, and borrowed some equipment from a 60`s tribute band. In all honesty we were rubbish, like two virgins on a wedding night we didn't have a clue.

The problem was when I got on stage I melted like an ice cream on a hot day. Had I been better looking I could have made it with a tiny bit of talent. Despite what people say, `looks` are very important in the world of celebrity.

Do you honestly believe if David Beckham looked like Wayne Rooney that he would have become a brand and an icon? Blondie made some fantastic records, but Debbie Harry being the best-looking woman in the world helped. If she looked like Angela Rayner, do you honestly believe she would have become a worldwide superstar? The Sex Pistols would not have worked with Elvis Costello as the frontman. That is why I can`t take posh boy Sir Starmer seriously because he looks like Lego man. I want a Labour Party leader who dresses like a Mod and talks like Danny Dyer. I can`t stand phoney people or fat women. I don't hate fat people and I`m not being deliberately offensive. But I ask you: Meatloaf or David Bowie? Gemma Collins or Kate Moss? I`m just saying out loud what most people say in private.

We all know that most women given the choice of David Beckham or Wayne Rooney would choose `golden balls`. What pisses me off is fat female celebs lying to young girls and telling them it`s cool to be `plus sized` ignoring the fact it`s not healthy. It`s not PC but obese women could spend a fortune on designer clothes and still look better wearing a Burkha. It annoys me because the first thing a female celeb does after dramatic weight less is appear on every TV show showing off her new slender body shape. She will often have a diet book or exercise DVD to promote. That isn't me being sexist, I am just telling the truth. It works both ways, as both sexes prefer slim partners. Let's be honest, the majority of women would prefer David Beckham to me (even in my prime). They'd rather shag Tom Hardy than the Punk Poet.

My showbiz career although unsuccessful and not making it onto Top of The Pops was a bloody good laugh. No-one can take away the fact that I discovered The Stone Roses, kicked a ball with George Best and shook hands with David Bowie. I infiltrated the wonderful world of showbiz and got away with it for 25 years.

Before joining Sounds I was a consciences objector to work, I decided at an early age that I wasn't cut out for work. I wasn't lazy, I didn't want to stay in bed all day. I've always been restless, hyper active and needed something to do. It's just that a 9 to 5 job never appealed to me. Never had what people would call a `proper job` but always made more than enough money to survive.

I was homeless for 15 years, from the age of Fifteen to Thirty but never went hungry. Punk Rock changed my life. I would not have become a journalist without it happening. The Sex Pistols, The Clash, The Jam and The Buzzcocks changed my life. I wouldn't be writing this book if it wasn't for David Bowie and then Johnny Rotten, Joe Strummer and Paul Weller. At first Rotten and Strummer were the look and attitude of Punk Rock but then Paul Weller became the main man.

He had the style, the songs and the haircut and unlike Punk Rock the staying power and talent to be the voice of many generations. Punk made me realise that most barriers in life are there to be torn down. I still believe in the DIY ethic.

When I outgrew punk I moved onto tabloids and reverted to being a Mod.

I was a ten-year-old Mod, a teenage Mod, a 30-something Mod and now I'm a OAP Mod. It never leaves you. There are certain people that make events happen, think about it. If Paul Weller had continued working on a building site and not picked up a guitar, would there have been a Mod revival in 1979? How different would it have been if Johnny Rotten and not Sting had passed the audition for Quadrophenia. If Bob Geldof hadn't become a Boomtown Rat then Live Aid would not have happened.

My point is had I not seen David Bowie on Top of The Pops how different would my life have been? I don't think I'd be sitting here writing my life story, there would be nothing to write about.

Meeting The Stone Roses I remember it so well, it's as if it only happened yesterday. They turned up in a big white American motor and we went to the pub, and then a big house on the outskirts of Manchester.

It was like a country mansion with a big bar and a snooker table.

We immediately hit it off and Tony Mottram and I stayed for the weekend. We all went clubbing Friday and Saturday night and we partied until the early hours.

We all did a lot of drugs, but I still managed to do an interview. The Feature was published within days and from then on I mentioned them in the gossip column every week. One night in a club opposite the Hammersmith Odeon, I talked our way into an after-show party for chart-topper Bryan Adams. I invented the story that the Canadian rocker had offered Ian £200 for his jacket, a lot of money in 1985. Another night, another party, this time in somewhere in Soho I came up with the story that Angie Bowie had been flirting with Ian, she did say "hello", but I rather embellished their brief encounter.

She did smile at him, but it looked to me as if she wanted to 'pull him' so I just wrote what I thought I saw. Like all good publicists I'd do and say anything to get my 'people' written about and known to the general public. I got pop fans talking about The Stone Roses before they were even famous in their own front rooms.

They would come down to London on a regular basis to play gigs and hangout and get noticed. I would take them around town and to a lot of parties. There was a big party at The Roof Gardens in Kensington where The Roses and others watched me having a quickie with my soon-to-be girlfriend Elle, who'd supplied me with the Golden invites. I had no idea we were performing in front of a two-way mirror.

A few weeks later I moved in with Elle the sexy press officer I called my Jewish Princess. She would introduce me to a whole new world of colourful characters and urged me to be ambitious. She was the first person to encourage me to be a proper writer.

The party was full of people I'd seen at other showbiz bashes in and around the West End. The A-listers Spandau Ballet and Duran Duran, new boys on the scene like King, oldies like Noddy Holder, Bucks Fizz and Status Quo.

Also present Bryan Adams, Paul Young, the usual page 3 girls and professional partygoer Chris Quentin. The following is kosher bit of chit-chat that ended up as a gossip column exclusive. Soul singer Leee John from chart stars Imagination tried to pull Ian Brown who made his excuses and hid.

Another night at The Sir John Franklin pub, next to Blackwell Tunnel and run by an old acquaintance of mine The Roses once again performed with Frankie Flame.

Read on, but it's not as exciting as it sounds. The East London pub famous for lunchtime strippers (Fri, Sat, Sun ) hadn't hired Frankie to make a mid-day appearance (thank god) but had booked him for a evening session. We popped along and Manchester United fan Ian joined Frankie for a rowdy, rabble-rousing version of the West Ham anthem 'I'm Forever Blowing Bubbles'.

This was also published in the gossip column. I did everything to get them noticed. I was a massive Jam fan and used my friendship with guitarist Bruce Foxton to try and secure a record deal. Bruce liked the demo and was interested in producing them. He'd done a great job on 'Turning Japanese' into a hit for new wave band The Vapors.

I arranged a meet. Ian Brown, an ex-skinhead, scooter boy and Mod was a massive Jam fan and really keen on Bruce producing. Future guitar hero John Squire was not. He was a Clash fanatic and wanted Joe Strummer or Mick Jones.

The Stone Roses co-founder wasn't impressed with the suit Bruce was wearing so refused to have his picture taken with Mr Foxton. I wasn't in any way embarrassed. This to me wasn't madness, rudeness or arrogance. It was a statement, an amazing show of self-belief and self-confidence. John Squire already knew he was going to be a massive star and would make it on his own terms.

As history proves The Stone Roses became the biggest band in the world and John Squire recently had a number one album with Liam Gallagher.

The funny thing is The Stone Roses, pretty much like Oasis became a lad's band loved on the football terraces, but early on it was the other way round.

Pat Stead and Joanna Burns at Sony and Epic liked them as did Patsy Johnson, Bernie Coyle, Chrissie Cremore and heavy metal Heather. But the blokes in A and R departments didn't want to know. I kept on going because I just knew they were going to be massive.

I took a tape along to my new best mate Hughie Gadson, one of the coolest blokes I'd ever met and introduced to me by Elle. He was one of her artistic and flamboyant circle, I know what you're thinking, and "yes" I did end up staying at his place, a spacious luxury flat in Paddington. Hughie went on to manage rave band EMF, who had a massive hit with "Unforgetable" and is now co-manager of Madness.

Hughie was one of the funniest blokes in showbiz, who liked me a lot, but I couldn't persuade him to sign The Stone Roses. I tried everything, even offered to sleep with him (joke) but he wouldn't budge. He'd just signed a band called 'Ring of Roses' (who died a death) and didn't want to manage 2 bands called the Roses. As history proves it was a massive mistake on his part, I still believe with Hughie in their corner The Stone Roses could have been as big as Oasis, or very close.

I would now be rich and famous because I know Hughie would have hired me to be Press Officer or some kind of assistant. Some London labels didn't want to know because of the way they looked and unfair reputation as 'bad boys'. The 'problem' was Ian had been a skinhead, pictures were circulating, and a gang of skinheads, scooter boys and football casuals from Manchester would follow them down to London.

The fans were great and there was never any trouble at any of the London gigs but once you get a bad reputation it's hard to shake off. I think the record label bigwigs were scared of another Sham 69 situation where 100s of skinheads 'The Sham Army' would smash up gigs. It was so unfair. As history confirms a bad reputation can unfairly last for decades. In 2016 at the Camden Roundhouse I was having a drink with Professor Matt Worley and joined by this arrogant champagne socialist who slagged off Ian Brown saying "I heard he was racist". Nothing could be further from the truth and this snobby bastard who'd never met The Stone Roses singer thought it was okay to abuse a working-class kid.

I tipped them to be massive and remember writing "The Stone Roses will have hit singles and a number one album within the next 18 months". I was spot on with that prediction but was two years too early.

At the time fellow journos were puzzled and kept asking why I raved about them so much. It was partly because The Stone Roses were the band I wanted to be in, the band I wanted The Buzz Kids to be. We shared the same attitude and ambition, but they had 4 things The Buzz Kids didn't have.

Talent. The charisma of Ian Brown, the guitar genius of John Squire and drummer Reni who Pete Townsend compared to Keith Moon.

I was gutted when I couldn't get them a record deal but so proud when they made it. It couldn't happen to a nicer bunch of guys. I was genuinely pleased when I saw them on Top of The Pops and have some great memories of hanging out with them.

As well as all the partying, doing drugs and chasing girls, when they stayed at mine I'd supply them with marmite, peanut butter and jam sandwiches and coffee for the drive back to Manchester. No-one can steal your memories and there ain't many people who can say they sung Mod classic 'Lazy Sunday' or West Ham anthem 'Were Forever Blowing Bubbles' with The Stone Roses.

# Chapter Five
# Every Day was Like a Film

As well as hanging out with working-class bands like The Stone Roses, after meeting Nicky I mixed with Bohemian types from the Chelsea Arts Club. Nicky was 12-years older than me with a massive flat, a young daughter and an au pair.

This was a new for me. I had never before knowingly been with a divorced woman who had a child. Every time we did anything I felt inhibited, like a virgin almost, because she was so experienced. But I recommend it, even the picnics in Hyde Park and boat rides on the Thames.

Nicky didn't have a title but she had the accent, was very posh, and took me to places I'd never been (in and out of bed). She took me to the Chelsea Arts Club, a reception in the Houses of Parliament, Sothebys and Avant Garde house parties in South Kensington and Notting Hill Gate. We even had afternoon tea in The Ritz.

Partying with rock bands was one thing, but at first hanging out with artistic types was kind of enjoyable once I got my head around it. She loved to take drugs and eat raw vegetables, and we were together for about three months, but only met up two or 3 times a week. It was perfect for me and no soppy hearts and flowers romance we were just friends with benefits.

The more I did it the more I liked, it became great fun with lots of free drugs, and plenty of sex with a posh older woman. So no complaints on that score, though part of me felt like a class traitor, but only a tiny bit because I was having so much fun and realised not all posh people are vile snobs like champagne socialist Lady Emily Thornberry. I even looked up to some of them, not in a forelock tugging way but admired their general knowledge and liked their decadent lifestyle'

We went to a sort of dinner party, minus a table and without food where people sat around talking and smoking weed. One of the guests was the younger brother of singer Lulu another was a Buddhist called Ziggy, no not Stardust, but a lesbian artist and reader of the Runes.

I pretended to believe, and she predicted I'd be filthy rich or dead by the time I was Thirty-five. Well, she got that wrong on both counts. A lot of these people also shared my fondness for David Bowie, Roxy Music and The Velvet Underground.

Before moving in these circles, my mates had always been more interested in football and girls than visiting art galleries and reading magazine articles about the Andy Warhol crowd in New York. Before discovering David Bowie, I was heading for a typical working-class way of life and looking for an escape route. Punk gave me that option. I didn't have the education of these people but I was more street smart than most. I survived on my wits.

Becoming a music fan than a music journo broadened my horizons. Inhabiting a brave new world that thrived on decadence was great fun.

I loved the wild side of life and the more I got involved, the more I enjoyed it. I was like a fish out of water but still able to swim. I wasn't sure at first and voices in my head were questioning my behaviour, but to me hanging out with this posh crowd was just another act of rebellion. Well that's how I explained the situation to myself.

At first, I enjoyed the company of decadent bohemians but partying without the rock and roll element got boring. There are only so many Buddhist meetings, chattering-class dinner parties and picnics in the park that a Cockney Rebel can stomach. I was missing my old mates at The Marquee and The Embassy Club.

As with everything in my life, apart from becoming a dad, it wasn't planned. I became great mates with a guy, let's call him Hugo, well it's something like that, but he'll know who he is. Nowadays he's a happily married man with 3 daughters but back then he was a 'player'.

He was Mr Sex, drugs and Rock and Roll and made me look like an innocent choirboy. Hugo, as were calling him was loaded, with a posh flat in the smartest part of Kensington who had access to beautiful women and vast amounts of cocaine. Like me he didn't have a 'normal job' but unlike me he seemed to be very wealthy. He was in and around the music scene and seemed to know all the 'right people' from record label bigwigs to drug dealers. He was my kind of bloke.

When I gave one of the bands he handled 'a five-star review' we became 'best mates' and ended up staying at his flat. I will never, out of loyalty, reveal his identity, but believe me he was the most mysterious person (in a nice way) that I ever met.

Hugo was much more than a 'Jack the Lad' and run of the mill 'man about town', he was like an enigma. He was interesting and secretive without being rude, and although I stayed at his flat I never knew exactly what he did for a living or how he got his money. In the East End you are brought up not to ask questions about certain subjects and I was just to his mate. He drove a flashy car, had top-of-the-range furnishings in his luxury flat and always wore designer clothes. He always carried a wad of notes and packets of cocaine. I knew he knew a lot of people who managed bands and owned night clubs and sometimes had a bodyguard for 'special trips'.

His lifestyle which included dating beautiful women and dining in London's top restaurants had to be funded somehow, but don't ask me how. A massive user of cocaine, I suspected he was also a major drug dealer or even a high-class pimp.

Why do I say this? Well the people who came in and out of his flat included fading pop stars, glam models, a gay friend of Freddie Mercury and some bodybuilder type who claimed to be a minder for Princess Diana's favourite dancer Wayne Sleep. Hugo was the biggest 'bird bandit' I'd ever met in my life, we are talking a different girl every other night, but also dabbled in a bit of bisexual action. I'd never met anyone like him before or since. The girls he hooked-up with were always wannabe singers, models, or actresses and mostly private school educated. It was he who introduced to me to Charlie, the girl not the drug, my last big crush before meeting the girl from South Afrrica.

Charlie ticked all the boxes, blonde and skinny who reminded me of a young Marianne Faithful, Hugo introduced me to her and she introduced me to her lifestyle which was wild. I'm not stupid and know I only got to meet her because of my friendship with Hugo and him 'bigging me up' as an influential person it was good to know. Charlie claimed to be a model but didn't work in the few weeks I knew her and never saw her picture in magazines. I'd bet my life she was some kind of escort whose now happily married and living in the suburbs.

I was still taking risks, bending the rules, taking illegal substances, posing as a kosher journo, but now I was doing it from a better postcode.

Like me Hugo was a massive Bowie fan and Nicky was into Lou Red, the New York Dolls and Patti Smith so you can only image our drug-fuelled conversations.

I really liked these people, but my old mate Garry Bushell disapproved, he found them too arty. Around this period I also met two women I'd grown-up watching on TV most Saturday nights.

Cilla Black, I met after at a recording of a TV show at LWT. I had to say "hello" because I'd always wanted to appear on Blind Date. Not to find the 'love of my life' but fancied five minutes of fame. I never got the invite, but Amanda Holden did, it launched her career. I still think "if only" and what could have been.

The scouse Songbird was very friendly when I mentioned her duet with Marc Bolan. Growing-up as a fan of T Rex, I loved their camp cheesy performance of 'Life's A Gas'. She remembered Marc as a very sweet guy, but sadly couldn't promise me a spot on Blind Date. I also met

Lulu, another famous singer from the Swinging 60s, at a showbiz reception and her younger brother at a Kensington house party.

He was friends with the Buddhist I'd met called Ziggy, no, not Stardust, but a Lesbian artist and reader of the runes. I've told this story many times and wrote about it earlier because I love saying the name "Ziggy".

She gave me a reading and I asked Lulu's brother about his sister working with David Bowie. Lulu didn't just sing with him, she fucked him, and years later admitted she was obsessed with Bowie, and distressed when he ended the relationship. Lulu had a massive hit with a version of his classic song 'The Man Who Sold The World'. Although I was hanging out with posh people, I never forgot my Cockney roots, but some might say my manners, when I asked "is it true your sister shagged David Bowie?" At the time Lulu, was so infatuated she behaved like an obsessed fan. She copied his clothes and even had a Ziggy Stardust haircut.

She recently published her autobiography and revealed all about her affair with The Thin White Duke. It was serialised in either The Sun or Daily Mail. As well as giving her his body Bowie he gave her the best record she ever made.

At times my life was like being in a movie, and looking back, even I find it hard to believe some of the things I got up to. Thank to moving in showbiz circles I was able to indulge all my fantasies and push boundaries. Had I been forced to get a 'proper job' or work in a factory I'm pretty sure I could have ended up in Broadmoor. I wasn't lazy or a scrounger but always a consciences objector when it came to work.

Around 1984/85 I met and 'fell for' a Jewish Canadian girl, it wasn't soppy love in a Mills and Boon kind of way. I don't do love, never been in love in my life, my dad warned me not to get involved saying "It's too dangerous and always lead to hurt". Apart from my children and grandkids who I love to bits, I've never loved anyone more than I loved my dad. Works both ways, because apart from my kids and grandchildren I don't think I've ever been on the receiving end of genuine love. I don't mind because I'd rather be liked by many than loved by a few. I was fascinated by Elle because of her confident character, 'foreign' accent and sexy personality. She was a top PR working for some of the biggest bands in the world. As with Hugo I won't reveal her true identity because like him she's now married with kids. Back in the day she was an exotic party animal who loved the sex, drugs and rock and roll lifestyle almost as much as me. Her being Jewish was also a main attraction, nothing to do with religion. It was all about my David Bowie obsession.

As well as owning every record, I've read every biography and such a expert I'd be a easy winner on Mastermind. I was well aware of Corrine

Schwab, known to the world as Co-Co. She was Bowie's lover, personal assistant and confidante, the woman who also saved his life.

She was also very smart and Jewish. I knew Co-co was American, but Elle being Canadian was close enough for me. Like Bowie's side-kick she was sexy, streetwise, highly intelligent, exotic and avant-garde. We spent a hot summer burning the candle at both ends. She was so special and different that I even introduced to her my mother. We spent the weekend in Cheshire and my mum was impressed saying "what a nice girl".

She hadn't a clue what we were doing in the bedroom, not that, we did do that, but I'm talking about what were putting up our nose. Another older woman, only by 4 years, but this is important when the lady looks like Joan Jett meets Susannah Hoffs.

Elle also had her own flat in South Kensington, a five-minute walk from Harrods and ten minutes from Buckingham Palace. She ticked all the boxes but for both of us it was more lust than love. She was special and changed my life in many ways, but I never allowed myself to fall in love, because we both knew it was only a fling and wouldn't last. We parted as friends and on good terms. That is why out of respect I will never reveal her identity, as her family would not enjoy reading about her wild past. The girl from North America was great fun, absolutely outrageous with no boundaries what-so-ever, though at times she was border-line bisexual. One night she tried to pull my friend Jenny Tee, made a pass at her in the back of a taxicab.

The next day I was taken aside by Jenny (the Debbie Harry lookalike) and told "your friend tried it on with me last night" adding "Please tell her that although I like her a lot, I'm not into all that". I thought "my life that would have been a threesome to die for" as I'd fancied Jenny for years. There was a happy ending as both went onto become best friends, and as far as I know strictly plutonic.

They say opposites attract but I liked Elle because she was a better-looking female version of me and made me laugh with her funny ways. We'd mock each other endlessly without either taking offence. She'd tease me for repeating myself and whenever she said something snobby I'd call her a "Jewish Princess".

At first I thought it was just another one-night-stand, and a place for me to stay, but somehow we were together for about 6-8 months, but both knew it wasn't going to last a lifetime. I'd read about women like her in books, seen them in movies, but not in the flesh. Sorry to mention Bowie again (no, I'm not), but her character reminded me of Angie Bowie, the accent, the mannerisms, the sexual aura. If you watch the DVD of the final Ziggy Stardust concert at The Hammersmith Odeon, you'll understand what I mean. The first few minutes is Angie holding court in the dressing room and sounding and behaving just like Elle.

This will shock you but Elle wasn't a blonde yet somehow I willingly fell under her spell. She was a cuter combination of Joan Jett and Susannah Hoffs. I broke the habit of a life-time and to this day remains one of my few non-blonde girlfriends.

I was sort of star struck, and in a drugged-up way in awe of her, but it wasn't a ginger prince/princess porky pies situation. I was impressed by the way she was on first-name terms with so many stars and all the top tabloid journalists.

I know what you're thinking, and 'yes' you are correct, I admit my original intention was to take advantage of the situation. As a streetwise operator I could always spot an opportunity. Elle introduced me to who at the time were the two most influential showbiz journalists in Fleet Street. This was before the Internet and mobile phones. She was on friendly terms with Martin Dunn at The Sun and John Blake of the Daily Mirror. As well as being the object of her lust, I was also her pet project. She was like a female Doctor Doolittle, forever telling me I should be on TV, writing books and working with the big boys in Fleet Street. She was very ambitious on my behalf.

I played the part of a kosher young journalist and must have been pretty convincing, as she had no idea an 'impersonator' was living under her roof.

Although we eventually drifted apart, which I knew we would, I have many happy memories of our time together and much to thank her for. Elle taught me to focus and be more professional. In our time together we partied hard, took plenty of drugs and hardly slept, but she never took a day off or missed an appointment.

Like me her brain was wired for cocaine and amphetamine sulphate. The only girl I've known who took more 'fast drugs' and handled them better was Jenny Tee.

I was never a smoker or heavy drinker and had no interest in weed, heroin or acid. At fourteen I discovered speed for the first time and I liked it, the little 'blue pills' shared my teenage years. They worked with my DNA and made sure I never suffered depression. They say drugs kill, but I genuinely believe they saved my life.

Fast drugs made me the man I am today.

After my dad fucked off to be with his fucking fancy women I used them for the next 15-16 years on an almost daily basis. I was never an addicted, just a user.

At first I took speed to be like my older mates. We'd go to Soho and buy bags of little blue pills. Then I sniffed sulphate and started snorting cocaine. It always worked for me and stopped me getting depression after being deserted and betrayed by my own dad. I never cried, not even once, but did suffer in silence, some form of emotional breakdown. It also helped me cope when my football career ended before it even got really started. I could not have coped with life if I hadn't had some form of 'fast drug' to use as a crutch. At first I used it to fight off depression, and it worked. Then to party, go to gigs and stay up all night. Then it gave me the confidence to sing in public, write songs and convince my brain I was educated.

I then replaced speed with cocaine and like Elle never had a day off work or missed a deadline. I can prove I was never addicted, as I gave-up overnight after 15-16 years of being a user. There was no pain of cold turkey, no drama or withdrawal problems. I had just become a dad. I had a son called Sam so didn't need any more help from Charlie. I was on such a natural high I didn't even need a tiny line of Colombian marching powder to make me happy. Stopping was the easiest thing I'd ever done with no negative reactions, except I put on weight, which I hated. So I started running with a bin big under my sweatshirt.

Elle was not only a major influence on my life, she made one of my schoolboy dreams come true by taking me to a recording of Top of The Pops. I've probably used this line before, but I was like a practising Catholic visiting the Vatican and meeting the Pope. She also introduced me to a guy called Hughie, who is now big name in the music business. He was a diamond geezer and another life-changing buddy. A legendary party animal in many ways similar to Hugo the toff, the guy I told you about earlier. But unlike him wasn't a gangster or a drug dealer.

He was a one-off and as with punk legend Garry Bushell loved him to bits in a non-sexual way. Not physically you understand, strictly plutonic, but had I been bisexual he'd be my kind of guy, only joking folks. Like most of Elle's friends he had a West End flat, a flashy car, and wore expensive clothes. He was always surrounded by beautiful women and not averse to a bit of Charlie. As with Garry Bushell I looked up to him but in different ways. Gal Bush was a renowned writer and Hughie an upper-class ducker and diver.

He'd discovered Wham and had interests in various record labels and music publishing. We became so close we were like brothers from different mothers. Maybe back in the day my love rat Romeo of a dad had known his mum.

He was charismatic, funny, intelligent and the ultimate charmer. It's no wonder women fell at his feet. Hughie told me he was the adopted son of posh parents and had tracked down his birth mum to a council estate in East London. A public schoolboy with a Toff accent and middle-class manners but had Cockney blood flowing through his veins. Like me his DNA was 100% working-class.

This explains why he oozed class but at the same time was just as streetwise as me. It was a winning combination. We hit it off immediately, so much so, when I split from the Jewish Princess I moved out of her flat and into his. I swapped Knightsbridge for Kensington. Without wishing to bore you, there is yet another David Bowie connection in my life. He introduced me to Angie Bowie at some showbiz bash, it was for me like being in the presence of Royalty, although coked-up to the eyeballs, I couldn't talk and become tongue-tied.

I was genuinely overcome and lost for words. This was Angie Bowie she'd shagged The Thin White Duke and had his child. I thought nothing will ever top this moment, but something did.

I went to some after show party for Tina Turner and DAVID BOWIE was there, I was in the same room as Ziggy Stardust and it blew my mind. They say you should never meet your hero, but he was more than a hero, he was fucking God to me (and still is). This is the man who changed my life. I eventually plucked up courage to say "hello". He smiled and shook my FUCKING hand. I couldn't talk for the rest of the night, and it felt like I was in a trance like state.

The next day I couldn't stop telling people and asking those who there "if that really happened". It did and not only do I have witnesses but press cuttings to prove it. Sounds magazine wrote about it saying "ten days and Garry Johnson still hasn't washed his hand", this became a running joke and went on for weeks.

Hughie and I became so close we shared everything from drugs to clothes to women He was `special friends` with Elle before I met her and then again after I had met him. One night in Stringfellows we both met Mauren a gorgeous young blonde au pair/child minder from South Africa. She looked like a young Susan George, when she dated Rod Stewart in the 70s, and we both fancied her. Strange but true, she'd moved to London with the hope of meeting Boy George, but instead she met us. Maureen had a horrible name and terrible accent but was stunning, drop-dead gorgeous. Not only was she out of my league, but also Hughie's. But marching powder boosts your ego. The three of us ended up at the flat of some bloke Hughie knew, the son of TV comedian Tom o'Connor. It was set in a private road somewhere in Fulham/Chelsea.

The funny thing is, I fell asleep, even though we were all snorting as I hadn't slept for 3 days and crashed out, so Hughie took advantage of the situation, not of me but of the South Africa stunner. When I returned to the land of the living, they both emerged from one of the bedrooms with big smiles on their faces. It was just another one-night-stand for Hughie but I didn't want to lose out as there was something about her. She was at the same time sexy and sweet.

A genuine 'innocent abroad' and that was a 'turn on'. Only been in London a few weeks and never been inside a pub or travelled on the London Underground. Her wealthy employees sent her everywhere in a taxi.

We met up a few nights later outside the Oval cricket ground, close to where she was living/working with this posh family. We went for a drink and not lying when I say 'every head turned when we walked into the bar'. It could have had something to do with her long blonde hair and golden tan but the dress she was 'just about wearing' also had something to do with it. For older readers she genuinely looked like Cameron Diaz.

It wasn't a one-night stand, as she had to be home at ten, that came later when we became really good friends, so close in fact, she almost moved into my flat, and not as a lodger. We saw each other on and off for a while but she kept going back to Malawi in South Africa to see her parents. The last time we met up she came to my flat (the first I'd owned) and stayed a few days. Once again she went back home to South Africa and a month or two later I met my ex-wife.

The mother of my kids moved in almost immediately and then I received an Airmail letter from Malawi which was read by my ex-wife. She was not a 'happy bunny' as it said something like "be back soon and looking forward to moving in".

My ex-wife was jealous at the best of times and went berserk. We were married 15 years and if I had a pound for every time she mentioned 'that bird from Malawi' I'd be a rich man'. And while on the subject of having a jealous wife like the bunny boiler in Fatal Attraction.

My own bloody mum dropped me in it 'big-time' by ' innocently', I hope it was innocently mentioning 'what a nice girl that Elle was', believe me that didn't do me any favours. Elle was another name I had thrown at me throughout my 15-year marriage though to be fair I'd retaliate saying "young girl married man, oldest story in the book" referring to her previous boyfriend, a married man called Derek, difference being I was only joking. My ex-wife hated it when reminded she was named as the 'other woman' in the divorce.

Those who know me will know I said it to wind her up and because it made me laugh, and nothing to do with jealousy.

I wasn't living with Elle when my Paul Young book was published but we were still friends. She appointed herself my PR and arranged various press events to promote my book. The icing on the cake being a LBC radio interview, I'd been a listener for years and massive fan of presenter Steve Allen. A radio legend I'd chat to Steve in places like Stringfellows and hang on his every word.

Talking to Steve Allen was a great honour as, along with Radio 1's John Peel he's my all-time favourite presenter. I hoped he'd be doing the interview but it turned out to be Clive Bull, who years later is still working as a LBC presenter. It was quite exciting but could have been so much better. I'd not done any radio before but as with my first visit to Top of The Pops a great experience. I've always been a great fan of 'first times' except for sex. My first time (can't reveal her name) as I don't kiss and tell like Prince Harry, but it was not what I expected and all over in a splash. I was only Thirteen and none of my mates told me the girl had to be wet/damp. It wasn't good and only memorable because the same girl gave me my first blow job.

Aged thirteen, unlike kids of today, I didn't really know what a blow job was but as with 'fast drugs' it soon became a lifelong love and addiction. Elle said it went well and as always I respected her opinion, I was well happy.

From day one she encouraged me to aim high saying "leave Sounds and join the tabloids". When I listened back to the interview it sounded like I had a bad cold, I was sniffing almost as much as I was talking. It was the first step on the ladder and led to better and bigger things. I wasn't freeloading when I stayed at Hughies. I wasn't using him to get free drugs and a roof over my head. I wasn't poncing. In return for his generosity, I got his bands in the paper and always gave rave reviews and maximum exposure, but the truth is I would have done it for nothing.

This was a genuine friendship between the East End Boy and a Toff who stole the show at my wedding and danced with my bride.

What's so 'special' about that? Always the showman and although on the day he didn't upstage the bride, he upstaged everyone else. He turned up looking like Bryan Ferry (circa Virginia Plain) wearing eyeliner, black velvet shoes and a satin suit. My ex-wife was not amused, and her dad was fuming. I was 'over the moon' by his big entrance as he brought along a vast supply of cocaine which made Bruce Foxton, Garry Bushell and the groom 'very happy'. And yes, I did say "eyeliner and velvet shoes".

Apart from David Bowie, it was Gal Bushell, Elle and Hughie who influenced my life more than anyone else. Through them I got to meet various household names including a famous hoofer who one danced with Lady Diana. One night the three of us, had drinks in a trendy Notting Hill wine bar and were joined by a famous dancer who seemed unwell. He'd either missed his flu jab or had a habit. He was sniffing more than a police dog on a drugs raid. Hanging out with Hughie and Elle led to me hanging out with people like me never got to meet. Artistic types into fast drugs and sex without strings.

I then started hanging out with a genuine All-American girl, the human Barbie girl Cindy Jackson. Amazingly as I write this chapter she's appearing on GB News promoting her latest book. I'm not shy about naming Cindy, as without my knowledge she used me to pull off a scam that was featured on News At Ten, and got her on the front page of every tabloid. The super smart scammer pulled off a classic sting on the British media. She drove a white sports car, had a flat in Battersea, and for a few months we were an actual item. I can best describe our relationship as 'friends with benefits', a little bit of sex and a lot of drugs. I found her funny, and once again I was drawn in by the accent, but what really attracted me was her being a topless model who wanted to be a pop star. She was also a singer with punk/pop band Joe Public.

I'm doing a kiss and tell as an act of revenge because she betrayed me, not in love, worse than that, she damaged by reputation. I'm hoping rock star Noddy Holder reads and discovers what really happened that night in Soho. It was a long time ago but I still want to clear my name.

So here goes:

One night in Soho, Cindy and I were out and about having drinks with a few friends including Dan Higson, younger brother of Fast Show star Charlie, and a girl called Carmine.

Noddy Holder, the former Glam Rock star and drummer Don Powell joined us in the Beer Garden of a West End pub, there were others, but it was a long time and can't remember their names. The Slade singer was a great bloke, a legendary boozer with more jokes than Jimmy Carr. And until this night we got on really well. Over the years we'd met at various parties in London. I'd visited his Wolverhampton pub and stayed the night (with Elle).

Cindy asked to be introduced and as a favour to me, had his picture taken with the human Barbie sitting on his lap. He put his arm around her, no big deal and completely innocent. Well, it was on Noddy's part. Unbeknown to me Cindy was about to do the dirty on us both. Without my knowledge or that of Noddy Holder she sold a fabricated story to The Sun (I didn't get a penny), which really gave me the hump. Cindy claimed they were having an affair and the picture was splashed all over the front page of The Sun. They used the picture I'd arranged, to support her story, so couldn't really blame Noddy for thinking I was guilty, but I wasn't involved. I genuinely wasn't, have I mentioned I didn't earn a penny out of it?

I was pissed off on many fronts. After publication I didn't speak to Cindy and Noddy never forgave me. If we were in the same pub or hanging out in the same club he'd blank me. He was convinced I had to be involved, but I wasn't and have I mentioned didn't make a penny out of it. Soon after this incident my mate Dan lost his job after selling a kiss and tell story to The Sunday People or News of The World. He spilled the beans about his affair with Bucks Fizz singer and Eurovision winner Jay Aston. Dan was her Press Officer making him guilty of both personal betrayal and professional misconduct.

One night in 1984 I met page 3 legend Sam Fox, and her mum (Tony Mottram took the pictures). I fancied her mum more, always had a thing for older women. Sam was a genuine Cock Sparrer who I met over the years at various showbiz functions. In the 80s she dated Panny a guy I knew who owned The Phoenix Apollo night club in Stratford. This was before Sam came out as a lesbian. With the right handling, in the management sense I mean, Sam could have been the new Barbara Windsor.

She once told me 'my boobs have shrunk, but my bum is curvier, it's like a peach', which was nice of her to share. Sam's motto was "If you've got it flaunt it", and she had a lot to flaunt. I reunited with Panny in the early 90's when he gave me a star-studded party at The Phoenix Apollo. Not for me personally, as I wasn't that rich or famous. But for my magazine, I'd help set-up Zit Magazine with publisher Russell Church and he asked me to organise the launch party. Russell was a dead-ringer for Ricky Gervais who had a bit of the Arthur Daley about him. I was also rewarded for all my help with two new jobs, chief showbiz pundit and TV columnist.

I decided to bring the West End to East London. On the night The Apollo in Stratford was packed with soap stars, pop singers, page 3 girls, professional footballers, World champion boxers, East End gangsters, old friends and some of my mates from Basildon. Local girl Suzanne Mitzi the best page 3 girl of all-time and West Ham star striker Frank McAvennie were also in attendance.

My mate Cockney comic Mickey Pugh was Master of ceremonies and guests were greeted by a Saddam Hussein lookalike. The guests included Barbara Windsor, Sam Fox, Jim Davidson, Brian Conley, Jonathan Ross, Joe Pasquale, Billy Murray, Ross Kemp, Bradley Walsh, Jimmy Jones, Bobby Davro, some top Underworld faces who wouldn't want to be named and gangsters like Tony Lambriano and Dave Courtney who certainly would. Also in attendance were Andy Swallow, Cass Pennant, Keith Chegwin, Pete Way from UFO, Jenny Torring, some West Ham footballers, Leyton Orient manager Frank Clarke and Antonia Moore, known as the black Marilyn Monroe impersonator.

Some-time during the evening I went outside to The Beer Garden with Antonia to catch-up on old times, my ex-wife caught us talking, just laughing and chatting but was not happy. Unlike my close mate and West Ham fanatic Steve Newton who had his picture taken Frank McAvennie and was well happy.

When we got home I was wacked over the head with a shower rail. Unlike me, my ex-wife was a very jealous woman, In 15 years she hit me four times, twice for talking to black girls. I was slapped because of two innocent kisses on the cheek, can you imagine the reaction if she'd caught us having sex? The other time was for hugging my best mate from school in Southend High Street who looked liked a combination of Bob Marley and Eddie Grant. Anyone would think she's racist!

It was a great night and the highlight was not meeting Suzanne Mitzi or Kray gang member Tony Lambrianou, it was my old mate Hughie Gadson turning up.

I hadn't seen him since my wedding, when he turned up with a bag of Charlie.

I also met glam model Zoe Anderson for the first time and we hit it off immediately. She was drop-dead gorgeous obviously, but also very nice, sweet and extremely funny. Not just a pretty face, but also a member of MENSA and a Scrabble champion, who went onto do Page 3 and become a Daily Star favourite.

We kept in touch and a year later I was working for lads magazine Front and we met up for a photo shoot. The 21-year-old lap dancer from The Circus Tavern had done well for herself appearing in various pop videos and SKY TV's brilliant football drama Dream Team. I was well happy she'd done so well.

One evening we met at The Circus Tavern on my way back from London after interviewing James Whale at Talk Radio Towers. I'd been driven up to town by old school mate Vere already impressed by meeting James Whale and now things would get even better. We pulled up outside The Tavern where we'd hung-out as teenagers before it became a lap dancing club. As I was meeting Zoe the bouncers waived us through to the VIP area.

She sat with us in her sexy lingerie, and we arranged to meet the next day, not the three of us, just me and her. We went for a drink at The Five Bells pub in Vange and when we walked in heads turned. She was wearing a white mini skirt that could pass for a belt. I'd always worked alone but we worked together on a few stories and three appeared in the national press. My favourites being Zoe turning down a presenter's job on Blue Peter, to host a sexy game show on Channel 5, it was a splash with a great picture of Zoe. There were others I can't remember the details, but all of a sexual nature that ended up in the Daily Sport, one was about 'golden showers' and bloody hilarious. We became and remain plutonic friends

One evening she drove me home in her red sports car, it was a boiling hot day and her skimpy outfit was a crowd pleaser. As we stood chatting, most of the men in Chestnut Drive decided to come out and cut their grass.

I had a few pictures taken with Zoe for work purposes. In one she was naked, another standing next to me topless and a third sitting on my lap in her underwear. Those pictures are the reason my ex-wife hit me for a fourth time. Once again, she was not amused and ripped up two of the pictures.

Only the underwear picture survives and currently hangs on the wall in what my kids call "the showbiz room". Zoe was a right laugh and quite shy when she wasn't performing. But in front of the camera she had few inhabitations. Once during filming for Bushell On The Box we did some location shots for the DVD and the police tried to arrest her for indecent exposure.

She was naked in someone's garden and we told her no-one could see apart from the cameraman. We lied and a nosy neighbour called the cops. I'd think back at things like that and other funny situations whenever I was feeling down after my heart operation. Laughter really is the best medicine. I enjoy looking back and luckily I'm blessed with a great memory. Maybe I should have forgotten all about singing and gone on stage as a novelty act. Johnson the Memory Man.

My near-death experience awakened the freedom fighter in me. It breathed new life into the middle-aged wannabee, but I'm not a fake 'born again rebel' because the Cockney Rebel never went away. I never stopped being a maverick with attitude and something to say. I hadn't died I'd just been sleeping.

Dead men can't talk, so I'm telling my story now before it's too late. A raw romp and no-holds barred a kiss and tell that reads like a novel, but straight-up it's a true story. I believe you can either tell a good story or you can't. It's not something that can be taught. Like all great singers, actors, footballers and boxers a raconteur is born and not made. Punk legend Garry Bushell once called me the "Arthur Daley of Journalism".

A perfect description and one I would have paid good money for. Hopefully this book containing the truth, the whole truth and nothing but the truth will make people laugh and make my kids proud of me. It's also time my estranged daughter knew the truth. I could reveal graphic details about her mother. I could 'slaughter' her mother by revealing X-rated details but that would give her genuine reasons to hate me. It's bad enough my daughter hating me for things I haven't done. So let's keep it civilised as I have more than enough family, friends and legal documents to convince my daughter of the error of her ways. Without being rude she is so wrong to model herself on Megan Markle.

My daughter is 'out of order' to condemn an innocent man.

I was a bloody good Father. A devoted dad who always put his kids first, they were the most important things in my life. I have loved many things in my life and had a number of obsessions, but such is my character can only handle one obsession at a time.

My three children replaced everything else as the most important things in my life. Much to the annoyance of my ex-wife and her parents (the in-laws from hell) both Sam and Adam were 'Daddy's Boys' from day one. My ex-wife was horrified as day after day my daughter followed in their footsteps.

My little Princess was always at my side, sitting on my lap and sleeping on my side of the bed. My mother-in-law from hell would make half-joking and snide comments about 'how Lucy was getting just like the boys'.

Ma Taylor knew how to press all the right buttons to trigger her daughter and cause friction. I'm not crawling or begging my daughter to 'love me', I just want her to know the genuine truth before she comes to her final conclusion about her dad.

I've always believed you should never be afraid of the truth, sometimes it hurts, but the truth is the truth, it can't be sugar-coated or ignored. I hope one day she'll be big enough to accept the truth and admit she was a victim of vile and malicious brainwashing.

I can honestly say hand on heart I'm one of the most child and female friendly blokes she'll ever meet. If she finds a partner to love her kids as much as I loved mine, she'll be a very lucky woman.

Fact: I have never hit a women or a child in my life. You probably can't remember but I was like putty in your hands. You always had me wrapped around your little finger. I always liked a joke and made you laugh not cry. I told a joke when you was born not knowing that years later it would be used against me. It was an innocent joke although I half meant it. I repeat it was a joke but years later your mother used it against me to stop me from seeing you.

She told Social Services I was dangerous and intended to hurt you, one big fucking evil lie. Here is the joke, and for the avoidance of doubt, I repeat it was a joke.

When you was born I said: "Lucy will wear braces on her teeth and a shaved head until she's Eighteen". Adding "I know what boys are like".

At the time everyone at the hospital thought it was funny and 'just me being me'.

Fast forward six years and your mother told Social Worker Peter Brown and the court: "You can't let Garry see Lucy, he's threatened to shave her hair off".

Can you imagine how I felt standing in Court? I was never a threat to my daughter and believe me your hair was never in danger.

I was never mentally ill, a manic depressive or would-be serial killer. If I met my daughter there is no way I'd depress or bore her to death. I'm pretty confident I'd have her laughing within minutes. Lucy, this is turning out to read like a CV with me auditioning to be your dad.

I want that job and hope that one day you give me the chance to prove I'm a nice bloke. I'd pass any test you set with 'flying colours' and that's why the Taylor mob stopped you from seeing me. I know you don't want to believe it but I really am one of the 'good guys'. I'm a funny bloke ask your brothers and their mates. They'd film me commenting on TV shows, it was like a DIY version of Gogglebox. Why don't you ask to see the clips? Back to me being slandered and verbally abused in Court.

Your mother lied "He's planning to kidnap Lucy and take her out of the country". These disgusting lies were believed by the court. If you don't believe me then take the time to read all the Social Services documents. Why are you scared of the truth? There was even worse to come, she told the authorities I was dangerous and that you, Sam and Adam were all scared of me. She then told the police I was planning to kill her and her boyfriend, which was fair enough but untrue.

What wasn't fair and a wicked lie was the false allegation I was also planning to kill you, Sam and Adam. That evil lie got me arrested and banged-up in Bellmarsh top security prison. I was sectioned and told unless I convinced psychiatrists I was 'sane' and not 'dangerous' I could be held for Twenty years.

How much of this do you know about? I have all the legal documents if you have the time or decency to read them. Are you really that 'stupid' that you can't workout you was brainwashed to hate me? Let me repeat so you can take it in. Your mother told the police I was mad, mentally ill and planning to kill my own children. Unless I could prove my innocence and sanity, I was looking at an indefinite life sentence.

Are you happy with that? I'll return to this later and explain how I was eventually found innocent of all false allegations. It took me five years to convince the Police, Social Services and Family Court that I was not mad, bad or dangerous. So far it has taken 19 years (and still counting) to convince you I'm an innocent bloke and a decent dad. If my daughter doubts any of the above I have 900 pages of official and legal documents obtained from The High Court that she should have the decency to read before wishing me dead. I hope that one day unlike her hero Megan Markle she'll discover her moral compass.

# Chapter Six
# This is a Modern World

1973. Back to the beginning and easier times. I wanted a Ziggy Stardust haircut and for five quid got a half-decent attempt at the He and She Hair Salon in Barking High Road. I wanted to be skinny so became borderline anorexic. I bought, begged and borrowed Bowie's back catalogue. Hunky Dory, The Man Who Sold The World, Space Oddity and The World of David Bowie. Along with Ziggy Stardust and Aladin Sane they became the soundtrack of my youth.

There was one particular song I fixated on and became completely obsessed with it was `London Boys` from The World of David Bowie. It was speaking directly to me. That song captured my mindset and sparked my imagination. A bleak yet beautiful song with a story about teenage speed freaks in London. It proved to be a catalyst for one of the pivotal changes in my life. It chronicled my life and love of fast drugs. I'd already learned bits and bobs from older siblings of my mates. I was aware that little blue pills helped them to dance all night and talk fast. I was discovering what drugs went with what music. It was like matching wine with food, and I was feasting, gorging and absorbing all that I could about Bowie's music and lifestyle.

Growing up in the early 70's there was a limited choice of escape routes for working-class kids. Back then even Noel and Liam wouldn't have stood a chance.

1976 would change all that. In childhood all my early heroes were men with big ego's and massive personalities. Loveable rogues like my dad, granddad and Georgie Best. From an early age interested in reading about The Kray Twin and The Great Train Robbers and watching Robin Hood on TV. I was fascinated by showman like heavyweight boxer Cassius Clay who became Muhammed Ali. I was glued to the Telly watching his press conferences and at the time confused how a black boxer could look like Elvis Presley.

At school while the other kids caught the measles and played with toys I caught the fame bug and was never cured. I was like a modern-day TV reality `star`, I had no talent but from an early age wanted to be famous. It was a massive part of my DNA. I also had a massive imagination and would lose myself in books and films.

I was also blessed with good looks, massive self-confidence and thankfully never cursed with shyness. Some of the few things I inherited from my dad.

He also had various 'words of wisdom' that I've not always followed but never forgotten. Like "you can't please all of the people all of the time", "If you walk into a room full of people, there will always be at least one who likes you" and "never talk to fat girls on the street". Like him I had a Danny Dyer accent and a Ray Winstone walk, more of a swagger than a traditional walk. When I went to Detention Centre and Borstal most of the black kids had the same swaggering walk. Years later, both Ian Brown and Liam Gallagher would have that walk.

One of the many reasons my stepmother hated me with such passion is because I looked more like my dad then his twin brother. We talked and walked the same but 'thank god' we didn't think the same when it came to family values. I was a loyal fucker and he was a selfish bastard. As a young kid I wasn't really good at anything, but this never undermined my confidence. I always wanted to be good at something and impress my dad, but it didn't happen overnight. My first attempt was football. I had all the passion, but early on not the ability.

I was obsessed and always reading football magazines and watching it on TV but on the pitch didn't impress my dad or the PE schoolteachers. Aged seven, I was often a reserve, Aged 8 a fringe player, at Nine and Ten just a regular member of the team.

My dad was not amused. He decided to take action and coached me every weekend and it worked. Almost overnight he transformed me into a natural striker and prolific goal scorer. I went from fringe player to Man of The Match to 'Top Dog'. Aged Eleven I never looked back.

I couldn't stop scoring goals. Some would say I became a "big-headed bastard", including my mum, and I did. Becoming the best after so long being one of the worst was toxic. I already had an ego to start off with and now I had a genuine reason to show off so I grabbed it with both hands. Every performer needs a platform, and my first stage was a football pitch. They do say "every flat surface is a stage"

My first performance was as a cheeky five-year-old in the front room of my Nan's East London council house. It was a rousing-version of the Cockney classic 'Maybe Because I'm A Londoner'. I still love that song. Throughout the swinging sixties a major social event in East End life was the big 'family party' with a more the merrier open house policy that took place on an almost weekly basis.

The Johnson family held more than most and it was at these parties with boozy singsongs around the family where I found my earliest audience. Every family member did a turn, so even the toddlers got a chance to perform. The guest list included neighbours, friends, extended family and sometimes total strangers, with `bring a bottle` being the only house rule. Gatherings such as this became legendary. It was at these shindigs where every guest had to sing for their supper, and I found my first fans. They were a captive audience so had no choice but to listen and sometimes cheer. My dad always stole the show with his Al Jolson routine. I was crap and to be honest didn't have The X Factor, but luckily even at that age had more front than Blackpool.

My dad had dozens of relatives, and I was always known as "Charlie`s Boy` and spoilt rotten. So always had them eating out of my hand and pretending to enjoy my performance. As is my character whatever I lacked in talent I made up for with enthusiasm and ego, which is why criticism has never affected me. Luckily I`ve always been my number one fan and at the same time my biggest critic.

As I got older and more addicted to these family gatherings, I murdered songs by everyone from Elvis Presley to The Beatles. Unlike any music lovers in the room. I loved the sound of my own voice. Over the years my singing voice has been `slagged off` by everyone from Garry Bushell to Ian Brown of The Stone Roses and Bruce Foxton of The Jam.

Aged Thirteen and no longer the innocent Cockney Choirboy I was already falling out of love with the academic side of school, though I loved the sporting and social benefits of attending Hassenbrook Comprehensive. I was obsessed with football and girls. Like most working-class boys I was genetically programmed to play football and chat-up girls. My Irish Cockney DNA also made me a rebel from a really early age. At fourteen, I was always going to school less and less each month. Truancy was like an addiction as I was charming more girls into bunking off school. My parents were at work so between 9am and 5pm I had an empty house, many of my mates and quite a few girls lost their virginity in my spare bedroom. Near the end I was only attending school when we had PE or a school football match. I was transforming from part-time schoolboy into a feral teenager. Aged fifteen my schooldays and education virtually stopped when my dad left and killed off any chance of following in the footsteps of Georgie Best. I would semi-retire from football and months later hang-up my boots forever.

The truth is I never got over my dad leaving or quitting football, a huge part of me died. I was never the same again. I spent the next fifteen years self-medicating and blocking out the past. As a child my dad was my hero and it took me a long time my dad was a selfish bastard, more fake than Monopoly money and Sir champagne socialist Starmer combined. After leaving the Detention Centre and discovering David Bowie I spent the next three years waiting for something to happen. I had no idea what the future would offer but first had to come to terms with my past. I come from a mixed marriage. My mum was a Catholic and my dad was a bastard who couldn't keep his hands off anything in a skirt.

I've never been selfish, but admit when it came to women, we were very much the same. I used girls as a schoolboy and a teenager, because I was angry, they were the same gender as my stepmother.

I never used women in my twenties because I was mixing with females who inhabited and were successful in a man's world. When it came to sex and drugs they behaved like men. So in a way I did follow in my dad's footsteps, variety was the spice of life except when I got married I changed. I became a one women man. My children came first. I grew up but my dad never did. I still looked but never touched, not once did my roving eyes become wandering hands. My three children would never be deserted by me. I've always been an anything goes type of character, a working-class liberal who was into sex and drugs more than most.

Not bragging it was just the circles I moved in, so I'm not some stuffy old prude into all that religious bollocks, and even though I don't believe in marriage I did take my vows seriously. I could never cheat on my wife, because by definition I would be cheating on my children. I never even thought about betraying my children. Innocent kids should never suffer the pain and hurt of coming from a broken home. I don't care what anyone says and however good I was at being a 'single dad' and sole carer my boys both had their lives disrupted.

They didn't ask to be born and deserved a normal childhood and although I always tried to do my best for them, they grew-up different from their friends and missed out on family life. My ex-wife and former in-laws can never be forgiven for what they did, and I just hope karma gets them. In all honesty the jury is still out on my daughter. Is she a nasty, spiteful, hateful person or an innocent victim of brainwashing? I sincerely hope, even believe she's a nice person and wish her a long and happy life 'with or without' me.

But me being me and the character and personality I have I can't lie, I genuinely believe she should do the decent thing and either tell me to "fuck off" to my face or explain in a long letter or email what she actually thinks I've done wrong. Many might disagree but I genuinely believe she owes me an explanation.

I worshipped my dad as a kid but hated him as an adult. When it came to parenthood my ambition was to be the opposite of him. At the ripe old age of Thirty-three I wanted to be a family man, a great dad and a faithful husband and proud to say I became all three. Never played for West Ham or had a best-selling album and dated Kate Moss but more importantly I was a top dad.

When I was nineteen and starting out on my showbiz career I would happily have settled for that. Believe me those great memories of bringing up my kids beat any other high I've ever had. Nowadays I dream of those days much more than I do of the sex, drugs and rock and roll years. I look back on my life through the eyes of a granddad, a mod pop.

My mum was a Catholic and my dad was an atheist who worshipped in the mirror at his own reflection. Notches on his bedpost and extra-marital affairs meant more to him than his child. How they ever met or married is beyond me. They had nothing at all in common, not even me. My mum wanted me to be the studious school prefect type and my dad wanted me to be a footballer.

My mum was happy to be a wife and mother, whereas he wanted to be a 'Ladies man'. I don't do him the honour of being a 'bird bandit' as I prefer the description of 'dog bandit'.

My dad was no man of taste and more of a Poundland Casanova who always went for quantity rather than quality. My parents were like chalk and cheese. She wanted a happy family life, whereas he wanted a world of pubs, clubs and betting shops, The Sporting Life newspaper and bow-wows in his bed.

He was Arthur Daley with all the chat and no trilby hat, a Del Boy character always telling jokes and looking for a pound note. The truth is he was a con artist, a fake, a snake and a liberty taker. But as a child I didn't know that, and to me he was always a superhero without a cape. Admitting naivety is a hard bit of humble pie to swallow, but admit I was taken in, hoodwinked and conned.

He was a 'star' in the eyes of an impressible kid. He was a former footballer and song and dance man, with flashy clothes, good looks and more jokes than Jimmy Carr. The more I think about him the easier it is to remember how much I loved him as a kid and feel slightly 'guilty' about slagging him off. I'm quite emotional, almost tearful, but however much I worshiped him for almost 15 years at the end of the day he betrayed me. I can't re-write history but I can tell the truth.

And the truth is he loved his fucking wife more than he loved me. He thought more of that fucking bitch than he did his own son, his own flesh and blood.

In my book that is unforgiveable. He left without a word of explanation or even bothering to say 'goodbye'. The final encounter between us took place outside a fish and chip shop in Stanford High Street. There were no hugs, tears or form of apology. Just a quid each for me and my best mate Vere and then he was off. Vere and I shared a lot. We lost our virginity to the same girl and my last meeting with my dad.

The bastard fucked-off and didn't give a moment's thought to the consequences of his actions, the hurt he caused and the chaos he left behind. As long as he was happy, that's all that mattered. He was throughout his entire life, a self-centred and vain individual convinced that the world evolved around him. Sorry if I sound bitter, but the truth is I still am. He didn't just walk out on his family like millions of other men throughout history. I could have handled that.

He went much further than most men and allowed his f*****g wife to 'send me to Coventry'. She stopped him from watching me play football. When he left I was in pieces but refused to cry or show any weakness. I lost control of my life but controlled my emotions. Never forgive and never forget, that became my mantra, and something I've practised ever since. The only person I can't take a stance on is my daughter. I genuinely don't know if she's a 'guilty' or 'innocent party'. I'm not a hypocrite but she's the only person I'd give a second chance. I'd like to think maybe years of 'brainwashing' and the influence of the Taylor Cult are to blame, but she owes it to me (and herself) to hear the truth.

As is my character I'm prepared to give her the 'benefit of the doubt' but it takes two to tango. She has every right to hate me, but, to hate some-one you must have genuine reasons. I could not hate a person I do not know and never met unless they were a child abuser or serial killer. Unlike my daughter, I have genuine reasons to hate my dad. I knew the bloke and personally suffered at his hands.

Lucy hasn't even had a row with me or ever been on the receiving end of any verbal or physical abuse. We've never been in the same room or even spoken on the phone yet she chooses to hate me and behave like the Meghan Markle of Essex. I am living proof that time is not a great healer and neither should it be, all forgiveness does is let the 'guilty person' off the hook. You can't whitewash past events or turn back the clock, but the truth is I am a one hundred per cent innocent bloke. Just because I hate one woman, my so-called stepmother, it doesn't mean I'm some kind of woman hating male chauvinist. My daughter has been brought up on a tissue of lies and programmed to hate me. That's why the Taylor family stopped her from seeing me, because they knew the real me was the opposite of the monster they created.

More independent evidence from two women who've known me all their lives and who both grew-up around me. Toni King the daughter of my Godfather and Leigh-Anne Franklin the daughter of my Dad's closest cousin. I've always had women in my life, in both my personal and professional life.

The people who helped when Sam and Adam were on the run from Essex Social Services were mostly women. I could not have coped, and won, without the help of Justine, Diane, Sarah, Kelly, Jodie and Samantha. Why hasn't my daughter got the guts to speak with these women? Maybe as I suspect she's scared of the real truth. These women did not all help me because of my looks, I should know as every morning I see myself in the mirror. They helped because they liked Sam and Adam and knew I was 'female friendly' and innocent. I'm not being big-headed, well maybe a little bit, but I know my daughter would end up loving me to bits.

Why are you so scared to put my theory to the test? A fact of life you should personally investigate. Showbiz Journo Garry Bushell has interviewed all the comedy greats in his career but always calls me "the funniest bloke he's ever met". I am nothing like the picture you've been painted. I won't bore you with hundred of stories from my past but mention some recent events.

I did two shows with TV funnyman Phil Jupitus in 2019. A lovely bloke and we got on like a house on fire and he called me "a very funny fella". That is some comment coming from a top comedian. He was a team captain for ten years on Never Mind The Buzzcocks and has worked with all the comedy greats from Jimmy Carr to Frank Skinner. Not comparing myself to those comedy giants, not even me would do that, but can you guess how chuffed I was when Phil called me a "funny fella". We hung out together for a couple of hours and I wasn't drinking or taking drugs so must have been good company. I'm not showing off or bragging just for the sake of it, but doing my best to sell myself to my daughter.

I'm not crawling to her or begging for love, which is why I aint scared to slag off her mother and my ex-in-laws. I could publically and verbally destroy her mother but prefer my daughter to read the court documents in privacy of her own home.

I don't hold back, I have no filter, I just tell the truth. If she's scared of the truth then so be it. If she had genuine reasons, I could live with her hating me, but can't accept if it's built on a tissues of lies. I am doing my best to sell the 'real me', the person I've known all my life as my daughter was brought up to believe that I'm something that I'm not.

She might not like my use of drugs or non-PC view of the world, but that's who and what I am. But what I'm not is the 'monster' in her head that was created by her mother, the Taylor family and Ginger Prevost. I have never been mentally ill or a bad dad who hit his children. I would be perfectly happy to take the strictest of Lie Detector tests on Live TV.

When my so-called stepmother died, I boycotted the funeral and my dad called me a "nasty bit of work". I mean the bloody nerve and sheer arrogance of the bloke from Planet Ego. I might be many things but I'm not a bloody hypocrite.

I've always been true to myself and genuinely proud that 'rightly or wrongly' I've always stick to my guns. Never been a sheep, a follower or a leader. Dating back to schooldays I always preferred being the number two in a gang. The world for me has always been black and white and never grey. The funny thing is when my wicked stepmother finally died I didn't cheer or even smile. There was no positive or negative reaction. I felt nothing. I rung my mum and said "she's dead". I'd waited so long for this day and to say that, it was a dream come true, but couldn't celebrate. I felt kind of angry with myself because I just felt numb. My extreme hatred was for a living person who emotionally abused a 15-year-old boy and not for a rotting corpse. She was my 'hate figure' for forty years who lived inside my head and ate deep into my soul. Had I attended her funeral I'd be forced to grow a beard as I could never again look myself in the bathroom mirror.

I can't change the way I am. My mindset and DNA is built on old-fashioned values and working-class morals. I am all about trust and loyalty and none of that moral code applied to my stepmother. I thought of her in the same way Jews think about Adolf Hitler. The bitterness towards my dad and his wife ever faded. Unlike my daughter I had a genuine reason to hate. I carried my hatred all the way to her grave because of what she did to me as a kid. It was emotional child abuse, plain and simple. My happy world was turned upside down and the next 4-years would be like an extreme X-rated version of Eastenders. I'm not playing the victim but I was only a child, and didn't realise a glass is never half empty but always half full.

I became deeply depressed, and it was horrible, the first 3 or weeks were the worst times of my life. I soon realised that depression and self-pity was not for me and that anger is full of energy. All my life I've hated bullies, be they schoolteachers, coppers, social workers or playground trash. Any adult who hurts a child physically or emotionally should be severely punished. I was 'attacked', 'abused' and shown no consideration by two selfish adults who had no consideration for the feelings of a child. Overnight my dad forgot I was his flesh and blood. I looked and acted older, easily passing for seventeen, but my Birth Certificate stated I was still a child. They turned me into a time bomb waiting to go off. I became feral and a teenage tearaway. I survived by self-medicating, being naughty and putting it about like a male version of a tart. I admit I did treat some girls as shit but at the time I was a teenage boy and not a grown adult. I was completely out of control, running wild, wasting my youth and now (as a self-educated adult) realise I was looking for some kind of 'love and affection'. In my teens I decided that one-night-stands rather than relationships would ensure no other female would ever hurt me. I spent years making sure no-one could get close enough to hurt me. My dad never hit me, not even once, never physically hurt me, but fucked me up emotionally. I don't think it was lasting damage but it lasted 15 years.

Men like him shouldn't be fathers and give all decent dad's a bad name. They are not rapists or paedophiles but do almost as much damage to women and children. This might have sold old-fashioned and non-PC, but the majority of women are the weaker sex and all children are born innocent. I'm not a prude in any way, anything goes in my book in my book, as long as it's between consenting adults and doesn't affect the lives of children. I'm not a born-again Christian, or a bible basher and believe in all pleasures of the flesh except for adultery. As soon as I tied the knot, I became a one-woman-man. It wasn't easy and may sound an old-fashioned point of view, but if a bloke can't live up to his marriage vows then why get married? Remembering this traumatic part of my life is no fun and will probably give me nightmares. So let's go back in time and to a day that still haunts me. I had no idea at the start of 1974 it would be last time I was locked-up as a teenager. But not my last spell behind bars as in 2007 it happened again when I was banged-up in Bellmarsh top security prison.

1974 was a big year, the last time I met Lyn, and also the first time I saw a pop star in the flesh. The meeting with the blonde beauty from my schooldays took place in Central London and the showbiz connection in Southend-on-sea. I saw Lemmy and Hawkwind at the Kursaal.

I was up in court at The Guild Hall with best mate Vere, who as at my side throughout my teenage years. We popped out at lunchtime and randomly bumped into Lyn who was working at an office in nearby Liverpool Street.

I hadn't seen her for about 18 months and believe me she looked even more stunning than previously. She really was a combination of a young Susan George and Britt Ekland and I was still attracted. We had a laugh and a chat and agreed to meet when she finished work. Guess which one of us wasn't standing outside Fenchurch Street Station at 5'o'clock.

That afternoon the power mad judge put Vere on probation and sentenced me to three months in a Detention Centre. Was he a racist bastard? Surely, he had to be. We were both in the dock on the same charge, but my black mate was let off and I was banged up for being white. Well maybe not, I think he was influenced by my attitude. At the time I was a flash, cocky seventeen-year-old and shouted out "You wouldn't talk to me like that if I was Reggie Kray". My mate laughed but the judge was not amused. Not only did my outburst put me behind bars it meant I didn't get to meet up with the 'love of my teenage years'. Sadly, we never met again.

I didn't think so at the time but maybe the judge did me a favour as my enforced holiday inspired my poem 'Ballad of The Young Offenders'. I'm now thinking to myself had I turned up at Fenchurch Street my life could have been so different. I genuinely believe that afternoon was my Sliding Doors moment, like most people when I watch that film I always think of the various "what if" moments in my life.

In 1992 I went along to a school reunion and discovered she'd emigrated to Australia in her 20's. My early childhood was brilliant, with my dad more like a big brother than a father. The trouble was he always loved himself and other women more than he my mum or me. His hobbies were football, gambling, drinking and chasing skirt. Nowadays very few marriages are genuine 'shotgun weddings' with an irate father of the bride all 'tooled-up'. My own marriage was like an alternative modern day shotgun wedding. I was threatened by my girlfriend "if you want kids you'd better marry me".

I'd been anti-marriage all my life and always avoided it, but I was in my 30's and wanted to be a dad. I had no choice, and it was an ultimatum I couldn't ignore. My ex-wife had just turned sixteen, no not when we got married, when we first met.

The historic meeting took place at a family Birthday party, no she wasn't my cousin, I'm Irish not Welsh. She had long blonde hair, a tiny waist and was wearing black skin-tight leather trousers. I thought to myself "yeah well nice, I'll have some of that" (I've always been an old-fashioned romantic). I deliberately brushed up against her but thank god nothing happened. Let me explain. At the party I was speeding out of my head and spent the night in Leyton at my Uncle Johnny's.

The following lunchtime we went for a few pints at his local Irish Working Men's Club. Two pints down and guess who walked in, only the sexy blonde from the night before. I walked over said "hello" and asked if she wanted a drink, she said 'yes' and at this moment had no idea of her age. I'd have put good money on her being eighteen. Then 2 or 3 of her mates walked in and all looking about fourteen.

I said "Don't mind me asking but how old are you?" and when she replied "sixteen" I couldn't get away quick enough and made my excuses and left.

I said 'goodbye" to my Uncle Johnny and headed home thinking 'Good God that could have been embarrassing'. I thought nothing more of it. She was a friend of a cousin I didn't speak to so our paths never crossed. Another four years would pass before we were re-united. I was invited to a family wedding and once again she was there. The first time I was on amphetamine this time I was high on cocaine. The stars were aligned and if you believe all that bollocks it was fate. But the truth is had this wedding been held a week earlier I wouldn't have been there.

I was ill and would not have attended. Was it also fate that we both turned up alone? Maureen my friend with benefits, shame about her name, but nice face and hair was visiting her parents in South Africa, and at the same time my future wife was dating a married bloke called Derek, who couldn't get away to attend the wedding.

And more info to support the 'conspiracy theory' that our meeting was fate and written in the stars. Had the Wedding been a week earlier she too would not have attended as she'd be struck down with severe food poisoning, which is one of the reasons she looked so good. She hadn't eaten for a week so was at her skinniest and looked like a wasted Kate Moss. I mean come on, how could I resist. She was still ten years younger than me but also four years older. She was now legally and morally an adult. Maybe, maybe not, I'll later mention what happened next.

# Chapter Seven
# This is no Soap Opera

Now this part is a story I've been waiting to tell since December 2013
   Case Number CM4P00300
   Judge Roderick Newton was (forced) by a Higher Court to follow in the illustrious footsteps of Lord Justice Mumby and the law-abiding Judge Moloney.
   He removed the Gagging Orders, through gritted teeth on every aspect of my personal, private and public life.
   I could now legally tell the uncensored truth about my fight for justice and lift quotes and content from all legal documents.
   I was tempted to go public but because of the adult content decided to wait. I did not want to expose my then 13-year-old daughter to graphic facts about sex, drugs and rock and roll. Not my adult truth and the adventures of my youth but wanted to protect her from the X-rated stories and truth about her mother. She was too young and also wanted to spare my son's blushes. But now the time is right. I can write an X-rated kiss and tell about my 15-year marriage. So here goes, only joking.
   After a lot of thought I've reluctantly decided to leave out any sexual content that might embarrass my ex-wife. There will be no graphic references to sex, porn movies, her dressing up, or role playing. As far as I'm concerned whatever happened behind closed doors stays behind closed doors. I'm a Mod, a modern man, but also got a moral code. The former Mrs Julie Johnson has had a lucky escape. I know from my tabloid past that the public would love to read about the X-rated version of my marriage, it would sell more books, but I'm not going to do that.
   The picture of my marriage will be more airbrushed Walt Disney than X-rated pornography. More like Mills and Boon than Fifty Shades of Grey. I know fans of Babe Station, Ben Dover and Only Fans will be disappointed, but I want my kids to read this book. It will still be hard-hitting and tell the truth, but for me it's more important to amuse than shock. I also want my sons to be proud of how their dad became a Z-list celebrity. I didn't make it to the top, but I got out of the gutter and had a lot of fun along the way. These are the kosher memoirs of a Punk Poet and Tabloid Terrorist. Not a revenge porn paperback or sentimental rags-to-riches saga.

This is no soap opera, but the true story of a man who was born to do more than simply exist. I could never do 9 to 5 or settle in a dead-end job.

After a lifetime of breaking rules and being different, I wanted to do it my way. It's factual and told in the way I talk, combining conversations and confessions rather than a conventional autobiography. As in life, I'll probably repeat myself many times and maybe confuse you because I am a mass of contradictions. I am 99% of the time a working-class liberal, but when it comes to any form of child abuse or sex crime I'm a right-wing fanatic. I don't believe in the death penalty but do believe in thirty-years solitary confinement without parole for all sex offenders regardless of colour, race or creed.

This is a roller-coaster ride down memory lane, and unlike Prince Harry's fantasy autobiography it will be the actual truth, and not 'my truth'. I used tabloid terrorism to infiltrate the world of showbiz and rub shoulders with the rich and famous. One night early in my career, I went to a lavish after show party for rock superstars Iron Maiden.

It was held in the Function Suite at Chelsea Football Club and because of my Cockney DNA I behaved like an East End tearaway. I slipped out to explore the stadium and found myself on the pitch (years later my youngest son Adam would score a goal on that very pitch). I then sneaked into the First Team changing rooms and couldn't resist writing "West Ham Rules" on the White-Board. I want you to read about my antics and enjoy the anecdotes in no particular order. All names have been changed to protect the innocent, so only the guilty will be named. Don't worry I'm only joking.

I'm not Prince Harry, I'm not bald and ginger, thank God, so won't be naming the lucky girl who took my virginity, but can I be so gallant about the first girl to suck my 13-year-old dick (in my bedroom under a poster of George Best)?

All the boys (and some of the bitchy girls) thought she'd leave school and become a page 3 girl because she loved taking her top off behind the Youth Club or at the back of the local park. She was the talk of the school playground because one lunchtime she did an 'Erica Roe' on the football pitch (younger readers can Google Erica Roe). I won't name the teenage exhibitionist as I have no wish to embarrass her. I will be attacking my dad and his f*****g wife who made my life hell and also having a slight 'pop' at my daughter Lucy. I'll be holding back because I'm not sure if she's 'guilty' for treating me like dirt or the innocent victim of brainwashing. The truth is I would pass any number of Lie Detector Tests because all the official revelations are lifted from Police and Court documents. If it's facts you're after, you'll find them here. My memories are never dull or in black and white, but always vivid and in Technicolor.

As a showbiz journo I got to meet hundreds of famous faces and most of my rock and roll heroes.

It's not always a good idea to meet people you idolise so I avoided George Cole and David Jason. Just in case they wouldn't be the people I wanted them to be.

I idolised there alter-egos Arthur Daley and Del Boy Trotter and didn't want to risk being disappointed. The two biggest heroes of my life were and still are David Bowie and George Best. I was genuinely nervous when meeting both and felt like a devout Roman Catholic having an audience with the Pope.

I also met Sir Bob Geldof before and after Live Aid. Twice at record companies when he was begging and pleading with pop stars to sing on "Do They Know It's Christmas". The third time was in a Manchester hotel months after the concert. Bob had a virus and was drinking orange juice, under the weather, but still able to hold court in the bar. There were 7 or 8 of us including two PR girls from the record label. One of them the blonde was a Northerner who I'd fancied her for months. Her mum lived nearby so dropped in to say 'hello'. I was well impressed how Bob talked to me like a mate and made a fuss of her mother. He is a genuine man of the people.

There was no happy ending for me as the PR girl chose dinner with her mum over room service with yours truly. Weeks later I went to Dublin with her work colleague and stayed at a plush 5-star hotel all expenses paid. I smuggled three grams of speed through customs and one of the highlights was drinking green Guinness at 7am. The civil war was still going on in Northern Ireland and for my own safety was told to talk in whispers and not reveal my Cockney accent at the gig. I was thinking but I'm half-Irish my mum is Catholic and comes from the Dublin suburb of Blackrock. It's so hard not to talk when you're speeding so genuinely feared I'd be exposed and be shot by the IRA.

Also had a pint with Sex Pistol Steve Jones in a Fulham pub he was like a rock and roll Dave Courtney with more stories than JK Rowling. He's a genuine working-class hero who like me had been banged-up in a Young Offenders Prison. He now presents his own radio show Jonesy's Juke box in America. Bumped into Sid Vicious walking down the Kings Road and personality wise he was the complete opposite. Nothing like his image and in many ways almost shy.

Had a great Ziggy Stardust haircut with snake hips and skinny waist, really looked the part which is why girls loved him but his image was one hundred per cent fake. He wasn't vicious and softer than a baby's nappy. The media lied about Johnny Rotten saying he was thick but he wasn't.

The John Lydon TV interviews always show how smart and articulate he really is.

The Sex Pistols were brilliant and changed the world, but so wrong to replace Glen Matlock with Sid. Just imagine how good a second album would have been.

It was great meeting legends like George Best, Michael Jackson, George Michael, Whitney Houston, Ozzy Osbourne, Dale Winton and Barbara Windsor. A diverse collection of celebs and most were memorable and never to be forgotten encounters. One of the people I wish I'd never met is child abuser Gary Glitter. He always had the gift of the gab, and vast supply of cocaine but being taken in by that pervert makes my blood boil.

Would I speak to him again? Yes, through a medium. 2013:

Like our saviour Jesus Christ, I rose from the dead, only I went one better and did it twice. After 29 days in a coma and on a life support machine I returned to the land of the living. I came back for a second bite of the cherry. For the eternal optimist it was more than a second lease of life, I saw it as another shot at stardom. Most people would see it as the last throw of the dice whereas I saw it as another stint in the spotlight. I would write a book and then a film script, you're thinking "what drugs is this guy on" but I say read on.

At first it was strictly nostalgia and talking about the past like a guest on Radio 4's Desert Island Discs. But then, as with most things in my life, fate stepped in. I was contacted by Swedish rock star Soren Sulo Karlsson, who wanted the punk poet to write lyrics for his new album. I supplied him with a dozen new ditties, but knew my old stuff was much better. I was soon in the studio with Sulo, former Clash drummer Terry Chimes, singer Idde Schultz and top record producer Kevin Poree. The Swedish star gave my old punk poems a rock and roll makeover and music mogul John Dryland was blown away. Cargo Records released the album 'Punk Rock Stories and Tabloid Tales' which received rave reviews including a five-star rating in StreetSounds magazine.

I was soon doing TV and Radio interviews. So how do I tell you my story?

The answer to that is "my way" and not in the traditional and sometimes boring style of childhood, teenage years, marriage, divorce, death. Who today plays their favourite album in chronological order? Just as we select the Playlist for our MP3s, I've chosen a new and hopefully entertaining way to write a modern-day autobiography. First, a statement of fact, I am not and have never been what people would call a mainstream celebrity. I've been on the telly now and again, done a few radio interviews but never been approached to appear on Celebrity Big

Brother (I'd do it like a shot), or I'm A Celebrity (not for a million quid). I've performed as a punk poet, singer, written songs, impersonated a tabloid journalist, and other bits and pieces from stand-up comedy to rock and roll management. What I am is a born daydreamer. A celebrity is something completely different.

In the old days celebs were famous for having genuine talent or for actually doing something entertaining. A hit record, box office film or starring role in a TV series. Nowadays, if you appear on reality shows like TOWIE, or bake a cake with Mary Berry, you are called a "celebrity". The fame game is not what it was but I can't knock it, as it gave me everything I wanted. Sex, drugs and rock and roll lifestyle.

I was the 'star' of my own reality soap opera, a real-life drama, the only thing missing were TV cameras. I played the part of a Cockney wide-boy more times than George Cole and David Jason. I was doing it before Mark Wright was born.

I believe you can either tell a story or you can't. It can't be taught and with the help of 'fast drugs' I was pretty good. Like all great singers, actors, footballers, and boxers, a raconteur is born and not made. This is my life, written in a style that will soon be the only way to write a $21^{st}$ century autobiography. The old days of when I was born, where I grew up, my first love and what I did in chronological order are long gone. Welcome to the modern world. Punk writer and Tabloid Journo Garry Bushell described me as "The Arthur Daley of Journalism". A perfect description and one I would have paid good money for.

Hopefully this book will transform me from Z-list to B-List celebrity and gain me an invite into the Big Brother house. The first thing you should know about life as a professional scammer is that you're never off duty, like a Copper without a uniform and always looking for a lead, or a face to fit-up, even when you're taking the kids to a Christmas pantomime. One year we went to see EastEnders heart-throb Ross Kemp starring in Dick Whittington at Southend Cliffs Pavilion. There were almost as many mums as screaming kids in the audience. It was more like a Chippendales Convention, and this gave me a great idea. I invented a stalker. It worked because there was a germ of truth. I made up a story where Ross was being stalked by an obsessive fan. Women were hanging around the stage before and after every performance, I just enhanced it. I came up with the idea that Ross posted guards outside his dressing room and left every night by a different exit. My 'source' told me he was living in fear. I wrote she was hanging around the stage door after every performance and that every night Ross had to leave by a different exit. This clever piece of creative writing was a Sun Exclusive and paid for the panto trip and a Christmas present for my wife. I've always had a soft spot for panto and once appeared in my local amateur production of Jack and the Beanstalk. I danced like John Travolta in that movie, no, not Saturday Night Fever, or even Grease, but the scene where he was machine-gunned down in Pulp Fiction.

I've many great memories about panto but saved the best for last. My 1998 Wimbledon encounter with Swedish stunner Britt Ekland, a teenage crush and life-long obsession. She no longer looked like the stunning beauty hanging on Rod Stewarts arm. Her character rolling about topless on a bed in the gangster movie 'Get Carter' having phone sex in black tights is still one of the sexiest scenes in UK movie history, but she was still very attractive for her age. She was well past her sell by date, but still sexier than most women half her age. No wonder Rod the Mod fell in love with her. I will always have a soft spot (and a hard one) for Britt.

Another example of creating stories out of nothing we're my many showbiz exclusives about former Blue Peter star John Leslie and then girlfriend Abi Titmus.

It was her stunning looks and blonde hair that first got me interested in the naughty NHS nurse. In 2003, the hunky TV presenter was accused of rape and Abi became a 'star' by accompanying him to court every day. For what seemed like months they were the lead item on every news bulletin and front-page headlines in every tabloid. Leslie seemed to age in every picture, whereas Abi transformed herself from 'girl next door' into a genuine sex symbol. When a friend told me Abi was obsessed with American TV beauty Pamela Anderson, I couldn't resist the temptation boost her image and my bank account. I invented stories about her joining the cast of Baywatch, making a soft-porn calendar and being invited to Hugh Hefner's Playboy mansion.

When John Leslie was acquitted, I wrote he was rebuilding his career in America and auditioning for the role of James Bond. (If anyone doubts any of my content I've got the press cuttings to prove it). I'm not sure what happened to John Leslie but Abi ditched her nurses uniform and as I predicted became a 'porn star'.

She was, for a while the Number One pin-up in lad's mags Loaded, Front and on page 3 of The Daily Star. The naughty nurse went from giving bed baths to oral sex, starring in a sex tape and landed a presenter's job on an Adult TV Channel. She became the most famous nurse sin Florence Nightingale. For those who are interested Abi's finest hour is still entertaining teenage boys and dirty old men on You Tube. Not a word of this autobiography is a figment of my imagination as, like me, 27 scrapbooks containing newspaper cuttings, legal documents, sworn statements and medical records do not lie. The Punk Poet only deals in facts. It has to be the truth, the whole truth and, nothing but the truth. I would love to promote this book on national TV wired to a Lie Detector machine and observed by a panel of body language experts. So if Jeremy Kyle is reading this, please get in touch.

My story might read like a novel but believe me it's a 100% kosher factual account of my life. I grew up reading about the Underworld exploits of Reg and Ronnie Kray and the adventures of The Great Train Robbers.

Hero worshipping George Best and David Bowie and watching great British films like 'Get Carter', 'The Long Good Friday', 'Villain' and 'Get Carter'. Fact or fiction it didn't bother me. I also liked Robin Hood, Jesse James, Guy Fawkes and Dick Turpin. I don't know why, maybe because of my Irish heritage, but I've always been attracted to rebels.

I have always supported the underdog. The Jews in Nazi Germany, blacks in Apartheid South Africa, and the white working-class used and abused by Tory Toffs and champagne socialists. The British Establishment is more deadly than the American Mafia. I am not a follower of fashion, politically correct, a loonie-leftie or right-wing bigot. My view of the world is my vision. It might not make sense and admit I'm a mass of contradictions, but always honest and loyal to family and friends. I am at heart a working-class liberal with middle-class manners who dislikes the royal family and all it stands for. I'm not a traditional patriot, but at the same time don't like people attacking my country or praising their own.

I truly believe that nationality is an accident of birth and where you're born, unless it's Australia, doesn't make you superior or inferior to others.

I genuinely believe being born Australian is the greatest gift in the world and can't understand why Aussies swap Bondi Beach for Earls Court. When I win the Lottery I'll buy Australian passports for all my family. I am just an individual and not a paid-up member of any so-called society or tribe.

I am at heart an outsider who only cares about his friends and family. I have no interest in orthodox religions or party politics. I am anti-establishment (who genuinely hates all politicians) and would describe myself as a genuine life-long rebel. I've worn the T-shirt and 'walked the walk'. I am a practising rebel who dresses like a Mod with my own beliefs and code of conduct. I have the laidback character of a Hippy but will always think like a Punk and dress like a Mod. I deliberately repeat myself to make sure you understand what I am and where I stand. Wow – that was a bit of a rant, but I'm trying to paint you a picture and fully explain my personal beliefs and moral code. It's my manifesto, and unlike Labour and Conservative General Election Manifestos it's 100% true.

Fact:

In my day Working-class kids had football, boxing or rock and roll (if they were any good at) to save them from the dole. In the modern world today's teenagers also have reality TV and Podcasts. The hero of this book tried all the 1970s escape routes from boredom and poverty and failed at all three. You can also add marriage to that list. That is why I was once nicknamed 'the nearly man'. At Fifteen I gave up a promising football career because of a 'family bereavement', well that's what it seemed like at the time. The truth is my dad 'pissed off' with the latest in a long line of 'fancy women'. He was no longer cheering me on from the touchline. Not embarrassed to admit that I'm just as bitter today as I was back in 1972 but I hide it well. Nobody would ever guess I'm only one tablet away from depression.

Broken-hearted I hung-up my football boots but looking back I should have carried on being the 'Georgie Best of East London' and the 'white Pele of Essex'.

At the time I thought I was getting back at him for walking out, but it was a gross misjudgement on my part. He didn't care. It didn't bring him back and I never got to pull on the famous Claret and blue shirt of West Ham United. I lost all interest in football for the next twenty years. Boxing was just a passing phase, probably because I wasn't very good at it. I could take a shot and had a head like concrete, but I lacked the killer punch. I wasn't a Sugar Ray Leonard in the ring, or the great Mike Tyson on the cobbles. Then there was sex and drugs and rock and roll. No problem with the first two – I was a natural.

The problem was I couldn't sing and that's a big problem when you're the singer in the band. I formed a band called The Buzz Kids and our debut gig was also our last. I think that tells you how bad we were. We were contenders and the real deal performing and rehearsing in the garage but couldn't do it live. I was allergic to singing my own songs in public but loved doing karaoke. In the bedroom mirror I was a 'punk Ziggy Stardust' and 'the future of rock and roll' but on stage I melted like an ice cream on a hot day. I loved an audience when I was talking and holding court in the pub, but not when I was singing my protest songs. I've always loved protest songs and protest singers from Dylan to Lennon in the 60's to The Sex Pistols and The Clash in the 70s. All my adult life I've always hated politicians and Labour MPs more than others, from Blair to Sir Starmer they are all, pathological lying enemies of the Working-class.

Newspaper cuttings from 1976 confirm it was both Labour and Tory Councils who banned The Sex Pistols from playing in towns all over England. The Tories are the natural enemy, but they don't hide it, whereas the champagne socialists pretend to be the champions of the working-class. They haven't been on our side 1945. It was Labour politicians who ruined East London. They knocked down my Grandparents house and bulldozed the street they'd lived in for fifty years to build ugly concrete tower blocks. Punk Rock was the voice of the working class and Labour MPs tried to silence Johnny Rotten and Joe Strummer. Snobs like Sir Kier Starmer and Lady Emily Thornberry do not represent the Working class.

Like those born with silver spoons in their mouths all champagne socialists believe they were born to rule. What this country needs is a leader with a social conscience, with a sense of humour and genuine working-class DNA.

If I was a great orator like Nigel Farage or George Galloway I'd apply for the job. My slogan would be "Vote for me to end poverty and homelessness" and I'd campaign to abolish private schools, the Royal Family and House of Lords.

The hero of this book tried and failed at football, singing and all things showbiz. That's why I made sure I succeeded as a dad. I was committed to being a fun Father and best friend. None of all that discipline bollocks for me, I was more liberal than a hippy from a Greenpeace commune. But somehow lost my daughter who has grown up to be a UK version of Megan Markle. I'm nothing like Thomas Markle or any of those feckless fathers featured on The Jeremy Kyle Show. I am the complete opposite. So why does my daughter hate me and wish me dead?

That's the million-dollar question. We've never had a row, a verbal or physical bust-up but she hates me! It's hard to take for a bloke like me who sees things in black or white. To quote The Rolling Stones song "I used to love her but it's all over now". That's how I feel at my lowest, but such is my character I always bounce back. Of course I love my daughter. I have replaced some of the unconditional love I once had for her with the feelings I now have for my grandchildren. They love me more than my daughter can ever hate me. If that seems cold and heartless please let me explain. From 2005 to 2012 I was always ultra-loyal to my daughter and wouldn't hear a 'bad word' about her. I sent Birthday cards and Xmas presents every year.

Not once did I get a reply. I didn't want long letters of gratitude but a "thank you" would have been nice. She was just a kid so never felt betrayed or angry about her behaviour towards me. That came later. I expected more when she became a teenager. Part of me always thought she'd become curious about her dad and make contact. I remained loyal until she was 21 and became an adult. Maybe boys are wired differently to girls but if my dad had NOT walked out on me there's no way I would have disrespected him as she has me. Part of me because of the loyalty 'gene' that controls my DNA tries to make excuses for her and blame it on brainwashing. She's still my 'flesh and blood' so when I argue with myself part of me always defends her conduct.

Aged Thirteen and as my life hung in the balance she refused to visit me in hospital. I'd been in a coma for 29 days and when I was back in the land of the living the Hospital Chaplin contacted her on my behalf.

There was no visit or even a 'get well' card. The question is, was that because she's hard hearted like her mother or just a 13-year-old child? Or clutching at straws, and again giving her the benefit of the doubt maybe her mum didn't pass on the message. My daughter also ignored a request from my own mum and wouldn't co-operate with the Salvation Army. In 2016 she did not reply to my final letter and again in 2019 snubbed the intervention of the Salvation Army.

As is my character once again I gave her the benefit of the doubt, maybe she has no knowledge of any of the cards, presents and letters. Perhaps the information about my health condition was not given to her. I bend over backwards to give my daughter the benefit of the doubt. Then BANG a bombshell revelation. I was handed a legal letter from Essex Social Services stating in her own words:

"I don't want any contact with my dad" but doesn't explain why.

At the end of the day she's my daughter so I'll always make excuses for her, maybe just as part of my brain froze when I was fifteen, part of hers froze at the age of Seven. Maybe she looks at me through the eyes of a child who still believes the lies she was told as a toddler. On advice from Essex police officer Jenny Stedman, I went to court in May 2022 and won my last out-standing case. Amazingly it was her evidence that provided the final piece in the jigsaw. She supplied the 'bullet points' and I fired them.

The judge ruled I could legally approach my daughter in the street or knock on her front door. My ex-wife went ballistic and tried to overturn the ruling. A journalist friend the crime reporter Jon Austin was in court. He phoned that evening and said "When the Judge ruled against your ex-wife she stormed out of the court". I contacted my daughter, this really was for the last time, and informed her of the court judgement, and as per usual she ignored me.

That was the final straw. She's no longer a young child, she's a adult, a 24-year-old-woman with a boyfriend but continues to behave like a child and treat me as a stranger. In 2008 she was am innocent 8-year-old child brainwashed by her mother and vile grandparents to hate me. No way is that her fault and can't be blamed in any way. I can even understand why she was scared to see me, as god only knows what load of old bollocks and wicked lies she's been told about me.

Was she scared of upsetting the Taylor family and those lying bunch of bastards from Wales. The Welsh Mob who only met me half a dozen times in fifteen years were quite happy to brainwash my daughter against me. Then there was the truly evil ginger geezer bird Sally Prevost, one of the nastiest ugliest women on Planet Earth who got `inside her head`. Ginger was a genuine enemy and our mutual hatred for each other goes back 35 years. Between 1989 and 2005 we only met 4 or 5 times and maybe she saw my sons on three occasions. She was never invited to Christenings, Birthday parties, Xmas gatherings or summer functions as I couldn't stand being in the same room as her. Facts my daughter should know that will explain why she `brainwashed` you to hate me. And this is very important, PLEASE check these facts and if you disprove a single claim then using `the domino effect` it will rightly destroy my argument. I'll use Bullet Points to make it easy for you:

- When I met your mum she and Ginger had been best friends since school.
- Your mum was also her driver.
- I broke up their friendship
- I then married her best friend
- From day one see tried to split us up
- My mum said on our Wedding Day "you want to watch her, she'll try to break you up".
- She was right about that.
- Constant sniping and bitching.
- In 1992 before SAM was born I banned her from the house.
- No contact for about 10 years until a few months after she left her husband and got divorced.
- Ginger then got her claws back into your mum and encouraged her to have affairs.
- She provided various alibis when your mum was cheating.

Importantly and although I hated Ginger because of my character/personality when she turned up at her house with her ` kid` and short of cash I gave her either £700 or £800. I wouldn't piss on her if she was on fire or give her 50p for a cup of tea but couldn't see a little kid go hungry.

Lucy do a fact check on all the `bullet points` and I'll make a deal with you, if they all `stand-up` which they will, promise me you'll get in touch. You're not to blame as growing-up you had no idea of the history and `bad blood` between us. I'm happy to take a lie detector test anytime, anyplace, anywhere, but everyone involved in your upbringing refused the offer. Ginger didn't know Sam, Adam, you or me but told Social Workers I was a "bad dad" so `God only knows` what kind of vile bollocks she told you. I won't embarrass my daughter and write about what went on between 2004 and 2011. All she has to do is make a FOI request to Essex Social Services or borrow the 900 pages of documents I was given on the orders of The High Court.

My daughter is scared to meet me and of knowing the facts because deep down she knows I'm telling the truth about her mother, my former in-laws and that ginger Prevost? I've said to my daughter lets visit the police or meet the Head of Essex Social Services together but always declines my offer. As a journo and 'news junkie' I can't get my head around why some people are scared of the truth. My 24-year-old daughter should be smart enough to understand the bleeding obvious, if the Taylors didn't like me for the 15 years, I was their son-in-law, they aren't going to say anything nice when I became an ex-son-in-law. You don't need a University Degree to work that out. Let me tell you the truth about Mr Tony Taylor. He was the polar opposite of me and we clashed from day one. He was like something out of the 1950's. He was a small-minded racist bigot. Selfish, ignorant and hated everything about modern day culture. He was a fan of Bernard Manning, Alf Garnett and Benny Hill. To him any bloke who dyed his hair or wore earrings was gay. I did both. Have you got the picture? He had one view of the world, and it was his, a skinny little runt who had plenty to say behind closed doors but not the guts to repeat in public. Mr Taylor was a pathetic armchair general who sorted out the world's problems wearing cheap Tesco jeans, a string vest and tatty old-fashioned slippers. He was the spitting image of the George Roper character in the 1970s sit-com George and Mildred (check it out on YouTube)

Apart from beer and fags the only true love of his life was Adolf Hitler. The mass murderer was his hero and like the Fuhrer he wanted to gas all Jews, Blacks and Queers. He would say things like "When I was young there were signs in windows saying 'no blacks, no dogs, no Irish'. Those were the good old days"

Lucy are you aware my mum is Irish, I'm half-Irish so that makes you quarter-Irish.

Old man Taylor was always mocking the Irish.

Are you aware I'd wind him by getting your brothers to wear Irish football shirts and believe me he was not amused. He never liked me and, believe me the feeling was mutual, and anyone who is not as 'thick as shit' can't you work out why he and his brain-dead wife did a hatchet job on me? They spent 15 years enjoying every moment of turning you against me. I'd love you to admit I've painted a pretty accurate picture of him. Have you ever wondered why he hated black people? Let me supply the answer. Do you know he disowned his sister when she married a black guy? I'll bet my life you've never met any of your mixed-race relatives, or even knew they existed. He disowned his sister weeks before her wedding and they've never spoke. Now be honest did you know your mum had 3 or 4 mixed-race cousins?

Are you aware my best mate from school and throughout my teens was banned from attending my wedding because he was black? I can only imagine the sort of comments you were subjected to growing up under his influence. Again, I ask you to be honest and admit I've painted a pretty accurate picture of Mr Taylor.

As Sam and Adam got older I'd say to your mother "Please tell him to stop mouthing off in front of the boys". What can I say about his wife, apart from the fact she looked like Mrs Brown from that awful BBC comedy Mrs Brown's Boys?

I could say a lot, but won't as just thinking about her is depressing enough. I don't think my mother-in-law from hell ever laughed. The truth is your mum wasn't just scared about you meeting me, she was terrified. And with good reason, she knew my character better than most and that you would 'love me to bits'. That is why the Taylor family, the Welsh mob and ginger Prevost deliberately lied to a young girl. It was a form of child abuse.

The truth about your first five years on planet earth is this, 'you thought the world of me' and the feeling was mutual. You followed me everywhere and would never leave my side. Your mother was not amused and not a happy bunny. It made her insecure because Sam and Adam were 'daddy's boys' and you were a 'daddy's girl'. I have no idea what she's like now but throughout our marriage she was a very jealous woman. It must be a 'family trait' as Ma and Pa Taylor were jealous of my dad, because just like Sam and Adam you always flocked to him.

Maybe you're a jealous person I don't know. If you are you've inherited it from your side of the family, as it isn't part of the Johnson DNA. Like me your brothers haven't got a jealous bone in their bodies. Throughout my marriage I was hit over the head or verbally abused for looking at other women, I stress looking at other women. I couldn't break the habit of a lifetime, but never touched. I'm no Saint, far from it, but I am ultra loyal and always put family first.

Once I became a dad, it was a job for life, and no woman on earth would ever be desirable enough to threaten the relationship I had with my kids. And while we're on the subject of your mother and the rest of the two-bob Taylor family let me tell you a few home truths. I could sugar coat everything to crawl into your good books but not interested in all that old bollocks. I want you to like the real me not some fake version. At the end of the day I've always been a seeker of Truth and Justice. Maybe it's the journo in me or just a life-long obsession. Your mother had an odd relationship with her weird parents, and I always refused to join in. It's hard to explain, even for a 'people-watcher' like myself, but in a way, she was scared of them. Not in a physical way, as I genuinely don't think they ever hit her, but in their presence, she was always a different person.

In a nutshell the Taylor's were old-fashioned and boring. People rarely laughed in their company. I was expected to behave likewise, but as is my character, I would deliberately say things to shock them. It's the only way I could relieve the boredom of being in the same room. I loved getting a reaction be it a raised eyebrow or deadly silence but would never dance to their tune, and along with the 10-year age gap is why they never liked me. They molly-coddled and treated your mum like a child instead of a grown-up woman. Ma and Pa Taylor would always call her "Dear", never 'babe' or 'darling' but always "dear" which would really wind me up. Be honest, does any of this remind you of growing-up under their old-fashioned influence? Am I lying or telling the gospel truth? It's a really important question because if none of this rings true it makes me look like a liar and would rightly make you doubt any of my other claims.

I wouldn't take that risk as convincing you of my honesty is what this book is all about. Your mother wouldn't/couldn't show any emotion or talk about adult subjects in their presence. I'm a very tactile person and the Taylors were the polar opposites. Your mum was, how can I say 'very affectionate' when her parents weren't around. Always kissing and cuddling in private, showing affection in public but never in front of her stone-age parents, she was always an emotionless ice queen. If I tried to kiss her she'd flinch and pull away just like your mate Megan Markle does with the ginger Prince.

Apart from our Wedding Day, they never witnessed us touching lips. Whereas in front of my dad your mother would sit on my lap, show affection and roar with laughter. I could always make her smile in private, at parties and in the bedroom.

In the privacy of the bedroom, she was a different person. What would a psychiatrist make of her split-personality? I could tell you stories that would give her parents heart attacks and make you blush, but I won't. The X-rated stuff will not enter the public domain. As much as I'd love to embarrass your mother and her parents I won't do it. There was one thing I loved doing to wind-up Ma Taylor, if I'd spotted her heading towards our house, I'd wait ten minutes then come bursting through the front door shouting "I'm home, get your clothes off". That never went down well with the prude from the 1920s which is why I kept on doing it. Your mother would only laugh when I made the same 'joke' in front of my dad.

I'll say one thing on the subject of sex and leave it at that, without going into detail (though all the facts are in the court documents). It was my medical condition that started with circulation 'problems' and ended with a triple heart by-pass, that explains why she started having affairs. You might not like the truth but can't argue with facts. Your mum confessed on oath in a court of law.

For-the-record she admitted two affairs and denied a third. Again because of the 'Domino effect' I wouldn't risk lying to a daughter I wanted in my life. One false allegation or single lie would cast doubt on my testimony and ruin any chance of us being reunited. I am really not that stupid to take such a risk.

Moving on: Contrary to what the Taylor family have told you and brought you up to believe, I'm the least male-chauvinist person (apart from Football) you'll ever meet in your life. I'm telling you hand on heart if you meet a partner more female and child friendly then me you're going to have a happy life with a nice bloke.

Your middle-name is my tribute to the great plutonic 'love of my life'. The woman is a class act, smart, sassy, independent, and the most loyal person I've ever met. When I came out of prison (on trumped up charges) for 7 attempted murders she was the first person to ring me up. When I got out of hospital after my first heart op she sent a Fortnum and Mason hamper.

Rebekah employed and looked after me for over Twenty years. She also kissed and cuddled Sam and Adam as kids. I was also employed by many other females of the species. My great friend and Bowie fanatic Annette Witheridge was my boss at The Daily Star. She now lives in New York, but we remain in touch. Sharon Marshall (now the TV critic on This Morning) was my friend and boss at The Sunday People who gave me my own Showbiz column. I also worked for Jane Moore, now presenting ITV's Loose Women and Claudia Connell at The Sun.

My top showbiz contacts were mostly women. Pat Stead, Joanna Burns (both at my wedding), Patsy Johnson, Jasmine Kimera, Bernie Coyle, Chrissie Cremore, Jenny Torring and Erica Echenberg. Jenny was a 'Debbie Harry' lookalike, Bernie took me to Dublin for one of the best weekends of my life. I flew out the country with no passport and pockets full of 'fast drugs'. Pat introduced me to Michael Jackson and then George Michael at her Birthday Party. Erica I lived with, Chrissie I had a one-night stand with and Jasmine, who unfortunately I didn't have a fling with was a stunning Sade lookalike.

Patsy and I stayed up North in the same hotel as the Southampton football team when they were managed by the legendary Lawrie McMenemy.

When we came down for breakfast we shocked the entire team. She had shoulder length Bob Marley dreadlocks, and I was sporting a dyed-blonde Rod Stewart feather-cut. We looked an amazing couple, but this was 1984 and before professional football went cosmopolitan. Years later Patsy got me `beat-up` in East London. Lucy you should ask your mum about the time she attacked me in Walthamstow Market. I spotted Patsy at one of the stalls and called out her name. We said "hello" kissing and hugging in the street. Afterwards your mum went `mental` and slapped my face for embracing a black woman. I think she had a `problem` with black people. Months later in a Southend shop (think it was Next) I bumped into my best mate from school and your mum was not amused when I hugged him, and he hugged her. I had the silent treatment for the rest of the afternoon. One night I brought him home so she decided to have an early night claiming migraine, the funny thing is I knew her 16 years and that was her one and only migraine. Can having a black person sitting on your sofa drinking a cup of coffee really bring on a migraine? I`ll have to Goggle that.

Another very special lady in my life was Marie Bayliss, although only ten years older than me, she was like a second mum. She was an unsung hero at The Sun and luckily, we just clicked. One of the nicest and most genuine people I`ve ever met. She was a lovely and kind-hearted woman. Marie was from East London and had time for everyone. She looked after me throughout the 80s and 90s and in 2006 took Sam under her wing. She arranged for him to do his work experience at The Sun. He visited the Big Brother House, attended a England football team Press Conference and got the youngest-ever by-line in the papers history. Lucy you should read this very carefully as both Rebekah and Marie knew all about my fight to see you.

As did The Sun`s Agony Aunt Diedre Saunders who provided me with much helpful advice. If you don't believe a word what I say about `fighting to see you` ask these various women. Talk to the mums of your brother`s friends, or better still have the decency to ask Sam and Adam what I was like as a dad.

I must mention my old mate Annette Witheridge, now resident in New York and `best friends` with Angie Bowie. Annette is the journo who broke the story about the relationship between Prince Andrew and Jeffrey Epstein. It was her photographer who got the exclusive pictures of the pervert Prince and the child abuser hanging out in New York. She was my boss on the Daily Star pop column. We bonded in a Fleet Street pub over our mutual love of David Bowie.

The first person I met who could easily drink Garry Bushell under the table. Her liver was indestructible. If someone had chucked a Molotov cocktail at her, she`d have downed it in one. She was a great storyteller and good company. Annette once made a 300-mile round trip just to hold

Sam in her arms before flying off to America. I hope my daughter has noticed that these people are all women. I didn't just like women for sexual intercourse I loved them for being the nicer sex. If I was stuck on a desert island with just one person, I would always choose female companion. I've always liked women as friends with or without benefits. They smell nice and are more loyal. I went to four different comprehensive schools and many youth clubs but never saw another girl as good-looking as Lyn.

My schooldays and teenage years featured loads of lust, love bites, fumbling losing and taken of virginity, premature ejection and plenty of rejection but no experimenting with her. I was just happy to be her friend. Even at that young age I knew lots about women, I knew how their minds worked, a stunning 13-year-old girl would want 15 or 16-year-old boyfriends and not another 'kid'. At fifteen she would want an 18-year-old with a car.

I still remember the time her dad (who I fantasised about being a gangster) giving us both a lift home in his big flashy motor. I was so in awe, that unlike me I stayed silent all the way home. Not a word during the 15-minute drive from Blackshots Stadium in Sifford Clays to Stanford-le-Hope. I could normally talk for England, but not a word. It's funny and don't know what a psychiatrist would make of it, but in my life the four women I've felt closest to have all been 'plutonic relationships'.

In my schooldays it was Lyn, Toni in my teens, Jenny in my early 20s and Rebekah as an adult. Jenny was hand-on-heart a 'dead-ringer' for Debbie Harry circa 1979/81 and wore the shortest mini-skirts in history. It was lust at first sight which grew into friendship. I knew I had no chance. She was five years older and a top PR whereas I was just starting out. I knew my place in the pecking order. She dated pop stars and went on to marry a millionaire rock guitarist. I soon found out we had something in common, a love of Colombian marching powder and she became the twin sister I never had. The more I found out about her the more I liked, I loved visiting her flat in Baker Street and driving about town in her car. We were great plutonic mates for more than a decade and had some great times. But enough of her and back to me, well it is my story. I started the day as a fanatical 15-year-old football fan obsessed with George Best and went to bed dreaming of Ziggy Stardust. As with Lyn it would as with Lyn be a life-long love affair and although never consummated the closest thing to intimacy without taking your clothes off.

At a 15-year-old schoolboy I had no idea that one day I'd meet my hero in the flesh. It would be like a Roman Catholic meeting the Pope. I got so high on his aura I came close to levitating. I said "hello, and shook his hand, the running joke was I didn't wash it for a month. My hand felt hot and tingled, very much like my penis after losing my virginity. Unlike Prince Harry in his kiss and tell hatchet job `Spare` I will not be revealing the identity of the lucky girl. After my brief encounter with David Bowie, I would tell all future girlfriends, and my ex-wife, "you're being undressed by hands that touched David Bowie".

It's a line I'd trot out for years. It broke the ice and always put a smile on my face, and sometimes hers. But when I deliberately told that story to Ma and Pa Taylor neither of them cracked a smile. Becoming a Bowie fan proved a great distraction from the misery of my private life. It was the perfect escape route for a messed-up kid who'd lost his dad, his bedroom with many memories and all personal belongings. Although loving an Alien, which in 1972, is what some adults would call him did provoke a backlash. At times it wasn't always safe walking about as a `Bowie fan`. You could be attacked in the street or beaten-up on the underground.

The skinheads who hadn't grown up into Suedeheads or transformed into Glam Rockers would call you a "poof" for hero-worshipping a bloke in make-up. But I wore my Bowie badges and T-shirts with pride. Thick bigoted boneheads didn't understand that the more you looked like Ziggy Stardust the better-looking girls you attracted. I was so committed to the cause that if need be I was willing to die or at least take a severe beating to show my allegiance to David Bowie. I felt like a black man standing up to the National Front and the KKK. Years later I would get to play football with Georgie Best my other hero from that moment in time. In my opinion the Irish genius was better than both Ronaldo and Messi and still the greatest player of all-time. Off the pitch he was also a winner.

Don't forget he won the European Cup and also slept with three Miss Worlds and shared girlfriends with Rod Stewart. Who in 1972 would have predicted my future encounters with David Bowie and George Best? Ladbrookes and Paddy Power would have given better odds on a blind 3-legged horse winning the Grand National. Up until the age of fourteen, my life was pretty good. I was the local football star, had plenty of mates, girls liked me and I called myself the "White Pele" or "Cockney Georgie Best" than `bang` my world came crashing down.

# Chapter Eight
# Boy About Town

The first 14 years had been so easy. I went to school. I played football, and spent a lot of time in bed, on top for fun, under the covers to sleep. Becoming fifteen changed everything. Before that all I had to worry about was scoring on and off the pitch and worrying about my complexion. I was a young man trapped in a boy's body and because of hormones some days had more spots than a Dalmatian dog. I always craved excitement and luckily had a father figure I could look up too, but as they say love is blind. I enjoyed Sunday football over the park and learning my trade. My football-mad dad trained me hard and somehow transformed an average 8-year-old into a talented teenager. Something happened between my last year at Junior School and first year at Senior.

I still can't explain what happened. I still couldn't (still can't) do all the amazing ball tricks and juggling my sons do with ease, never done a 'Cruyff' turn in my life, but my dad had turned me into a lethal goal-scorer. All I wanted to be was a 'fox in the box'. I never tackled or headed the ball (in case it mucked up my hair) but I scored in every game. I could also dribble a bit and make a decent pass, but my main ability was putting the ball in the back of the net.

It turned out I weren't a great footballer but was a natural goal scorer and that's all I wanted to be. It's the number 9 who gets all the glory and I loved it. This meant it was my name read out at School Assembly. Being a centre-forward is a bit like being the lead singer in a band, let's be honest whoever mentions the drummer? I enjoyed visits to Colchester Zoo and day trips to Southend-on-Sea. In those days Southend was the jewel in Essex's crown. Today the place is a dustbin and a bit like East London by the sea. But back then I loved the place. The amusements, Rossi ice cream parlour, Peter Pan's playground, candy floss, the smell of the sea.

Like the taste of Southend's doughnuts life was sweet.

Then BANG my dad fucked off without even saying "goodbye" to set up home with his latest bit of skirt and her fucking son. The truth is he never said "goodbye" or ever apologised. My once happy life spiralled out of control and overnight, I changed from a cheeky kid with the world at his feet to a teenage terror who mum's warned their daughters about.

I was the best footballer in the area and picked to represent the District Team, believe me I was really good at scoring goals. I was spotted by

West Ham, QPR, Orient and Southend United and played in various trial games. Weeks before my dad left I was spotted by Ipswich Town but 'bit of stuff' wouldn't let him take me all the way to Suffolk. You can bet your life that had it been her son than my dad would have driven him all the way to Mars.

I went from being the apple of my dad's eye to being second best, her son had everything, but I got fuck all. I learnt a childhood lesson that in adulthood has never left me. Never do anything to your own children that will haunt them in adult life. I can still remember all the horrible things I suffered a kid. I would not allow history to repeat itself. My sons had a 2 year age gap but were always treated like twins, got the same toys, football kits and clothing brands. I'm proud to say I never ever hit them, not even a slap, and don't think I ever shouted at them. I didn't appreciate it at the time, but in a way the selfish behaviour of my own dad, helped me become the dad I became. After being expelled from Hassenbrook I went to a nice school in Stifford Clays where the boys were nice and the girls were pretty (those obviously none as nice as Lyn). In a way because of my football ability, I was welcomed with open arms. I had always scored against them in previous years and now they had me in their team.

It was only a brief encounter but great fun. Sadly, I left after a month but stayed long enough to play games 4 games for my new school team. My debut was a 5-2 win against Geoff Pike's school in South Ockendon and I scored Four. The next day my name was read out at School Assembly, and I was congratulated by the Headmaster. Then another win against a school from Aveley and two more goals from the new boy.

Followed by a 1-1 draw against my old school and the only game I didn't want to play in. From the minute our coach pulled up outside the sports hall I didn't want to be there. I was 'spooked' by seeing friendly faces, familiar school buildings, teachers I knew and old mates. It was my first time back and I hated it. I didn't like being in the Away dressing room and wanted to be wearing my old football strip.

I really didn't want to score against my old mates and when I did deliberately didn't celebrate. I was double-man-marked and hardly got a kick, though to be honest my heart wasn't in it. I spent the entire game in second gear and talking to old mates in the middle of the pitch. Once I'd scored my goal I'd done my bit and just concentrated on stopping Hassenbrooke from scoring. It turned out I was quite a good defender but no glory in booting the ball up the pitch. The game ended in a 1-1 a draw and I was happy with the result. My $4^{th}$ and last game was a cup match which thank to my hat-trick we won 3-0. That was my last-ever school football match as days later I was sent to another school and left on day one.

At 16 I hung up my boots for good after being substituted at half-time in my comeback match. A decision I have regretted every day since. There is a funny side to this. I hadn't played football or done any sport for about for about 6 months and was talked into coming back by the dad of some girl I used to know.

It was a fluke meeting. I popped into see my Nan and she had the painters and decorators in, this bloke goes to me "you're Garry Johnson" and talked me into playing for the Under 18 Team he managed that Saturday. I didn't train I wasn't fit but I had a massive ego. On the way to the game with his daughter and her boyfriend he asked, "how many will you score today?" Still thinking I was the dog's bollocks I replied something like "at least 2 maybe 3".

If a week is a long time in politics, six months out of football without training and living on a diet of amphetamine sulphate is a lifetime. I was off the pace, dead slow, breathing heavy and pulled a muscle so was happy to come off. My big mistake was not getting fit and giving myself a proper chance. I stopped playing to punish my dad (he didn't care) but ended up punishing myself. I was a f*****g mug because I mugged myself off.

January 1970 was the start of my first year as a Teenager and England, including London was a dull and boring place to grow up. All the shops would close at 1pm for an hour and nothing opened on a Sunday. There were only three TV channels and a single radio situation that played pop music. At the beginning of the 1970s Radio One was dominated by talentless, stone-deaf Disc jockeys like Tony Blackburn, Diddy David Hamilton, DLT and the child-abusing Jimmy Saville. These middle-aged morons were all-powerful and decided what music teenagers were allowed to listen to. Saville was a pervert, but Blackburn was a wanker. This cretin slagged off everyone from David Bowie to The Sex Pistols and wore what looked like a Michael Fabricant wig. Before the arrival of Ziggy Stardust everything in the UK for teenagers was grey, bland, boring and duller than dishwater. England like our TV screens was black and white, without a splash of colour.

The daily diet was beans on toast, fish and chips, rubbery beef burgers and tasteless pot noodles. Our parents were stuck in a rut watching mindless moronic mush like Crossroads and Opportunity Knocks on weekdays and religious rubbish like Songs of Praise on Sundays. Every Sunday was boring and seemed to last forever. London might have hosted the swinging 60s, but by 1972 the party was well and truly over. There was no pleasure dome and then along came David Bowie.

Along with Roxy Music, Marc Bolan and Rod Stewart he re-invented teenage culture. The 10-year-old Mod, 12-year-old skinhead, 13-year-old-

Suedehead grew his hair and became a Glam Rocker. I had a Rod Stewart haircut, because we shared a love of blondes and the same nose. My barnet would later become a combination of Mick Ronson and Rod Stewart. I lacked the beauty of David Bowie to look good with a Ziggy Stardust, but my extreme use of fast drugs and rarely eating did give me his sunken cheekbones. The truth is I looked bit like Johnny Rotten years before he became a Sex Pistol. My dyed blonde feather cut with red streaks got me funny looks off old ladies in the street but thank god lots of attention from young girls.

I was born in East London and grew up in Essex. So, I am a genuine Cockney born within the sound of Bow Bells. My dad said I came into the world at the same hospital as pop legend Marc Bolan and The Kray Twins. Maybe that explains my life-long fascination with East End gangsters, rock stars and rebels. Medical experts do say childhood influences what we become in adult life. My dad was a good-looking bloke, a loveable rogue, notorious womaniser, football fanatic, dedicated gambler and well-known in Hackney. Like Cockney gangster Reggie Kray my dad was a twin, but unlike Reg his twin Alfie was the normal `quite one` who never broke rules in his entire life. My dad was always the `star` but his twin brother had the last laugh on his loud, cocky and big-headed brother. He briefly made it as a professional footballer.

My dad played for Spurs and Millwall reserves and the Brentford Youth team but unlike his brother and best mates Derek King, (my Godfather) and Alfie Stokes (his best mate) never turned professional. He was a prolific goal-scorer, and his exploits always featured on the sports pages in the Hackney Gazette. His team was The Albion who played over Hackney Marshes and three of the boys signed for Spurs. The winger Alfie Stokes became a first team star before moving onto Chelsea and playing for England. Defender Derek King played 20-odd games for the first team before joining Cardiff City for £28,000. My dad only progressed to the reserves before moving onto Deal Town in the Southern League. Today that would be like playing semi-pro for Canvey Island. His twin brother Alf who grew up in my dad`s shadow played 12 games for Leyton Orient before emigrating to Canada.

In every aspect of his life my dad was famously cavalier with his cash, didn't like it burning a hole in his pocket or gaining interest in his bank account. He did not attach merit on creating a nest egg and never thought about saving for a rainy day. All his life he routinely blew all his money on wine, women and song, a perfectly good thing to do, if you`re a single bloke with no responsibilities. What he didn't waste on those lifelong vices he spent on clothes and gambling. I`m pretty sure he modelled himself on Michael Caine`s bird bandit character in the Alfie movie.

My first 14 years didn't feature David Bowie so I'll speed through this period of my life. In my youth kids had football, boxing or rock and roll to save 'em from the dole. Nowadays you can add Reality TV and Podcasting to those options. I was a genuine 'wannabee' but didn't know what I wanted to be. I wanted sporting stardom and then showbiz fame but ended up as a guttersnipe on the streets. Football, boxing, crime and singing, I tried and failed at all four, and you can also add marriage to that list of failures. Five losses, five defeats like a talentless punch-drunk boxer but never knocked out. I always bounced back and never gave in or admitted defeat. I could defeat any feelings of self-pity or depression without help from Andrew Tate or Jordan Peterson with the help of fast drugs.

To quote the Chumbawumba song "I get knocked down but I get back up again, you aint never gonna keep me down". I did come close to losing everything in December 2013. I 'died' twice and my kids were told I might not survive.

But after 29 days in a coma and on a life support machine I woke up and lived to fight another day. I won't ever run the London marathon or last pace at a suburban orgy but can get out of bed and walk to the shops. My near death experience awakened the freedom fighter inside me, it breathed new life into my Cockney rebel DNA. I wasn't throwing in the towel, my fight for truth and justice, was back on the agenda. In hospital heart surgeon Dr Eghan Khan called me his "Christmas miracle". He was a fantastic bloke who looked like movie star Omar Shariff and once dated The Princess of Wales. My own nickname is "the nearly man", with a bit of talent and a lot of luck I could have been a champion but spent most of my life as a contender. All I lacked was the ability to succeed at any of my chosen professions. I could easily have been a traditional rock star. No problem with the sex and drugs. I was a natural at both, but couldn't sing. That's a big problem when you're the singer in a rock and roll band. I looked the part and could pose with a hairbrush in front of the bedroom mirror, but that wasn't enough.

The public are never wrong which is why The Buzz Kids debut gig was also our last. I think that tells you how bad I was. As for crime I gave it my best shot, but I was no Reggie Kray or Al Capone. I was prolific as a kid and fearless as a teenager but wasn't very good and kept getting caught. I was locked-up in violent institutions like children's home Boyles Court Brentwood (twice), Little Heath Remand Home, East London (twice), Redhill Special Unit in Surrey, Kidlington Detention Centre Oxfordshire and a Borstal in Hertfordshire. It wasn't a 'piece of cake'. It was bloody horrible and a waste of my precious time. I had new allies to break rules with but not many I'd want as mates on the outside.

The truth is being locked-up as a youngster is not clever, you're a victim of violence, boredom and petty discipline. I was Seventeen before the penny dropped and realised what looks cool in the movies isn't any fun in real life.

Now I understand my acts of rebellion were a form of self-abuse in the same way teenage girls self-harm or develop Anorexia. I pushed the self-destruct button, went on a crime spree and the only loser was me. In 1973 nobody talked about mental health or showed their emotions. I was my own worst enemy and today a shrink would say I was craving attention and looking for love. Aged Seventeen I finally saw the light. It was a combination of David Bowie, fast drugs and growing up that convinced me to be the real Garry Johnson. I ditched the teenage tearaway act and reverted to being a loveable rogue. Never again would I let other people or the voices in my head control my emotions.

I also developed a social conscience and started writing the song lyrics which would soon become my punk poems. Even as a mixed-up teenager I'd never been a fan of petty criminals or low-life lawbreakers. I was always attracted to Al Capone and Robin Hood. It's not politically correct to admit such things, but still have a soft spot and fascination for The Kray Twins and The Great Train Robbers.

I enjoy reading all about the exploits of Bruce Reynolds, The Adams and Hunt Families and celeb gangster Dave Courtney. Before 1972 and discovering David Bowie, I was a disillusioned mixed-up teenager without a dad. I got my supply of affection from a menu of lust by shagging lots of girls and having one-night-stands. I was starved of love but didn't go hungry. I also removed my-self from food and lived on a diet of 'fast drugs' as like David Bowie I wanted to be skinny.

Even David Bowie himself couldn't put into words the effect of discovering Ziggy Stardust had on my life. It was so life-changing, that even he, myself, Charles Dickens and JK Rowling combined couldn't do it justice. They say people never forget where they were when JFK was shot, or John Lennon murdered. Well, I'll never forget the first time I saw David Bowie singing 'Starman' on Top of The Pops in the TV Room at Stanford Youth Club. Those three minutes of magic in a bleak and grey world gave me what can only be described as a religious experience. A genuine Godlike figure came into my life but wasn't wearing white robes or a sporting a Jeremy Corbyn beard.

Also watching with me that Thursday night on July 6th 1972 were future pop stars Gary Kemp, Boy George, Holly Johnson, Steve Strange, Morrissey, Jarvis Cocker and Gary Numan, no, not in Stanford Youth Club, but all over the UK. He had red spiky hair and was more beautiful than most women. It was the start of my musical education and life-long obsession with all things David Bowie.

It wasn't the governments short sharp shock sentences that kept me on the straight and narrow, I didn't want to risk being banged-up and losing my Bowie haircut. You couldn't be a Glam Rocker with short back and sides haircut.

I immediately turned my back on following in the footsteps of Reggie Kray and Georgie Best and decided I wanted to be a pop star. But how? I couldn't sing or play guitar, and this was four years before Punk Rock and The Sex Pistols

I used those four years to transform my mind and body. I also dumped my girlfriend because she didn't look like Angie Bowie. I'd read that models and  jockeys used amphetamine to lose weight so stopped eating chips and increased my intake of little blue pills. Years of playing football and running had resulted in me having an athletic build and I wanted to look wasted. What I'd used for fun on Friday and Saturday nights I now used on a daily basis. I desperately wanted to be skinny and when one of my mates elder sisters told me about the power of speed I upped my intake. And it worked. I felt great, ultra confident, full of energy and started to look just how I wanted. I even had sunken cheekbones which became my pride and joy. I quickly noticed the skinnier I got the better-looking girls I attracted. It was the start of my 15-year love affair with fast drugs. At the time I was seeing a girl I didn't really like that much, she wasn't my type but had 3 things going for her.

An empty house because her parents worked, a Jane Fonda haircut, like her character in the movie Klute, big boobs and it's know it's not PC but I'm describing the 70's. She was what teenage boys would call "easy". It was better bunking off school in her warm bedroom than hanging about in the cold over the local park. I dumped her because she didn't share my love of David Bowie. I sound a right bastard, but I was only fifteen. I wanted a girl who looked like Angie Bowie, skinny and blonde with a Twiggy physique. Then I found one in a neighbouring Youth Club. She looked great and like me loved David Bowie, but there was a problem. Her name was Brenda. She looked the part but I couldn't go out with a girl called Brenda. Even before Ziggy Stardust entered my life I knew I was different from the other kids at school. I didn't just daydream, I believed. I knew from an early age I could die of boredom; I always needed a high to function and enjoy life. I was born with an addictive personality. I always craved excitement and needed an obsession. Before Bowie it was football, clothes, (Fred Perry Shirts, Levi Jeans, Crombie Overcoats, Monkey Boots) and Georgie Best. I was so obsessed with the longhaired Irish genius I even cheered when he scored against West Ham.

I soon realised crime was a mugs game and not really my cup of tea. The truth is if you're not from a kosher crime family, or related by marriage to a top villain, one of the chaps and a proper face, then a life of crime doesn't pay. Even more so nowadays with CCTV and no longer a code of silence in the underworld. Without first-class connections you'll always be second division rather than Premier League.

At Boyles Court, Little Heath, Redhill, Detention Centre and Borstal I got to mix with a lot of black boys from all over London. It wouldn't happen today because of segregation but we mixed. Like me, most were natural rebels. At school my best mate was black, a kindred spirit and a rebel, so I related to their anti-authority attitude. We broke the rules whenever we got the chance and challenged the bullying authority of the screws.

I got bored with being a teenage delinquent and looked for something else to occupy my time and control my pent-up anger. I moved away from being a skinhead and got into the early days of Glam Rock. Marc Bolan, Rod Stewart and Slade replaced my Trojan Ska collection on the record player. My taste in girls also changed. Like most thirteen-year-old boys what first attracted me were boobs, but as I matured it was legs, bums, blonde hair and cheekbones. I was never a typical Page 3 fan, always preferred models with nice hair to big boobs. I always fancied Suzanne Mitzi and never Samantha Fox.

No education. No qualifications. But luckily God gave me the gift of the gab and cheek of the devil. My story begins in the music press when I reviewed a gig I didn't attend because I missed my train. Along the way I managed The Stone Roses and predicted they'd become the biggest band in the world. I ended up with TV and showbiz columns in both The Sun and The Sunday People. I was part of the tabloid world for more than 25 years and sold stories to every Fleet Street newspaper. Along the way I met and worked for the biggest beasts in the red top jungle. The cream of the crop Piers Morgan, Rebekah Wade, Garry Bushell, Andy Coulsen, Peter Willis, Nick Ferrari, Matthew Wright, Annette Witheridge, Sharon Marshall, Martin Dunn, Claudia Connell and Kirsten McKenzie, the daughter of Fleet Street legend Kelvin McKenzie.

I was a one-man press association flogging stories on everyone Princess Diana to Maggie Thatcher. My CV includes published world exclusives on legends David Bowie, Madonna, Kylie Minogue, Tony Blair, Rod Stewart, Mick Jagger, Sade, The Kray Twins, Michael Jackson and George Michael, and so many more I should write a book. Random highlights include Maggie the Movie, with Madonna as the Iron Lady, Mick Jagger to spend £60,000 on new lips, and Michael Jackson making a pop video with Princess Diana. David Bowie's breath being sold in jam jars off a stall in Petticoat Lane. I was never sued or asked to retract a single word from one of my thousands of world exclusives or showbiz stories.

The East End boy who dropped out of school and struggled with grammar became a top showbiz tipster. The Punk Poet ended-up rubbing shoulders with A-List, soap stars, film actors, TV presenters, Page 3 girls and genuine music legends like David Bowie, Paul Weller, George Michael, Johnny Rotten, Sade and Sir Bob Geldof and many more. Sometimes my imagination got the better of me and I'd spice-up stories to get more traction in the tabloids, but unlike war criminal Alistair Campbell my 'sexed-up' creations never led to the deaths of millions of innocent people. No celebs ever complained because I always made people appear more exciting than they actually were. Did I ever get rumbled? Yes. But only once, and I was the "star" of the story. Private Eye magazine turned me over and I loved it. The Sunday People published a 'sexed-up' story about me. I never complained and found it hilarious, almost a career highlight. I'd claimed in another World Exclusive that pop superstar Robbie Williams was learning Cockney rhyming slang to star in a movie version of an East End crime novel. I forgot to mention that I'd written the book and claimed the name of the author was a Gal Jackson. According to my source the Take That singer had been sent a copy and was learning to talk like Ray Winstone. Before Private Eye 'outed' me, The Sunday People were unaware that Gal Jackson was Garry Johnson. I wrote Till Death Us Do Part and used the paper to boost sales. I thought 'on no, the game is up', but talked my way out of it and never lost my showbiz column. I not only had the luck of the Irish and more front than Blackpool, I also had more lives than a cat.

This is that PRIVATE EYE story (word for word)

In a SENSATIONAL EXCLUSIVE, the People revealed a few weeks ago that Robbie Williams is learning Cockney rhyming slang because he wants to play an East End gangster in a film. The pop superstar wants to ditch his Stoke-on-Trent accent to play an ex-boxer turned East London 'Mr Big', it reported. A source said "Robbie read about the character in a book called 'Till Death Us Do Part' and it blew him away. But he knows he's got to sound like a Cockney if he wants the part". The by-line on the story was GARRY JOHNSON, by an amazing coincidence, the author of 'Till Death Us Do Part' is Garry Johnson, a pseudonym of the self-same Garry Johnson. His novel is published by New Breed Books, a firm run by a bulking bouncer named Jamie o'Keefe. Unusually for a publishing house, it also offers classes in combat skills and self-defence. Still, the book comes with an ecstatic tribute from our old friend Garry Bushell, TV columnist for, er, the Sunday People.

"Bloody brilliant...if there's a better revenge novel around I'd like to read it".

Johnson has been a mucker of the other Garry since the days of New Punk in the early 80's, when Bushell was lead singer of The Gonads and Johnson sang in The Buzz Kids. Alas, Inspector Knacker isn't as impressed as Bushell by 'Till Death Us Do Part', which seems to be based very loosely on Johnson's own marriage break-up, the main difference being that the protagonist enlists the help of the underworld to extract revenge on the unsavoury character who threatened his children. Two weeks ago Johnson was arrested at his home in Wickford, Essex, and hauled off to Basildon Police Station, since Knacker had apparently interpreted the book as a 'death threat'. We trust this silly misunderstanding will soon be cleared up before Robbie Williams take fright. But he may still find Johnson's publisher a bit scary.

In an interview four years ago with (inevitably) the People, Jamie o'Keefe declared, "If you road rage me while I have my children in the car, then, I would not hesitate to come tearing through your front door at five 'o'clock in the morning and break every bone in your body before you could wipe the sleep from your eyes. I've done that a few times when it was deserved".

As Garry Bushell would say, "Bloody brilliant".

It still makes me laugh and always have enjoyable flashbacks when I see the brilliant Ian Hislop on Have I Got News For You.

The funny thing is I appeared in Private Eye two more times but genuinely can't remember what for.

I want my daughter to know the real me which is why throughout this book I pull no punches. There's no sense in writing an autobiography unless you're prepared to tell the truth, the whole truth and nothing but the truth.

I reveal many things about myself that some people will consider 'bad taste' and say things about my daughter that could be considered 'own goals' but I say them because that's how I feel about her. I genuinely don't know why she hates me, there are no reasons, and 90% of me believes she's the innocent victim of propaganda and concerted 'brainwashing'. I will do anything but lie to see my daughter. I want her to judge me on the facts, the absolute truth and not a pack of lies. If she doesn't want to know the truth, so be it, that's her personal choice, but before making her mind up she should at least have the decency to listen to the facts.

From where I'm sitting her position is like the jury reaching a verdict without listening to the evidence or attending court. Lucy must be the only girl/woman in the world who doesn't want to know who her dad is. If we met and she genuinely didn't like me I could honestly accept that. I wouldn't be happy but I'd shake her hand and wish her well. All I've ever wanted is the chance to state my case and ask "why do you hate me" and "why are you scared of the truth?"

And who knows I might not even like her, it's not out of the question, just because she looks nice it doesn't mean she is nice. I look like 'trouble' but that doesn't mean I am. I wouldn't be keen if she supported champagne socialists and didn't want children, but I could handle it. I wouldn't be impressed if she took drugs or swore, believed in corporal punishment, or was a bit of a snob who looked down on the working-class but I'd cope. I wouldn't be pleased if she was religious and liked the Royal Family, but I could live with it. If she was any of the above I wouldn't disown her but would find it hard to share a Xmas dinner.

Instead of pulling crackers we'd be having rows.

Maybe she'll read my opinions and think "good God what a horrible bloke I don't want to know him". I could live with that, as at least she'd have genuine reasons to hate me. It's her silence and the not knowing that's so hard to handle, it's as if she has power over me and enjoys dangling me on a piece of string. Just because she doesn't look anything like her mother, it doesn't mean she hasn't inherited her personality. I can only hope for the sake of any future boyfriend/husband that she doesn't end up anything like my former mother-in-law. Then she really would be a vile human being with more wicked ways than Adolf Hitler. Over to you daughter darling, had my say, the ball is now in your court. Am I angel or devil, hero or villain? You decide.

Dead men can't talk so I'm telling all in a kiss and tell romp that reads like a novel but believe me it's a very true story. It's completely uncensored apart from the removal of all the X-rated content relating to 1990-2005. I'm going back in time and re-visiting my past to help readers understand how my background influenced my character. I hope it explains why despite the odds stacked against me I refused to give in. It wasn't just a fight for justice it was also a class battle. All my life I've been at war with authority.

I've been sent to a Detention Centre and a borstal where I was severely punished and beaten-up by bully boy screws. They punished me at Redhill special unit by locking me in a tiny room with no window, no furniture and no food. Things like that damage the mind of a 14-year-old boy for the rest of his life. In those days the staff in any Government run institution had a licence to abuse and dish out corporal punishment. Burly bully boy screws had permission to kick the shit out of skinny teenagers and really enjoyed their jobs. The first time I was sent to Boyles Court

Children's Home in Brentwood, Essex I was only 12-years-of-age. What happened to me was reported to Essex Police and the NSPCA.

My head was mixed-up from an early age, and I coped by self-medicating with amphetamine. First the physical of abuse by institutions followed by the emotional abuse from my dad and his wife. Inside I was hurt and broken but never cried. I never allowed the pain to get the better of me. A lot of the pain went away, unlike the hatred for my stepmother, have I mentioned she stopped me from becoming a footballer? She was just like the evil stepmother you see in films and read about in books.

The one-time District footballer (star striker) who had trials with West Ham, QPR, Leyton Orient and Southend United ended up behind bars. I ended up spending more time in various courtrooms than I did on football pitches. After the divorce my mum moved to Congleton in Cheshire and my dad set-up home in Plaistow, (five minutes from Upton Park) with his latest fancy woman. I was fifteen and homeless with no money and just the clothes I stood-up in. It's hard to believe I know but 100% true. If you don't believe me call my bluff and organise a Lie Detector Test. I am willing to be hypnotised and subjected to regression therapy. We are talking about 1972 and things were different back then. There was no army of social workers taking teenagers into care and back then kids could just disappear into the shadows. My dad went down market in all aspects of his life. He swapped a 3-bed semi with a garden in Essex for a 2-up and 2-down East End slum. Most people move from East London to Essex but his wife forced him to do the opposite.

If you're wondering why? His f*****g wife didn't want her son moving to a new area, changing school or leaving his mates. She moved him about 500 yards and expected me to move 30 miles, or did they? I repeat they moved to a 2-bedroom house. I say again my dad and his 'new' family moved to a tiny two-bedroom house. Could they not do maths, where was my bedroom? Sorry, but no room for me at the inn, but the truth is even a ten-bedroom mansion would not have been big enough for me. I became a non-person who in their eyes no longer existed. I was replaced in his life by her son. The snide was a year older than me and as with his mother it was instant hate on my part. It then became mutual after I verbally attacked his mother at every opportunity. An escalating feud that started with me and Vere breaking into their house and ended with a 'fake bomb' placed under her car. Plaistow police were called, and they sealed off both ends of Kingsland Road.

The truth is on top of losing my dad. I lost my home, my bedroom, my clothes, my chopper bike, my cat Smokie, plus all my football medals. Like snow on a sunny day, they all disappeared. All I had left was memories and friends. I was fifteen when I started sofa surfing and sleeping on floors in bedrooms. I spent nights sleeping in a caravan at the back of a girl's garden and unknown to her parents. My lowest point after exhausting all other options was sleeping (trying to sleep) in the Waiting Room at Stanford Station. This is where amphetamine came in, so I could stay up all night wandering around Soho.

She stopped my dad from watching me play football. She knew he couldn't be in two places at the same time so, under her orders, he watched her son and forgot about me. Never again would he stand on the touchline giving advice or cheering me on. At the same time the fake 'father and son' from the family I never recognised attended West Ham games together. It would be another 25 years before I watched a football game with my dad. I invited him along to watch my son Sam, his grandson play, as long as he came alone. So why did his fucking wife hate me so much? My old friend Toni King, daughter of my Godfather Derek, who I've known all my life told me years later: "She was jealous of how close you were to Chas and how much you looked like him" adding "She never liked him talking about you". She also said, "My mum and dad were disgusted by how she came between you and Chas".

Adding "He would only talk about you when she wasn't in the room". My cousin Leigh-Anne Franklin who I've also known all my life said, "my mum thought the world of your dad, but didn't like the way she controlled him and made him choose between you or her". Maybe my dad was 'weak' but that's no excuse.

Aged fifteen I was like a orphan and became bitter and feral, but rather than sulk or wallow on self-pity I went on a teenage rampage. It's not PC to say it out loud but drugs saved my life. I went wild for a few years and scummy social workers and posh middle-class probation officers tried and failed to make me behave.

These vile breed of champagne socialist posh people with patronising accents and Mickey Mouse degrees behave like paedophiles without committing actual sexual abuse. It's a form of grooming as these University educated Guardian readers try every trick in the book to try and control your life. They use various techniques to hide their deception and can't hold a conversation unless they are talking down to you. All are a bunch of middle-class wankers who live in the suburbs and know fuck all about real life. A sharp East End boy like myself could outsmart these bastards in a fair 'fight' but they bend rules and make-up lies for a living. In 2007 when I put the truth into the public domain, they got me locked-up in top security Bellmarsh Prison, the toughest nick in England. I was arrested on trumped up charges and threatened with life behind bars.

Let me explain how the Punk Poet found himself sharing a landing with a Muslim terrorist. My ex-wife went to Basildon Police (the most corrupt force outside the Met) and told them I was about to go on a killing spree. She `twisted the knife` by saying I was mentally ill and a danger to my three children. She lied that I was planning to kill her and murder her boyfriend.

No member of Basildon Police had the decency to read my crime novel Till Death Us Do Part or question her tissue of lies and I was arrested. They considered me so dangerous that eight Officers turned up at my home and surrounded the front and back of my house. I was handcuffed and dragged into a van.

On arrival at Basildon Police Station, I was surrounded by members of the Mental Health Team who usually deal with psychopaths and serial killers. My ex-wife on the advice of her solicitors told the police I was planning to become a serial killer.

She provided a Hit List that included her boyfriend, my in-laws, her solicitor, herself and my children. There was no Hit List. I hadn't written a Hit List, it had nothing to do with me, it was complete bollocks, but Basildon Police were not interested in the truth. I hadn't written a Hit List, but I had written a book. I told the book I'd written a crime novel, just as the week before I told my local newspaper as part of my publicity blitz. I'd written a novel but the so-called Hit List was not written by me. I asked the police to contact a handwriting expert, but they refused.

They considered my book a death threat even though they hadn't read it or even seen a copy. Had they read my book they would have seen only one character was doused in petrol, tortured and then shot in the head. He was described as 6ft tall with no front teeth and a baldhead, as much as I hate my ex-wife she's looks nothing like Shrek. But somehow, she convinced them I was planning to kill her.

Her allegation contained more fiction than my novel, but Basildon Police bought it hook, line and sinker. I'd not seen or spoken to her for well over a year but they hung on her every word. She convinced them I was planning to kill my children, the worst crime in the word. Basildon Police without a shred of evidence decided I was Public Enemy Number One. The corrupt bastards then took away my clothes and forced me to wear a white anti-suicide boiler suit, like the outfits you see on TV. It was like something from `One Flew over the Cuckoo Nest` with me in the Jack Nicholson role. The cops said were detaining you under the Mental Health Act. Your wife claims you suffer from violent outbursts and that she fears for her life and that of your children. She told them I heard voices to which I replied "that's news to me" adding "but they do say you learn something new every day". The cops did not like my attitude, but the whole thing was so ridiculous I couldn't take any of it seriously. A flash cocky cop threatened "we don't have to prove your mad, you have to prove you're not".

Adding:

"You could be locked-up for the rest of your life". At first, I was handcuffed and surrounded by three or four cops and a member of The Mental Health Team at all times. My ex-wife had really done a number of me and convinced them I was the Hannibal Lector of Essex.

I was taken to another room and handed over to two plain clothed cops, a moronic male and a pretty female of the species. Mister Plod was Fred Flintstone without the loincloth, and it soon become clear that Lady cop modelled herself on the Helen Mirren character in Prime Suspect. I am face to face with a caveman cop and a wannabee Charlie's Angel.

They tried to engage me in conversation but for almost an hour I stuck to "no comment" and amused myself by imagining the female cop in a black Baby Doll nightie. Fred lacked the wit and charm of Sir champagne socialist Starmer and she lacked the brains to go with her good looks. We are talking dumb and dumber.

She was dead cute but he was brain dead. Cutie played good cop and Fred acted like a heavy from The Flintstones, but I wasn't impressed with their performances. The odd couple couldn't separate fact from fiction. God help us if there ever asked to investigate a proper crime. For over an hour on the advice of my brief (bad advice), looks as if you have something to hide, I answered "no comment" to every question. But as the questions got more bizarre couldn't remain silent any longer. I tried to explain that 'Till Death Us Do Part' was a novel and reminded them my name was not Harry Harris. I was not a East End gangster. The pretty but thick female crime-fighter said, "Mrs Johnson says you have a Hit List". I replied Harry Harris does, not me".

Adding:

"I'm not Harry Harris and I'm not a underworld hitman".

I won't bore you with all the details, but this went on and on, round and round in circles for about an hour". The truth is they didn't land a glove on me. There was no knockout punch, and I won every round on points. But as we all know with recent World title fights in boxing some verdicts are rigged.

I wasn't expecting a draw or even a split decision. It was so bent and on a par with a FIFA World Cup venue selection being decided by Sepp Blater. It was a Kangaroo Court with me in the dock and convicted on no evidence, I was considered as guilty as Adolf Hitler, Boris Johnson and Donald Trump.

The CPS is run by champagne socialists like Sir champagne socialist Starmer and never on the side of working-class blokes. If I'd been middle-class with a posh accent there is no way Basildon Police would have arrested me. I would not be banged in a freezing cold cell for five days. What happened to the rule of release or charge after 24 hours?

I'd done nothing wrong and was locked-up for five days under the Mental Health Act. Sir Starmer's posh mates at the CPS considered me so dangerous that I couldn't be released. Basildon Police took away my clothes and then my glasses, claiming I could use the lenses to slash my wrists. They were making it up as they went along. I was denied access to my children and a phone call to Rebekah Wade.

Dumb and Dumber came into my cell saying, "Were doing a dog search of your house". I asked "why?".

The female cop said, "Were looking for evidence". Why did they need a sniffer dog to find a book? It wasn't hidden, it was on my desk. A few hours later they returned with a copy of Till Death Us Do Part by Gal Jackson and still available on Amazon. This was two days after I was arrested, thus proving they had no evidence when eight members of Basildon plod surrounded my house. The female cop who got less pretty by the day said "I'm taking this home to read with a glass of wine"

That is a direct quote and the gospel truth. Once again for any doubters out there dare me to take a Lie Detector test. You pay and I'll do as many as you want.

The next day I was re-visited by Dumb and Dumber, despite having read the book but refusing my request of a review for Amazon, she still refused to believe I wasn't Harry Harris. A man was stabbed, tortured, doused in petrol and shot dead between the covers of my book and not on the streets of Wickford.

But Basildon Police had no interest in the truth. They were all powerful and both judge and jury. They had no interest in the facts. Surely it wasn't hard to realise my book was a novel and that I wasn't Harry Harris.

Till Death Us Do Part, although based 99% on actual incidents, the other one per cent was a work of fiction. It was the 1% that got me arrested and sent to prison.

If every cop in Essex had invaded Wickford for a month, they wouldn't find a rotting corpse, there was no body to find. But Dumb and Dumber insisted I was 'extremely dangerous', and a 'risk to the public'. Facts Basildon Police could not accept. Not only was I not 'mad', but I also wasn't 'stupid' either. What sort of idiot would make so-called 'death threats' in public? My book was not a secret. It already had 50-plus rave reviews on Amazon and a write-up in my local paper. The article even had a picture of me holding a copy of Till Death Us Do Part. I would say hardly the actions of a `guilty man` or the actions of a top East End gangster.

A week before my arrest Till Death Us Do Part was already in the public domain.

As I told Basildon Police, and, if they deny any of this, they have my permission to release the interview tapes. The facts dumb and dumber ignored. My name was not Harry Harris and I wasn't a 35-year-old night club owner. Just as the characters in EastEnders are not real, he did not exist. Basildon Police handled the case like a combination of characters from the `Keystone Cops` and `Carry on Constable`. But it was no joke or laughing matter.

I ended up in Bellmarsh top security prison for writing a book containing a fictional murder and naming real-life social workers and a self-confessed paedophile. Was there corruption? Should Basildon police re-investigate my arrest? I say the answer is "yes" to both questions. Instead of arresting my ex-wife for perjury they gave her a job as a Special Constable and let her boyfriend off with a caution.

If that don't stink of corruption what does? As proved by the recent cases of Wayne Couzens and David Carrick the police always look after their own.

She convinced the police I was `mad, bad and dangerous` and I was remanded to Bellmarsh maximum security prison. The last person sent to prison for writing a book was Oscar Wilde. I was in good company as he wrote The Ballad of Reading Jail and I wrote my poem Ballad of The Young Offender. Like me Oscar Wilde had Irish blood and was also an innocent victim of the British Establishment.

There is no such thing as `British Justice` for the working-class. Young single mums are sent to prison for not buying a TV Licence as are OAPs for getting behind with their Council Tax.

I ended up in Bellmarsh facing life behind bars. I'd been stitched up by my ex-wife and framed by Basildon Police, not only for a crime I didn't commit, but for a crime that hadn't even happened. It would take 15 years and thirty-plus court appearances (2007-2022) to finally clear my name.

The stress of being framed and having my `good name` dragged through the mud brought on five heart attacks and two triple-heart bypass operations and eventually lead to a mild stroke. Was I really close to `death`? The honest answer is "yes". I `died` twice and my children were told to prepare for the worst, but don't take my word for it. Ask world famous heart consultant Professor Eghan Khan, the former boyfriend of Princess Diana saved my life. I found myself handcuffed and locked in a windowless van on my way to Bellmarsh Maximum security prison in

Southeast London, home to some of the most violent prisoners in the UK, including gangsters, drug dealers, terrorists and murderers.

The cell inside the prison van was about half the size of a phone box and bit like a upright coffin. Although I was going to the UK version of Alcatraz I couldn't wait to get there as five days of solitary confinement in a windowless cell was does your head in. It was a deliberate act of torture by Basildon Police designed to break me and false a confession. I hadn't washed or eaten for five days and survived on cups of tea and water.

I had been denied phone calls, access to my children and had my clothes and glasses removed. I'd been unable to sleep as every thirty minutes the flap on my cell door would be opened and slammed shut. I had no human rights, and a Ukraine prisoner of war would get better treatment in Russia. I was deliberately tortured by Basildon Police. One Hundred and Ten hours without TV, Radio, Music, conversation or knowing the whereabouts of my children. I had no idea if they were safe. I was up against an unholy alliance of my ex-wife, Basildon Police, the CPS, the Essex Criminal Mental Health Team, Social Services and The Family Courts.

They all conspired to kill me. The scumbag alliance almost pulled it off but hadn't bargained on my fighting spirit. I always knew that one day the truth would come out, but didn't imagine it would take so long. Arriving at Bellmarsh was a bit like being in a film, so mentally transformed myself into the Ray Winstone character in Sexy Beast. The former boxer is one of my favourite actors. Whenever I pile on the pounds people say I look like him, so if this book becomes a movie I want him to play me. On arrival and although handcuffed I'm surrounded by half a dozen mouthy screws and 3 or 4 growling Alsatian dogs. As I step out the van a police helicopter is buzzing around overhead.

I was the innocent author a book being treated like a convicted terrorist or a serial killer. The Reception area is deliberately daunting and I thought back to the funeral of Ronnie Kray when Reggie arrived flanked by the biggest screws in the prison service to make him look small. There were big burly bruisers everywhere. A motley collection of growling giants, dog ugly tubs of lard with beer guts, flat noses and cauliflower ears giving it large.

This is the screws I'm talking about, not the prisoners. They all looked like a combination of Pitbull terriers and bar-room bullies in Gestapo-style uniforms.

Like Basildon Police officers these cowards would have volunteered to be guards at Nazi concentration camps. Intimidation was the name of the game, but to be honest, they weren't very good at it. They weren't convincing or genuine `experts` in the art of menace. These guys were nothing like legendary boxers Mike Tyson and Tyson Fury or underworld legend Dave Courtney.

All they had was strength in numbers and felt safe with odds twenty to one in their favour. Cowards by nature and in reality, like most coppers, they were the little fat kids who got bullied at school. This was their playground, and they loved the power and the Nazi-style uniform. Away from the prison jungle where they ruled with threats and intimidation and silly rule books, they wouldn't dare say 'boo to a goose'. But as prison guards they could play the big man and swagger about as 'Billy big potatoes', but in reality they were nothing more than two-bob traffic wardens and jumped-up jobworths.

Like Basildon cops a motley mob of second-rate stormtroopers with the brains of a scarecrow and the arrogant attitude Sir Kier Stalin and other Communist dictators. I wasn't scared and wasn't impressed, not being big-headed after the event, but I'd seen their sort before. As a young kid in Boyles Court Children's Home, and as a teenager in Little heath Remand Centre, Redhill Special Unit, a Detention Centre and Borstal back in the 1970's. I'd also met many genuine hardman and various tough-guys from the world of boxing and London's underworld.

Last year (2023) one of my old mates featured in a Channel 5 documentary about Whitemoor Prison. He's a 'name' and genuine A-Lister in the criminal underworld. In 1987 he hijacked a helicopter and sprung East End gangster John Kendall and a Scottish hitman from Gartree Prison. In 1994 he escaped from top security Whitemoor prison along with five IRA terrorists. When captured the bully boy screws didn't lay a finger on the Irish gang, they were terrified of reprisals. But ten of the 'ever-so-brave' screws beat Andy Russell (skully) to a pulp.

That shows the true character of prison officers, most are cowards in Nazi-style uniforms. There was another reason why I wasn't in the mood to be intimidated by the bully boy thugs. Five days in solitary confinement without food and hardly any drink had drained me. I don't know where she came from but found myself talking to a nun who enquired about my welfare. She had the compassion of Mother Theresa and the warmth of Lady Diana. A screw waived a piece of paper in my face, obviously from Basildon Police and asked "are you mad? Adding "It says here you're mentally ill, violent and hear voices".

So, I started frothing at the mouth and bite him. Warning for woke readers I'm only joking. I then sarcastically replied "so they say" and removed from Reception quicker then Walt Disney could hum 'Loony Tunes' and put in a cage. I felt like one of the monkeys at London Zoo. This was happening in modern day England, 2007 and not Soviet Russia before the fall of the iron curtain. I'd committed no crime yet here I was being tortured and looking at a life sentence. And people ask why I hate my ex-wife, Basildon Police and Essex Social Services.

I imagine being locked-up and losing your freedom is bad enough when you're actually `guilty` but when your innocent it's a `nightmare situation`. The saying is "if you can't do the time don't do the crime", but what about when you've committed no crime? I was the latest in a long line of British miscarriages of justice.

Who can forget The Guildford Four, George Davis, Colin Stagg, Barry George and The Birmingham Six? All were pardoned and released after serving a total of over 100 hundred years in prison. I'm thinking to myself, I'm now a member of that club and how many years would I be spending in prison? The nun in the Mary Poppins costume and one of the screws who could actually read and write booked me in.

I was immediately treated differently from other inmates, unlike normal remand prisoners I could not wear my own clothes or keep my glasses. I was issued with a bizarre prison outfit, like something Vivienne Westwood would have invented for Johnny Rotten in 1976.

It was a combination of a white anti-suicide boiler suit and orange Guantamano-style overalls. I was put back in the cage and given a cheap carton of orange juice and stale bruised apple, and felt like asking "what no banana?"

I was then taken under escort to a mini prison within the prison. I was surrounded by three burly screws all dressed in black and carrying batons. They all wore army style headgear and body armour. At the time I weighed about ten stone and was handcuffed so was hardly a threat yet they treated me like Charles Bronson. God only knows what lies Basildon Police had told Bellmarsh Prison about me.

After what seemed like a mini marathon walking down narrow corridors and passing through endless security doors I was handed over to three new screws. Without the riot gear they were more my size and had the ability to walk and talk at the same time. Not that well, but a vast improvement on the caveman grunts. The Neanderthals had left the building. Was this really the elite squad? More like a bunch of beer gut geezers who on the outside would just about get jobs as shelf stackers in Tesco.

I felt like one of those Jewish activists I'd seen on TV being handed over to the Americans by the KGB. We went down more silent windowless corridors and walked through more security gates. The place had more steel doors than Fort Knox. No wonder Bellmarsh is said to be escape proof.

I'm thinking `in a minute they'll kick the shit out of me`, but for some unexplained reason they didn't. Maybe I had a friendly face or did they really believe I was mad, bad and dangerous? Was I really the Hanniball Lector of Essex?

I found myself in a special secure unit with half a dozen cells. I was still kept in solitary with no shoes or glasses. It was soon explained I'd been sectioned and could be held indefinitely under the Mental Health Act. I had to prove my sanity before even being considered for release. I was 100% innocent of any crime and at the same time 100% sane, I was also smart enough to know the odds were against me. Once you're caught up in the system it's almost impossible to get out.

You're one man up against civil servants, police corruption, the CPS and every department of a potential fascist state. The first prison psychiatrist said "we can keep you locked-up until you convince us you're no longer a danger". It wasn't a level playing field, and completely against the common belief that people are 'innocent until proved guilty'.

I would be fighting with both hands tied behind my back and a 'firing squad' looking forward to firing the bullets. The odds were well and truly massively stacked against me. But like most working-class people I've always loved an underdog.

It was almost midnight when I was banged-up in this single cell with a tiny, frosted window, it let daylight in but I couldn't see out. It reminded me of the punishment cell from my teenage days at Redhill. It was about 12 foot long and six foot wide containing a bed, desk and toilet. This was no weekend break at Centre Parks or anything like a Butlins holiday camp. Noman Stanley Fletcher was nowhere to be seen.

I ate my rotting apple and drank what was left of my flat cheapo orange juice trying to get my around the situation I'd found myself in. Nothing added up. All I'd done was write a novel where a fictional character put three bullets into the head of a real-life self-confessed child abuser. I sat in my cell thinking I wish I had killed the fat bastard because the punishment would have been the same. I would later repeat this statement to the prison psychiatrist.

I'll never understand why Basildon Police and the CPS considered writing a gangster novel to be equal to the crime of murder. But as is my character I'll always tell the truth. I told the prison shrink then and repeat now. "If I'm ever diagnosed with cancer and given just months to live, if my death was 100% certain, there are two people I'd do my best to kill before I went to heaven". I said it with a big smile on my face as I've always believed in capital punishment for child abusers, be it physical or emotional. I added "As a precaution I would get a second diagnosis and confirmation of the date as I don't fancy a life behind bars. I would only become a double killer if I had a medically confirmed diagnoses/death warrant from 2 doctors, I'd want a genuine 'get out of jail free' card".

I won't name my intended victims, but pretty sure those who know me will know who I'm talking about. One a fat bald bastard who looks like Shrek with no front teeth the other a ginger geezer-bird who looks like Angela Rayner's twin sister.

A Trigger Warning for Basildon Police and for the avoidance of doubt. It's not a Hit List, it's a Wish List. And for the-record most people with heart problems don't usually get struck down with cancer. So the odds on me carrying out my fantasy Wish List are very slim.

The first 24 hours in Bellmarsh felt like 48. It might not be politically correct, but I take my hat off to top gangsters and bank robbers doing 25 years. How do they survive the boredom? As a 12-year-old I'd been to Boyles Court and as a teenager Little Heath, Detention Centre and Borstal but this was a big step into a dark and dangerous world.

That was then and this is now. My first impression was the constant noise. It was non-stop shouting, screaming and the banging of doors. I thought then and think now, how do teenage killers addicted to a criminal lifestyle cope with 25 years behind bars? There'll be no more girls, designer clothes or night clubs. The plastic gangsters will soon lose their swagger as they walk about in cheap tracksuits and go month after month without sex.

All their mates on the outside will be shagging, dancing, playing football, having fun and having kids of their own, and they will be growing old and rotting away in a concrete coffin. They'll soon discover the days are long and extremely boring with lots of lows and no highs. Will they still believe that crime is cool?

The truth is prison is nothing like Porridge the classic TV comedy. It's a f*****g shithole and dustbin of a place. I should know I've been there.

I woke up at 7am and then spent five hours sitting on my bed staring at the bare walls. Throughout the night and during the day the flap on the cell door would open every half-hour and I'd see a creepy pair of eyes staring at me.

Unbelievable but I'm telling the gospel truth, the happy-go-lucky guy who never got down in his life was on 'suicide watch'. It would be a few days before I found out why. Looking back now it was pretty hilarious. In the space of five days, I'd gone from being a doting dad and caring single parent into a would-be serial killer with a death wish. I only found out why and how this all happened after I was released.

Unbeknown to me at the time my ex-wife had somehow been granted what is called an ex-parte Court Hearing. It's not only held in secret and behind closed doors but the 'other side' me is not informed and my legal team risk prosecution if they tell me about it. This explains why Basildon Police arrested me.

My ex-wife misled the court and lied to the police that I was planning to kill her and my 3 children. When people ask why I hate her, I reply how would they feel if they were falsely accused of being a 'danger to their own children'. I honestly believe it's unforgiveable. She also hoodwinked some psychiatrist who I'd never met that I was 'mad, bad and dangerous'. And there's more, she convinced the Judge that my three kids were terrified of me and lived in fear. Any number of Lie Detector Tests would confirm I never ever hit any of my three children. In fact I rarely raised my voice.

Months later my Legal team said "No offence Garry but look how you look compared to her. Basildon Police were always going to believe her".

My cell door opened, and three screws kitted out with truncheons, pepper sprays and walkie-talkies escorted me to the Medical Wing. The three bulldog looking thugs in military style uniforms, looking like the over-rated and unfunny comic pub landlord Al Murray, handed me over to the medical staff.

I waited in the freezing cold corridor wondering what would happen next. Was I going to be sedated and force-fed a diet of mind-altering drugs and transferred to a padded cell? I wasn't even close. A prison doctor summoned me into his Consulting Room and said:

"It doesn't look good Mr Johnson, (he actually called me Mr Johnson), unless you can satisfy me you're not mentally ill, you are not going home".

Adding "if you fail to do so, we can hold you indefinitely". In other words I was looking at a life sentence. I replied, "I don't understand, you're joking, there's been no trial and I've not been found guilty of anything".

He replied, "There doesn't need to be if we consider you're mentally ill".

I was examined and asked a never-ending number of questions and the answers could determine the rest of my life. Around a hour later the three goons escorted me back to my cell. I sat in silence with no TV, radio or books and entertained myself by re-living great events in my life. Like most of the memories you'll read in this book. Considering I was banged-up in a tiny room without a view it wasn't a bad night in. The next morning, I was taken back to the Hospital Wing, this time two shrinks in white coats asked similar questions from different angles.

Questions were fired quick and fast from both directions. It felt a bit like being interviewed at the same time by Piers Morgan and Jonathan Ross. It seemed to go well with both quacks smiling at different moments. Then it was back to the cell and another week of being locked up 24 hours a day without a single hour of recreation/exercise. Time went slow but then a friendly looking screw came to my cell and asked if I wanted a TV or Radio. I chose a television to see some pretty faces on the box. Hopefully a sighting of Patsy Kensit on Emmerdale Farm. A few glimpses of her and Amanda Holden would lift my spirits. I was hoping he'd bring me a nice flat screen TV, but he returned with the smallest black and white portable I'd ever seen.

It didn't have SKY Sports, but it still felt like a gift from heaven. I'm a born optimist and thought maybe the doctor or psychiatrist had put in a good word for me.

I was pretty confident I'd passed the medical examinations and jumped through all the hoops. I would spend another 48 hours in limbo watching rubbish programmes on terrestrial TV which is only slighter better than staring at bare walls. Solitary confinement scrambles your brain and plays tricks on your mind. It dulls your senses so much you consider watching Eastenders and Coronation Street a treat. Food was brought to my cell twice a day and I was given a big bag of sweets, tea bags, packets of plain biscuits (no Jaffa Cakes), cartons of milk and some cornflakes. Was this food for good behaviour or because they knew I was innocent? I just needed a upgrade on my room, a mini-bar, and a sexy blonde to share my bed.

The next day I was offered a change of clothes (but not my own), and the chance of a shower. But still no razor, comb or mirror. I still looked like a tramp but at least I smelt nice. My conditions were improving, and the screws were treating me like a human being, but at the end of the day I was still in prison

Even soft conditions seem harsh when you've not done anything wrong.

At times Prison life is like TV's Porridge, there's no Norman Stanley Fletcher, but there are plenty of Mr Mackay's walking around. Since my arrest I'd been denied any phone calls at Basildon police station and received no visits at Bellmarsh prison. I had no idea about the safety or whereabouts of my children. That was the hardest part of my incarceration.

The day of my arrest started like most weekday mornings. I woke my kids up for school, prepared breakfast and said "see you at half-three". Not knowing I wouldn't be seeing them for a month. From day one Basildon Police and the Mental Health Team tried to break me by keep repeating "you won't be going home". They had no chance of breaking me, not being big-headed but my mind is unbreakable. They had power over my body but not my mind. I'd survived my dad leaving and breaking my heart so Basildon Police didn't have a chance.

Was it just my imagination? But I felt like a political prisoner being tortured and treated as Public Enemy Number One. I don't know if it was meeting that Nun, and no I didn't start praying or became religious, but I did become more Irish.

I felt like an Irish Republican being bullied and abused by the British state.

All I had done was write a book, name a child abuser and upset a friend of Basildon Police. I spent ten days in solitary and was treated like a freedom fighter in Nazi Germany or Soviet Russia. In the cell next door was a Muslim terrorist who like me wasn't allowed out, one of the screws told me he'd been in there for months.

My only visitor was the Irish nun I met on my arrival. She spoke to me through the flap in my door and offered me a bible. I said "no thanks" explaining I couldn't read anything because the screws had taken away my glasses. She was a nice lady and although I didn't discover religion, I did keep thinking of Marianne Faithful and the time she performed `I Got You Babe with David Bowie dressed as a nun.

Why so memorable? She was naked from behind. Marianne Faithful not the nun.

Then without warning I was taken back to the Medical Wing, I won't bore you by repeating details of the long walk. This time I met by a big black doctor with a Kojak haircut and Sir Trevor McDonald accent. The gentle giant said, "Garry there is nothing wrong with you". Adding "To be blunt I can't understand why you were sent here".

Adding: "There are no signs of any mental illness. I am recommending your immediate release".

He asked me one last question.

"How would you feel if the boyfriend of your ex-wife was hit by a bus and killed?"

Without hesitation I replied:

"Well happy".

He smiled saying "A perfectly normal reaction". Adding: "The various examinations we carried out on you went well, which is why were authorising your release".

Me "What can I go home now?" He laughed saying:

"This is a prison not a hotel, you can't just checkout. There are forms to sign and paperwork to be completed, so could be 24 or 48 hours before you're released.

Within hours my glasses were returned and the next day I was on my home. The case against me had fallen apart like a cheap suit.

Forensic Psychiatrist Dr Sian Llewellyn Jones, who usually deals with murderers and serial killers wrote: "Garry Johnson is a flamboyant personality, with spiky hair, a marked Cockney accent, talks very fast, wears dark glasses and has a strange dress sense, but is not mentally ill". And what of Dr Best the psychiatrist I'd never met, recruited by my ex-wife to get me arrested? He withdrew his report, apologised to the Judge and asked to be taken off the case. On the morning of my release, I was taken back to the zoo like cage I'd sat in on my arrival.

For a people watcher like my-self it was an interesting place to spend a couple of hours. This time the Reception Area looked like a crowded dancefloor in a Gay night club. There was no music, but the noise was deafening. Hundreds of blokes all suited and booted and all talking at the same time. Some were being released but most were waiting to hear their fate in courts all over London. The last time I'd seen so many men in their 'Sunday Best' was at a Wedding Reception. It was like a meeting of the United Nations with old men, young men of every race, creed and colour. I noticed that the various racial groups did not mix, the only thing they had in common was the fact that they were all prisoners.

You could cut the atmosphere with a knife. It's only a matter of time before a full-blown race war erupts throughout the English prison system.

# Chapter Nine
# Growing Up and I'm Fine

Unfortunately, that wasn't the end of the vindictive hate campaign against me by my ex-wife, Basildon Police and Essex Social services. My dad walking out meant my childhood was stolen and that I lost my home, mates and any chance of being a footballer. I was also parted from my clothes, chopper bike, cat and all my football medals. The only way was up and life did eventually get better but it took almost five years to become 'the old me'. I know my life reads like an X-rated decade of EastEnders but unlike the BBC soap there were a lot of laughs along the way. Times were different back then and 15-year-old boys could stay under the radar as there was no social media or mobile phones. My parents left an empty house, like them most of the furniture had vanished but I still had a key.

As I've always said 'every cloud has a silver lining' and I would take full advantage of the situation. The next few weeks at 9 Fairview Chase would be 'party time' for me and my mates. It really was girls, girls, and more girls for all of us. There weren't orgies, we were too young, but we always invited the 'right girls' if you get my drift. When my dad left I went into meltdown, didn't know it at the time, as back then people didn't talk about their emotions, they just had a breakdown or turned to alcohol. I chose 'fast drugs' and lived to tell the tale.

What happened made me anti-marriage all my life and only succumbed because I wanted kids. Unfortunately, the girl I met had old-fashioned parents who didn't believe in kids outside marriage. I can't really say that getting married was the biggest mistake of my life because it gave me two sons that I love and a daughter who hates me. Just as I hated my dad for walking out on me I hate my ex-wife for walking out on her sons. I believe in 'sex equality' and got no time for men or women who walk out on their children. I've got no respect and pure hatred for both sexes. When my wife left it brought back vivid flashbacks to when my own bastard of a dad walked out on me. I remember it as if yesterday, a Friday afternoon and coming home from school to an empty house. My mum was nowhere to be seen, and my dad was home much earlier than normal. He was on the phone and whispering, didn't know at the time, but obviously talking to his fancy women. I had no idea at the time and only interested in who was doing my tea. I just wanted to get washed and changed and head off for the Youth Club disco.

There were three `go to girls` in my school, if you get my drift, they were known as the `Cup Final Girls` because they went all the way and that night, I was meeting one of them over the local park before meeting my `proper girlfriend` at the Youth Club. Remember I'm describing what happened in the 70s in the dialogue of that period. You could say `Like Father like son`, except I was only fifteen and didn't have a wife and child.

The next morning there was still no sign of my mum and that afternoon my dad was gone. There was no kiss, cuddle or even a proper `goodbye`. All I got the next day in Stanford High Street was a couple of quid and a "see you later".

I guess that was his version of the tacky carriage clock you get when your time is up at the factory and you're no longer wanted. He never had the guts, decency or moral code to say "goodbye". When I found out he was never coming back my head hurt, my stomach ached, and my body shook. At the time I was a promising footballer and if it weren't for his terrible act of betrayal, I could have been a contender.

After five years of watching me play football every week, rain or shine, he stopped coming. I was always proud to have him standing on the touchline barking orders and shouting encouragement. With him gone part of me `died`. I became slower and stopped scoring so many goals. My head wasn't right and my heart wasn't in it.

When my boys started playing football, I attended every game even though at times it was difficult. Two years on-the-trot both got to School cup Finals, not only played on the same day but kicking off at the same time. I spent 90 minutes running from pitch to pitch, but well worth it as both times they were on the Winning Side. I was a good player in my day but both boys were better than me, far more technical and they headed the ball. I was just a `prolific goal-scorer` to my friends and a `glorified goal-hanger` to my enemies. They had all-round talent and could do `keeppie-uppie` and tricks with a ball that I could only dream of.

I wanted this to be a light-hearted book and promised myself not to mention my ex-wife, but it has to be said that despite my best efforts in a way history did sadly repeat itself. The selfish actions of my dad (and his wife) stopped me becoming at least a semi-pro footballer as did the selfish behaviour of my ex-wife prevent my sons from becoming professional footballers. After my dad left I'd spend the next few years as a messed up, mixed-up homeless kid running riot. An angry young man involved in various and illegal scrapes indulging in various substances.

I didn't really enjoy being a teenage tearaway, the only good thing about being a `bad boy` is how many girls find it attractive and want to shag you. Sadly, there is a downside, once you've got a bit of a reputation it's hard to shed, and you become a marked man. Boys from other towns who you don't know want to fight you and cops know your face. The novelty soon wears off and that way of life becomes boring. The truth is my heart wasn't in it, it was never in it.

I was/am more of a rebel than a criminal. I don't even like two-bob, low-life criminals. As with everything be it showbiz or crime I'm always attracted glamour. My `favourites` are The Great Train Robbers, the Kray Twins and celeb gangster Dave Courtney. Read so many books on The Krays I could go on Mastermind and have them as my qualifying round special subject. Then easily win the final answering questions on David Bowie.

At fifteen I gave up football and became the teenager most parents would n want their daughters to mix with. My roller-coaster journey into petty crime, underage sex and drugs would be a bumpy ride. There would be lots of laughs, mental torture but never tears. Somehow, I knew from an early age that the happiest people who see life as the glass always being half full rather than half-empty.

The story of the boy who was thirty before he grew up starts with my birth the 21$^{st}$ of January 1957 in the East End of London. My mum was eighteen and Irish and my dad cockney and ten years her senior. Not sure if I was planned or really wanted, but once I was born it was too late to send me back. The first fourteen years were great and have nothing but happy memories. I then became another innocent victim of what middle-class hippy social workers call `a broken home`.

1972 was a big year. My dad left home, and I discovered David Bowie.

Before Ziggy Stardust my life was all about playing football and kissing girls. But after seeing David Bowie on Top of The Pops I wanted to be a rock star, but didn't know how. It would be another four years before Johnny Rotten and The Sex Pistols showed working-class kids how to break into showbiz. Along with The Clash and The Jam they didn't just open doors they kicked them down.

Looking back on my schooldays and before I became a teenager there were two incidents that made a lasting impression on me. Both took place on a Sunday evening and led to a life-long hatred of child abusers and sex offenders. The first incident took place on the last weekend before my first year at Senior School.

A gang of older boys undressed a teenage girl at the back of the local park. I did not witness the attack but arrived after it had happened. Months later I would be 'molested' in a Children's Home. Those two incidents influenced my hatred for child abusers. I was taking a short cut home through the fields and saw a load of older boys gathered in a circle, as I got closer, I recognised some as older brothers of my mates. On the ground was a half-naked girl a couple of years older than me. They had her pinned to the ground in the long grass and were removing the rest of her clothes. I was only 12 and shocked as they grabbed and groped her. At the time I didn't know her name and hadn't knowingly seen her before.

I wasn't yet a teenager and, although I'd seen pictures in magazines this was the first time I'd seen a naked girl in the flesh. Even at Twelve I knew it was wrong and a cowardly act but didn't know what to do. Some of the older boys knew me and warned "don't tell anyone". I didn't for two reasons, one when your 12, 'big boys' of 15 and sixteen look like giants. Plus, I was mates with their younger brothers. On my first day at Senior School, I saw the same girl hanging out on what looked like 'friendly terms' with the same gang of boys. I didn't feel so 'guilty' then about keeping quiet. I don't usually get embarrassed but couldn't stop blushing when they called me over because I knew she recognised me as the skinny little kid who'd seen her naked. Even as a streetwise 12-year-old my young mind couldn't work out how a 'victim' was friends with her 'abusers'.

I was also a 'victim' during my first stay at Boyles Court Children's Home in Brentwood Essex. My abuser was not a gang a teenage boys but a Ronnie Corbett lookalike, a 1970s TV comedian, and by coincidence also occurred on a Sunday evening. I wasn't stripped naked, but I was 'touched'. The bastard came into my dormitory and sat on my bed. Without saying a word put his hand under my duvet and touched my private parts. Unlike the 'gang strip' of that girl at the back of Stanford Park this was reported to Harlow Police and the NSPCA.

I can still see his face and smell the stench of Brylcream in his hair. A year later I returned to Boyles Court looking more like a man than a boy. I was now a mouthy teenage tearaway and sought him out. The nonce was still wearing the same checked jacket and sporting an Elvis Presley style quiff. I gave him my best 'if looks could kill' stare and let's just say he never came back for a second grope. Those two incidents hopefully explain my lifelong hatred of all child abusers and sex offenders.

Hopefully it also explains why and how I reacted to certain events that occurred in 2005 when my ex-wife, her parents and ginger geezer-bird Sally Prevost 'sided' with a self-confessed child abuser. After leaving school first un-officially and then officially I decided that when it came to work, I was a consciences objector. I was only interested in skinny blondes, fast drugs, David Bowie and going to gigs. I couldn't conform to a 9 to 5 lifestyle and wanted to walk on the wild side. At sixteen I was hanging out in the West End and Soho Clubs and sleeping wherever I lay my hat.

My 'teenage years' with no responsibilities lasted longer than most people's but once I passed twenty-nine, I decided to grow-up and be a dad. All my mates had children, and I wanted a kid of my own. I gave up drugs overnight but giving up my 'Teenage Wildlife' proved to be much harder. Since leaving school and joining Sounds music magazine and then Fleet Street not much in my life had changed. I'd upgraded my choice in fast drugs with cocaine replacing amphetamine. Adult female women had replaced teenage girls, but I was still thinking and dressing like a Mod.

Hawkwind at Southend is the first gig I can remember. They'd had a hit record with 'Silver Machine', Lemmy played guitar, and a naked female danced on stage. I went with a gang of older boys who gave me some pep pills. This was before discovering David Bowie/Ziggy Stardust but after I discovered Mod as a ten-year-old Toddler. One of my earliest music memories is seeing The Small Faces performing 'Lazy Sunday' on TV. Even as a young kid I could tell a good tune, plus I was excited hearing a great Cockney accent. It's the first record I bought from a stall in Hackney Market, quickly followed by The Who's 'Substitute'. So proud to know I was a pre-teen Mod.

I was always into fashion and the best dressed kid in town, not boasting and only thank to Billy Lane my dad's best mate. A wealthy 'ducker and diver' who could get his hands on anything. Luckily for me he had two teenage sons into Mod and I got all their expensive 'hand-me-downs'. I went to school in the best Ben Sherman shirts, sta-press trousers, and aged Eleven had my first Crombie overcoat with a red top pocket hanky. Aged thirteen I was going to Monday and Friday night discos at Stanford and Gable Hall youth clubs wearing authentic 501 Levi jeans, Fred Perry polo shirts and two-tone tonic mohair suits. Girls who liked me as a skinhead, loved me more as a Mod with a suedehead haircut. This was because of my 'biggish' nose longer hair has always suited me. I was a dedicated follower of (second hand) fashion who couldn't dance but still loved dance records.

Apart from football it was music that ruled my life. I loved reggae and collected Trojan SKA compilation albums. A special song for teenage boys in 1971 was Max Romeo's 'Wet Dream' with the chorus of "Lie down girl let me push it up, push it up, lie down". It was banned by the prudish BBC but still got into the Top 20.

From the age of twelve I was never short of female attention, not entirely because of my 'good lucks' but like all teenage boys across England benefited from being the 'star of the school football team. In my day teenage girls always liked a footballer or a `bad boy` so I became both. In 15 years I`d taken vast amounts of drugs, slept with many women, made and spent a lot of money but something was missing. I`d been the favourite `Uncle and a Godfather but more and more I wanted a family of my own. I wanted to be a dad. I just needed to meet a female of the species who ticked all the right boxes. Blonde with a pretty face, long legs, and a sense of humour who like me wanted kids. I met my Patsy Kensit `lookalike` who unfortunately for me had old-fashioned parents who`d brought her up to believe that `kids and marriage` must go together like fish and chips.

We met at a family wedding and on the day it was perfect timing. We were both sort of single. She was finishing an affair with a married man and the Children`s Nanny I`d been seeing was visiting her parents in South Africa. So maybe it was meant to be happen, but unlike all the best Hollywood movies there wouldn't be a happy ending. On the day she reminded me of Suzanne Mitzi, owned a car and laughed at all my jokes. As Del boy Trotter would say "get your coat you`ve pulled". We went onto have three beautiful kids, but our marriage was always doomed from Day One as I never got on with her parents. They were not happy because I was unconventional and worse ten years older than their daughter. The day my Sam was born was the proudest day of my life and I took to being a dad like a duck to water. He was an emergency caesarean and almost died. The first week of his life was in extensive care. I stayed at his side night and day. Apart from the medical staff I was the only person to see him for five days.

I was terrified when the nurse told me to put my hands inside the incubator and change his nappy. My hands were shaking, and I was drenched from head to toe in sweat. I was so wet you`d thought I`d just got out of the shower.

I became addicted to parenthood and as is my character wanted more. Being a dad was better than sex, drugs, rock and roll. We were married for fifteen years and never stopped loving her or disliking her parents. Ma and Pa Taylor were like excess baggage in our relationship a pair of pathetic old dinosaurs whose minds were still stuck in the 1950`s. Had I known when I married my ex-wife that her parents would move to a house 300 yards from mine there would have been no wedding. Despite all this stress I`m proud to say I never cheated or `gave in` to any form of temptation. I loved being a dad more than anything. Sam and Adam sort of came on demand. No problem, no delays, but scoring a hat-trick wasn't so easy. My daughter had to be one of the most wanted and tried for babies in the world.

It took five years to get lucky. At first it was no hardship as most days we were going `at it` like rabbits. It was great fun to start with, but as the months dragged on I became weary and it became a worry. There was so to speak no `Bullseye` moment, we were not hitting the target. I was getting `stressed` and my ex-wife was losing patience. Like me she was desperate for a daughter to complete our perfect family. She stopped drinking and smoking and changed my diet. She added various things to her `dressing up box` (censored).

My ex-wife had charts pinned to the fridge and circled dates on the kitchen calendar. I was ordered to stop drinking tea, start wear loose-fitting pants and force-fed Zinc tablets and to have cold baths before coming to bed. Eventually it worked and on October $3^{rd}$ 2000 my daughter was born. I was a dad again at the ripe old age of forty-three. We now had three kids, but both wanted more. My ex-wife took control of `Project Four`. I found myself living on a strict diet of tuna fish, salmon, prawns and bananas.

I was also back on Zinc tablets and Cranberry juice. I took so many tablets that I rattled when I walked. Nothing was working so my ex-wife persuaded me to visit my GP who referred me to Basildon Hospital. To make matters worse and more stressful my ex-wife had already been tested and passed with `flying colours

The pressure was now on with embarrassing visits to Basildon Hospital which involved porno magazines and medical containers. I failed the medical. Unlike my ex-wife my re-production organs were not in `mint condition`. The earth-shattering results destroyed my confidence and although not `medically qualified` I'm convinced they led to my heart problems. I would soon become temporary impotent and unable to perform which resulted in my wife having two affairs. I told later that the damage to my heart and hardening of my veins was the reason why blood was not getting to my `private parts`. As if to rub `salt into the wound` my ex-wife went on to get pregnant by one of her boyfriends.

What done my head in more than her `adultery` was how a woman who hated me for not getting her pregnant than get rid of the baby. Her body, her choice but why the sudden change of heart? I was truly shocked when I read her confidential medical records obtained by my solicitor. The results from Basildon Hospital regarding the hardening of my arteries although `life-changing` at the time would eventually save my life. Although to put it bluntly "I couldn't get it up on demand" the medication did save my life. I went onto survive five heart attacks, two, triple heart bypass operations, and a minor stroke. And in 2023 and again in 2024 I had a new pacemaker connected to my heart. The truth is at my age I'd rather have a working heart than a functioning dick. Though both worked perfectly well in Blackpool, was that because of the sea air or the beauty of a girl called Carly?

My former father-in-law would mock me for being virtually teetotal. He'd say "it's just my luck, my daughter gets herself hitched to the only Irish bloke who doesn't drink". Mr Taylor thought it was 'unmanly' and 'wimpy'. The annoying thing was I was more of a genuine 'Jack the Lad' then he could ever dream of.

I felt like telling him all about the drugs, sex parties, the one-night-stands and all sorts of other illegal activities. Had he ever been to an orgy or done anything illegal?

Mr Taylor was so straight he wouldn't even watch television without owning a TV licence. I didn't need to drink pints of bitter in The British Legion Club to prove to him I was a 'real man'. I'm not boasting, well maybe a little bit, but I've had more women in a month than he's had in a lifetime. Taken more illegal drugs then he's taken aspirin and I'd say Stringfellows and The Playboy Club trump a working man's club. It was my choice to be stone cold sober and drug free. I wanted to be a 'great husband' and the 'best dad in the world' not his drinking buddy.

1974 was a good year. Ziggy Stardust slept with middle of the road pop star Lulu and in January she released her version of the Bowie classic 'The Man Who Sold the World'. He produced it and she had a hit record. That April I had my first line of coke and Bowie released 'Diamond Dogs'. Away from the routine of school I wanted to swap my teenage wildlife for a career in showbiz but didn't know how. But convinced 'finding out' would be a lot better than a 9 to 5 job on a building site. I was okay at chatting-up girls but unless you work as a gigolo you're not going to get paid for it.

1975: The Tory Party chose a female leader. David Bowie went funky and I became a white soul boy hanging out at The Goldmine on Canvey Island.

An escape route from routine and boredom was only 18 months away. Opportunity was about to knock. Something was occurring in the upmarket area of Chelsea and the downmarket squats of Ladbroke Grove and Notting Hill.

It was a new music scene linked to the fans of Ziggy Stardust and maybe I could be part of it. Down at the cheap end of the Kings Road Malcolm McClaren opened a clothing store Called SEX. He also managed a band called The Swankers, who would become The Sex Pistols. 1976: David Bowie released 'Station To Station' his musical masterpiece and revealed another new image. Ziggy Stardust was now The Thin White Duke. At the same time Punk Rock was growing and now consisted of The Sex Pistols, The Clash, The Buzzcocks and The Jam.

The Fab Four could never be bettered, so although tempted I remained a fan rather than a participant. Everyone has their `moment` and this was not mine. I couldn't do anything better than Johnny Rotten Joe Stummer, Pete Shelley or Paul Weller so bided my time.

Every town in England had a tacky two-bob version of the fab four and I didn't want to be a second-rate impersonator. Time would prove me right. A few like Generation X, Sham 69, and X Ray Spex who jumped on the bandwagon were good, but the rest were crap. I kept going to gigs as a fan but decided to be a writer. I reinvented myself as The Punk Poet and with no qualifications became a music critic. Punk Rock made me realise that most barriers in life are there to be torn down. I took on board the DIY ethic and transformed myself from a teenage tearaway into a tabloid terrorist.

There were three women who stood out in the Punk Rock generation.

Debbie Harry from America was the best-looking woman in the history of the world. Siouxsie Sioux and Viv Albertine were both smart and attractive and in many ways more arty than angry. To me, Punk was all about shaking things up, with exciting music and a cool attitude. I saw it as modern rock and roll for the Ziggy generation. I first saw The Jam in 1977, on a bill with The Clash and The Buzzcocks. What a night. Always loved Paul Weller and the way he didn't follow the punk rock rule book. Weller was always his own man and a MOD.

He was born a Mod and `upset` the NME by daring to rip up a copy punk bible `Sniffin Glue` in the middle of a concert. The Jam was always more Mod than punk which is why Weller outlasted both Rotten and Strummer and is still going strong.

I did for a brief moment flirt with the idea of forming a band but didn't want to be the $100^{th}$ clone of Johnny Rotten. For a brief moment in time Chrissie my hairdresser took my mind off Punk Rock. She was a bit older, only by a few years but older, so in mind qualified as an older woman and had her own flat. I've always had a thing for older woman, nowadays the ones I liked are all either dead or in care homes. It`s frightening and makes me feel old. It started when I was sixteen. One night I stayed at a friend`s house and the next morning after he`d gone to school and her husband to work she came into my room. His mum was about 40-42 and in her way quite sexy. She had bottle blonde hair scrapped back, no make-up but to an impressionable 16-year-old boy like me she was a Hollywood sex bomb. In fact, when she removed her dressing gown and the headband she was very attractive. I stayed three nights that week.

Chrissie was a brief encounter but continued to cut and bleach my hair for a few more years. I was writing a few poems and songs without tunes but still hadn't got round to forming a band. Then I saw Gary Numan on TV and was 'dead jealous', not in a nasty envious way, but more in admiration. The guy was doing what I'd always wanted to do. He was impersonating David Bowie on TV. Most music critics and Bowie fans were not impressed and slagged him off, but not me.

I thought he was great and genuinely thought good luck to him. The history books prove I was right as he went onto sell millions of records. Seeing Gary Numan made me think again about forming a band. Days later I saw David Bowie at The Wembley Arena and he convinced me to give it another go. I thought maybe I could bluff my way into becoming a pop star, so I formed The Buzz Kids. It was fun but a complete waste of time. Our debut gig was also our last.

Although I grew up admiring East End gangsters and boxers I've always hated bullies or people who hit or hurt children. I've always considered smacking to be a form of bullying. I hate it when I see other parents hitting their kids in the supermarket or over the park. I am the most easy-going liberal dad in the world, my sons love me, my grandkids love me, but for some unknown reason my daughter hates me. As a single dad I was like a 'mum in y-fronts' and did everything. I never said "no" and tried to spoil them rotten because it was a pleasure to do so, it gave me a buzz. My ex-wife once said to me:

"If you came in and I told you the kids wanted a donkey in the garden I know you'd say let them" It's true, I would have agreed instantly without a moment of hesitation". My character, personality, morals and values are a million miles from the films and music that entertain me. I love Punk Rock, British gangster films, the Ziggy Stardust/David Bowie lifestyle, Mike Tyson, Oasis and all things Mod, but when it comes to family life and children I'm a Mister Softie, a militant liberal who loves kids believing in Father Christmas.

At times my story will read as if it's being told by both halves of my character, or a showbiz source or someone else. It's for you and you alone to decide whether I'm a loveable rogue or a flashy fraudster? At the end of the day, which is worse?

The Punk Poet impersonating a tabloid journalist or Sir champagne socialist Starmer pretending to be on the side of the working-class? I made up stories and infiltrated showbiz parties. Blair and Campbell 'sexed-up' documents that led us into an illegal war. I admit to being a tabloid terrorist, but will Starmer admit to being a class traitor and Blair to being a war criminal?

No matter how many people I duped, conned or hoodwinked there is no blood on my hands. I embellished stories but none of my fabrications made women widows or children orphans. I'm confident the court of public opinion will judge me kindly. I plead guilty to being a professional scammer and wind-up merchant, but innocent of criminal deception. The truth is I'd rather be tabloid journalist (professional or amateur) any day of the week then a corrupt money-grabbing politician. I infiltrated Fleet Street because I wanted a fun and glamorous life,

I was the Peter Pan of Punk Rock and then I grew up. In March 2013 I was given five years to live and in 2024 the Mod Pop is still here. I refuse to throw in the towel and will never stop dreaming. In May 2016 at a friend's Birthday Party I got chatting to Football Factory writer John King. The best-selling author was a fan of my early poems and asked if I still wrote. I answered "no" but was too embarrassed to explain why. I stopped writing because I didn't think I could do it without 'fast drugs'. On the drive home however much I tried, I just couldn't get the conversation with John King out of my head. He didn't convert me to vegetarianism as I have been a non-meat eater for years, but he sparked my appetite to start writing again. What did I say about fate? Days later Swedish rocker Soren Sulo Karlsson made contact. A massive fan of my poetry book 'Boys Of The Empire' he wanted to work with me. Within months I was re-writing old poems new songs and then a novel. Soren recorded three of my new songs 'Punk Rock Stories and Tabloid Tales', 'Newton Brown' and 'Father's Day'. Without sounding big-headed they are, without doubt, three of my best songs, written straight from the heart and full of emotion.

The first time I heard 'Father's Day' I had tears in my eyes, written for the daughter I'd not seen since 2008. What else happened after my life-saving heart operations? I made my stage comeback in Blackpool, stayed 3 days and met a woman called Carly. I hung out with Steve Diggle one of my punk heroes from The Buzzcocks and was interviewed live on stage by my old mate Garry Bushell.

Back in London this led to various radio interviews and a TV appearance. And Paul 'the Mod' Hallam published an updated version of my punk classic poetry book 'Boys Of The Empire'. I also appeared at The Roundhouse in Camden sharing a stage with TV star Phil Jupitus. I got £200 for a thirty-minute spot, but more importantly got to stand on the same stage David Bowie first performed some of his Ziggy Stardust songs. I was fifty-plus and still going strong. I was living proof that people should never give up or stop dreaming.

In 1980 after a couple of years doing 'bits and bobs' on various punk publications I got my first break at Sounds music magazine wowing Editor Eric Fuller with my original Mod Crombie and barrage of live reviews. Eric who walked, talked and dressed like a Mod had no idea he was praising re-writes of old Record Mirror and Smash Hits reviews. I was posing as a hot young gunslinger and in my mind following in the footsteps of Tony Parsons and Julie Burchill. Before joining Sounds I always feared that one day I would have to get a `proper job`.

Although more or less a fraud within months I would become a proud member of the National Union of Journalists. And to this day, getting my NUJ card is still one of my proudest achievements. I felt like a regular soldier becoming a member of the elite SAS. The treasured NUJ card was my version of the red beret. I can still remember going to a meeting in Holborn where I couldn't get out of the room quick enough, in case they changed their mind. I really can`t explain how proud I was to become a genuine member of Her Majesty`s Press.

I prepared well for my interview with Eric Fuller, an original North London Mod from the 1960s. I`d seen him in and around his Covent Garden office, this was before the invention of emails, when all copy was delivered by hand. He`d published a few of my Reviews but this was my chance to become a regular member of the team. At the time Garry Bushell was Live Reviews or Features Editor. Eric liked my writing style (and my clothes) or should that be my art of copying?

I handed him a copy of Boys of the Empire` and he hired on the spot. Again, as with the night I obtained my NUJ card, I couldn't get out of the room quick enough. My journalistic career wasn't all a scam. I genuinely did discover The Stone Roses, became top tipster for Piers Morgan at the Sun, and right-hand-man to Rebekah Wade at News International.

My first live review published in Sounds was The Business playing at some scummy South London pub and my debut feature was former Jam star Bruce Foxton. I can`t explain the thrill of seeing your name in print. It must be like a footballer scoring the winning goal in a FA Cup Final or adding Kate Moss to your list of conquests. It gives you a rush and a buzz you can`t describe. Working for Sounds was a dream gig, but writing for The Sun was something else. With my background it felt surreal at times. The truth is, my family and friends all read The Sun and, whatever the champagne socialists say, it was at the time the genuine voice of the working-class. I don`t just mean politics, I`m talking about the coverage of showbiz, TV, football, boxing and it also had Page 3 girls. I loved all the celebrity stuff by Garry Bushell and the sport from Colin Hart and John Sadler. The truth is what I lacked in education I made-up for in having an active imagination. I was the best in the business, and it was more like `painting pictures` than fraud. My job was to make people laugh at the breakfast table and smile on their journey to work. My stories were lucrative but harmless and, in all honesty, tomorrow`s fish and chip paper. I looked the part, dressed to impress and like a Deliveroo driver always delivered the goods. However much white powder went up my nose I always stayed in character. When out drinking I would get merry but never drunk, to ensure I never let my guard down.

The name of the game was impressing influential people. It was all about being in the right place at the right time and never going off script. When it came to smoke and mirrors and 'sleight of hand', I was right up there with Penn and Teller and David Blaine. I don't deserve to be ranked alongside great writers. I know I'm no Clive James or Tony Parsons. But it has to be said, I do deserve a place, just a small place, in the history of British Journalism. A film of my life would be more exciting than an England team managed by Gareth Southgate, as it had more ups and downs then a game of snakes and ladders. Tony Blair got it wrong with weapons of mass destruction, Sir Winston Churchill with his promise of a land fit for heroes. I was like a postman and always delivered.

Nine times out of ten I always got it right. I predicted eight years before it happened that Carry On star Barbara Windsor would be joining the cast of Eastenders. The Kemp brothers would play the Kray Twins in a movie and Maggie Thatcher the movie. If you disagree with my comparisons to Mystic Meg or Charles Dickens as a great storyteller, you can't deny me a place alongside Jeremy Beadle as a great wind-up merchant. Most people who've met me describe me as self-effacing, funny, friendly, loyal, mischievous, charming and humble with no airs and graces and as down to earth as an East London fish and chip shop, and that's just my enemies.

I'm more than happy with those descriptions but will always describe myself as a "working-class liberal with middle-class manners". I readily admit I'm mass of contradictions, I'm a Mod but whose moral code is strictly old school. I'm proud of the fact I never swear in front of women or children. The accolade I like best is when friends or family say "He's a great dad", and when you're a single dad that means the world. In 2005 I became a housewife, a mum and dad without doing a Frank Moloney or dressing-up like Eddie Izzard. Housework, although not rocket science is in no way enjoyable, but, as with eating and breathing it has to be done. I won't reveal the joys of washing up, doing the laundry, ironing or making beds, because there aren't any. The only enjoyable part is the Tesco weekly shop and being surrounded by yummy mummy's pushing trolleys. In 1985 I predicted the addiction to phones before mobile phones had even been invented. I got the Sun Features Editor to believe I was addicted to my landline telephone. According to my so-called 'medical condition', I would wake up every ten minutes to check my answer machine messages and to talk on the phone with one installed in every room. This resulted in a full page exclusive with genuine medical experts commenting on my `condition`. Nowadays millions of people all over the world share my `illness`.

My love of a wind-up was responsible for a number of `world exclusives`, such as bottles of air breathed by David Bowie on sale in Petticoat Lane`. I don`t know how my rise through the ranks happened, but it did. There was no master plan, but to quote some old Tory politician, "events dear boy, events".

The promotions just kept on coming. My creative stories were being read by millions and published all over Fleet Street. I don`t feel any `guilt` because I always wrote nice things about people, that`s how I got away with it for so long. In those days, before everything was computerised, stories would be phoned-in to a team of, mostly women who I`d flirt with on the phone. Getting stories published was great but the social life was better. At Sounds it was one long round of drink, drugs and pretty girls. Working at the Sun meant more money and access to flashier parties, better quality drugs and prettier girls.

I met the cream of tabloid journalism. Piers Morgan, Andy Coulson, Nick Ferrari, John Blake, Matthew Wright, Matt Bendoris, Martin Dunn, Annette Witheridge to name but a few. The Sun was not perfect and made two massive mistakes like backing war criminal Tony Blair and of course Hillsborough. They got it terribly wrong after being fed a tissue of lies by a rogue News Agency and corrupt coppers. I enjoyed working in Fleet Street and being an imposter, it was a right buzz because I didn't have the qualifications to edit the Beano. But somehow through a combination of luck, charm and taking chances I got away with it.

Despite working in a middle-class world packed with Oxbridge types and public schoolboys I never betrayed my class. At heart I was still the same bloke who as a homeless Teenager slept on rock hard wooden benches at Stanford railway station, there was no CCTV in those days. I never forgot having to jump up every 15 minutes to pull the chord to get some heat. You don`t forget things like that, which is why I`ve never appreciated middle-class suburban rebels and champagne socialists.

Labour MPs are the enemy of the working-class, it`s always do as I say and not what I do. The truth is the sons and daughters of Labour MPs play on grass and our kids play on concrete. I started at Sounds with `nothing in the bank` and after 35 years of writing punk reviews and tabloid stories I still have fuck all in the bank.

Did I waste all my money on wine, women and song? No. I got married and then divorced. Was getting married the biggest mistake of my life? I can forgive Garry Bushell for ending my singing career, but why didn't he talk me out of getting married? I was let down by my best man, why didn't he lose the ring or stop the service? Though on the day, he gave a great speech. It wasn't a total disaster because it gave me my two sons, the best thing that ever happened to me, which would lead to me becoming a Granddad. (Mod Pop). I also got an estranged daughter who hates me, but who said life was fair?

Without sounding like a wimp, which I'm not, I'm a million miles from that, but I am a big softie when it comes to kids. I am not ashamed to say I miss my daughter, even though she hates me and I've shed lots of tears over the years.

I think of her most days but Christmas Day is the worst, followed by Birthdays (hers and mine). In twenty years, she has not once sent me a single Birthday or Father's Day card and genuinely believe she's been brainwashed to hate me. There's no other explanation. The only excuse for hate is if somebody has done you personal harm and I've never harmed a hair on her head. Those who know me will confirm as well as being a punk poet and life-time Mod I'm also an old romantic who likes films with a Happy Ending. I'm hoping the real-life feud featuring me and my daughter also has a happy ending.

Trust and loyalty are two little words that mean a lot to me, "Bollocks" I hear you shout. Adding; "You were a scammer". Some might even say "a professional liar" but nothing could be further from the truth, always hated liars with a passion and in real-life can't even do 'little white lies'. If I'm asked to give an opinion I give it, when it comes to saying things (as my daughter-in-law) says I have very little filter. I always shoot from the hip. I 'bullshitted' people and exaggerated stories on an industrial scale when it came to work, but that was my professional life and not my personal. But in my defence there was never any malice in anything I said or did.

It's not in my nature which is why I was so disgusted when my friend Cindy Jackson did the dirty on rock star Noddy Holder. After Cindy I had a massive crush on a blonde PR who was a dead-ringer for Dempsey and Makepeace star Glynis Barber. I fancied her from a far, close-up, fast asleep and wide awake. Out of respect I won't name her because she is now a wife and a mum.

But God, did I fancy her or what? She wore the shortest skirts with the best legs I've ever seen. A speed freak and a cokehead (she was just my type), but unfortunately a best friend without benefits. I stayed many times at her flat, but only once did we share a bed and nothing happened. We'd been up all night partying and at 6am it was too late/too early to consummate our friendship.

We were both too shattered for anything to happen, but not complaining as we got closer than I ever imagined and remained 'good friends'.

We had some great nights on the town with all our clothes on at places like Stringfellows, The Embassy Club and The Video Cafe but no more than a kiss and a cuddle with our clothes on. I loved hanging out with PRs as they always had great stories and much wilder private lives than a humble journo.

My friend Dan was a dead-ringer for 70's pop idol David Essex in his prime, he was a legendary bird-bandit and man about town. I often stayed at his flat just off Leicester Square and placed feel-good stories about his acts in various papers and magazines. I knew all about his affair with a chart-topping pop star and we often discussed it but never told a soul. It was 'strange' seeing her on TV and knowing all about what she liked getting up to in the bedroom.

Without tipping me off in advance Dan went public about his fling with Bucks Fizz singer Jay Aston. He was paid £10,000 for doing a Kiss and Tell on the Eurovision Song Contest winner. Spilling the beans to the Sunday People about their 'sex romps' had massive life-changing consequences for 'Dan the Man'. He lost his job and moved to Australia. I last heard from him on social media in 2016 and pleased to hear he'd made it big down under. Today he's very successful in the world of business. While we're on the subject of trust and loyalty it gives me the opportunity to prove I practise what I preach. I was invited to the home of a very famous English actor.

A genuine East End Boy made good, who's starred in some of my favourite films and appeared in episodes of Minder, my favourite TV show of all-time. In my opinion he also played Televisions best-ever on-screen cop in ITV's The Bill.

I visited him at his Essex mansion for a Christmas edition of News of the World. As a fan I considered it a great honour to be invited into his home and be introduced to his wife and family. They do say you shouldn't meet your heroes, but he didn't disappoint. I found him a perfect host and great company. After an hour we retreated to his Snooker Room where he produced drinks and some letters from behind the bar. He placed them on the green baize saying, "these will interest you".

They didn't just interest me, they f*****g impressed. They were personal letters from Reg and Ronnie Kray and I was holding them in my hand. I am thinking to myself "if my friends could see me now". (and my dad). I was blown away when he said, "between you and me the Twins are great friends and paid all my Drama school fees". These were dynamite quotes and front-page fodder for every UK tabloid, I could have earned a lot of money, but in my mind it would have meant breaking my moral code and betraying a trust.

I was a stranger in his house and also a guest, but more important we were both a working-class Cockneys. There's no way then or now that I would betray a confidence. If he'd said "you can go public" I would of done so, but only with his permission. It is not in my nature to give away secrets even when the person is dead so won't name the underworld boss who protected my family from a child-abusing pervert who threatened my children. What the TV cop revealed was pure gold, but I was a guest in his house. There is no way then or now that I would ever betray a confidence. It's not in my nature to give away secrets. That's why I survived so long in the wonderful world of showbiz. There is funny side to this story, as a few days after the interview was published, I got a phone call asking, "Why didn't' you mention the Twins?" I replied, "You didn't give permission". He laughed: "but you're a journalist so assumed you would". Joking: "I was a bit disappointed when you didn't, it would have done wonders for my street cred". I think that anecdote explains why I lasted so long in the Fleet Street jungle, as with Cockney culture it's all about trust and reputation, always better to build bridges rather than blowing them up. That's why I only name people who done me wrong or those who did me a favour. I never revealed or source or betrayed a confidence.

# Chapter Ten
# Standing in the Dock

Although my full-time career was as a showbiz journalist addicted to `truth and justice` I had many varied strings to my bow. What prudes would call vices I considered to be adult hobbies. I liked `fast drugs`, punk rock, the East End Underworld with a interest in porn movies.

No, I didn't star in them but did write a few scripts. My ex-wife told Essex Social Services I once lived with a `porn star` to discredit me as a parent. I admit I do have a colourful past but the only person to call me a criminal, a drug addict, a would-be serial killer and a porn star is my ex-wife. I was seventeen when I gave up crime and twenty-eight when I briefly hung-out with a porn actress and thirty-two when I gave up using drugs on a daily basis.

I was thirty-two when I married my ex-wife, but why let the truth get in the way of a good hatchet job? I thought what next? Will she claim to be a member of my Cup Final Winning football team or the drummer in The Buzz Kids? My ex-wife was advised by her legal team and my former in-laws to destroy my reputation. In court I was accused of being mentally ill, a serial killer about to happen, a danger to children and a pornographer. Fake news, blatant lies and slander.

I stood in the dock feeling like a black man at a KKK rally, I was without doubt the most unpopular man in the courtroom. The disapproving looks on the faces of the middle-class social workers said it all. They were all looking at me as if I was a combination of Hannibal Lector and a dirty old man who'd swapped his dirty raincoat for a mohair suit. My ex-wife had me on the ropes but sadly for her had failed to land the fatal knockout blow. I glanced across the courtroom at my smug-looking ex-wife who was thinking to herself "I've got him this time`.

She hadn't. The blood drained from her face when I stood up to defend my character. The judge asked, "what kind of films Mr Johnson?"

I replied in my best Arthur Daley impersonation "Good honest porn Sir, nothing more nothing less. There was nothing dodgy or perverted. Just what I'd call your everyday porn". He was not amused when I asked, "are you aware of the adult films made by Ben Dover?" Adding: "I admit to writing scripts and co-directing various films in 1986-87 but didn't meet my ex-wife until 1988 so what has my colourful past got to do with her, you or Peter Brown? Nothing I did before meeting my ex-wife or getting married has anything to with my parenting skills". Even brain-dead social worker Peter Brown smiled at my Oscar-winning performance. As is my character I was on a roll and wouldn't shut up asking "Have you seen any of my films? The hairstyles and the underwear will confirm they were made in the 1980's and not the 90s." I repeated "I did not know my ex-wife in the mid or early eighties". I reverted to the character I played at The Guild Hall Courts when I upset the judge by praising the Kray Twins.

The funny thing is although I enjoyed writing, directing and filming adult movies in my mid-twenties, I'm not a fan of porn, I don't see the point. What's so great watching other people doing what you'd rather be doing yourself? It's a bit like going to a restaurant and paying to watch other people eat.

My name is not Sherlock Holmes, and I never attended the Hendon Police Training College, but even I knew that unlike Essex Police that a Family Court and Essex Social Services would require evidence. For-the-record the 'star' of my 1980s movies had dark hair, (downstairs and below) and my ex-wife was blonde. The only 'porn connection' I share with the former Mrs Johnson happened in 2000. We were watching a C4 documentary about Essex porn star Lee Anne McQueen who came from nearby Canvey Island. It was uncanny because without her clothes on she was identical to my 'friend' from the eighties and my ex-wife.

My Arthur Daley performance in the Witness Box convinced the Judge I was not a pornographer, so my ex-wife didn't have a leg to stand on. The Family Court as with Basildon Police and Essex Social Services admitted I was not a danger to my children. Before my starring role in the Witness Box Social Worker Peter Brown, a dead-ringer for Principal Skinner in The Simpsons was convinced I was guilty of everything from the Iraq War to the 'troubles' in Northern Ireland. If Brown had his way I'd be arrested for the murders of JFK, John Lennon and Martin Luther King. My first contact with Essex Social Services was when a scruffy unwashed social worker turned up at my front door. The visit was unannounced so I had no prior warning, and this would work to my advantage. The middle-class woman who looked like the daughter of a trendy vicar waived a ID card in my face and growled "I'm from Essex Social Services" (she should have said "Nazi Party")

Adding; "Can I come in?" I replied "why"

She said, "You wife claims you're not feeding your children and that their undernourished and living in squalor". Remember, this visit was not planned, I had no prior warning. My ex-wife with the help of Social Services was out to get me, but as I had nothing to hide, I let The 'Gestapo Officer' through the front door. She asked to look around. It was more like an army inspection and a Police search than a casual browse. All she needed was a magnifying glass and a sniffer dog. She inspected both boys bedrooms and I'm talking inside wardrobes and under beds. The vile woman even checked my bed, the bathroom and the laundry cupboard. I could see the disappointment on her face when everything was found to be spotless. She then checked the lounge, dining room, kitchen, conservatory and was far from happy to find them all neat and tidy. I asked, "anything else?"

She replied, "Oh yes Mr Johnson". Adding: "I want to inspect the content of the fridge, freezer and the kitchen cupboards". Me: "Why?"

She sneered in her posh snobby middle-class accent "Because according to Mrs Johnson you are not feeding the boys". I was at the same time both fuming and smiling. I was angry because of the false allegations but also happy as unlike the posh bitch goose-stepping in my kitchen I did the shopping and knew the contents of the fridge. My ex-wife in her eagerness to smear me had forgotten both my boys trained two nights a week at a professional Football Club. They ate a healthy diet by following a lifestyle sheet provided by the club. The social worker found a fridge full of chicken, tuna, pasta, fresh fruit and vegetables.

The fascist female was not happy and left in a huff but without a word of apology. A month later I received a letter from Essex Social Services which stated, "No further action". They'd forgotten to include an apology, this was the beginning of my six-year war with Essex Social Services. The arrogant bastards would soon learn they'd picked on the wrong innocent person. I learnt between 2005 and 2011 that Essex Social Services do not like saying "sorry".

That's why I fought like a war hero until I got what I wanted. It would be 2010 before I got a verbal apology and 2013 before I got it in writing. It wasn't easy as the six-year war destroyed my health as I took on the combined forces of Basildon Police, Essex Social Services and The Family Courts. Essex Social Worker Peter Brown conspired with my ex-wife to cover-up the truth and the bastard who bragged in 2005 "we never lose" lost. He took a hell of a beating.

I wore him down with my defiance and the help of two MPs. I became more of a `pain in the arse` than the stalker in Baby Reindeer. I sent him twenty plus emails every day of the week, jammed up his voice mail and made numerous phone calls. I wore him down `bit by bit`, month by month, year by year, I became the most hostile parent he'd ever met. Over the years he went from him calling me Mr Johnson to saying "Garry, pleases can we talk?" and then asking for my help.

At first dealing with Peter Brown was very frustrating as unlike the Police he refused to allow any of our interviews to be recorded. He relied on notes from my ex-wife which were always a figment of her imagination full of lies and innuendo. From Day One I hated Mr Brown and believe me, the feeling was mutual. At first because of my thick Cockney accent and anti-authority attitude he treated me like a working-class criminal. It didn't help that I looked like Ray Winstone and spoke like Danny Dyer. My ex-wife had briefed him that I was "mad, bad and dangerous" and without a shred of evidence he hung on her every word.

He was 'putty in her hands' and it took five years before Mr Brown would see through her lies and came begging me for help. He turned up on my doorstep requesting a favour. "Garry will you please get Mrs Johnson off my back" Adding "She's still making allegations against you". I started laughing as seeing him so stressed really amused me. Mr Brown was being pressurised by his boss Nicky O'Shaughnessy to finally bring my case to a conclusion. He wanted me to see a high-profile Forensic Psychiatrist who specialised in serial killers and psychopaths.

He said, "I know there's nothing wrong with you, but it will really help me out".

Adding: "If you can convince a Forensic Psychiatrist that you're not dangerous it will get Mrs Johnson off my back". I wasn't keen as I'd already convinced a Bellmarsh Prison psychiatrist, Dr Best a Harley Street shrink hired by my ex-wife, a psychiatrist from Basildon Police Mental Health Team and Dr Black a psychiatrist appointed by Essex Family Court (3 times) that there was nothing wrong with me.

I'd already suffered five years of mental torture, persecution and successfully 'clearing my name' only for my ex-wife demanding the Family Courts ask for another opinion. She was determined I wouldn't see my daughter. Mr Brown assured me this would be the final hoop for me to jump through.

I'd heard it all before so said "No". He begged me to sleep on it. I decided to seek advice and contacted three people involved in my long fight for justice. Jerry Lonsdale my legal advisor. Ian Ashby an old friend from my youth and a former Met Detective and my MP John Baron. They all advised me to do it for the same reason. I had nothing to hide so nothing to lose. But was that true? What if Essex Social Services rigged the result or refused me a copy of the report.

I told Mr Brown I would only agree if certain conditions were put in writing.

The Forensic Psychiatrist in London selected would be independent of Essex Social Services. I would get a copy of the report. The verdict would be final. I got written assurance so agreed to be examined. The interview/examination was held in a high-security hospital in East

London, which according to John Baron MP cost Essex Social Services between five to seven thousand pounds.

The examination was intense and lasted close to three hours. I waited a stressful eight weeks to get the verdict. It was hand-delivered by Mr Brown and confirmed what 'the world and his wife' (and my ex-wife) already knew. I was not mad, bad or dangerous so asked "is that the end of the matter?"

He would not be drawn but it certainly changed the dynamics of the relationship as my sons were now 'free' of interference by Essex Social Services. I only ever saw him when I went to court for contact with my daughter, which he now SUPPORTED, but my ex-wife refused to co-operate. My daughter was told she could see me but under the influence of the 'Taylor family' declined the opportunity. So what did Essex Social Services get for their money?

A nine-page Report by Forensic Psychiatrist Dr Sian Llewellyn-Jones which started:

"Mr Johnson has spiky hair, a friendly smile, wears dark glasses and has odd dress sense. He speaks very fast in a marked Cockney accent. He has an expansive character and big personality. He is a little eccentric but not mentally ill".

The top Forensic Psychiatrist had virtually agreed with fellow shrinks from Bellmarsh Prison, Harley Street quack Dr Best, Basildon Police CMHT Joe Delaney and Dr Black from the Essex Family Court. Much to my amazement (and relief) Peter Brown and Essex Social Services kept their word and as with Basildon Police left me alone. In fact it was Essex Police who told me to return to court in 2022 and advised me of my 'rights'. They also supplied a lot of information I knew nothing about. So me being me I requested a Hearing at Southend Magistrates Court where I represented myself and won the case.

In 1992 I decided I was going to stop drinking and taking stimulants two or 3 weeks before Sam was born. I wouldn't need 'fast drugs' to make me happy anymore, I would be happy on life. I can still remember when and where I was when I quit taking substances. It was May 1992 in Manchester.

I'd been sent up North to review Bryan Adams concert at Maine Road, the then home of Manchester City FC. His act was the same but I wasn't the same person who saw him at the Hammersmith Odeon in 1985. That night I went to the after-show party and was buzzing out of my box. It was a good party and 1985 was a great year. I weighed 9 stone, had dyed blonde hair and cheekbones to die for. I took vast quantities of cocaine that night and went home with Joan Jett lookalike Erica

Echenberg. I loved being on the road and partying was a perk of the job. Who wouldn't enjoy hanging out with rock stars, models and groupies?

But that night in Manchester everything changed. The last thing I wanted was another night of sex, drugs and booze. I really didn't want to be there. I was missing my son and wanted to go home. I went to bed early and got up earlier and caught the first train back to London. That was also the night I quit as a music journo and re-invented myself as a TV pundit. There'd be no more long distance travelling and nights away. I enjoyed being a dad and never being more than thirty miles from home.

My ex-wife was determined to stop me from seeing my children and recruited Basildon Police and Essex Social Services with the sole intention of ruining my reputation and then killing me. I am not being over dramatic because my ex-wife knew I'd die without my children. They wanted me dead.

She surrounded herself with the sort of people I'd hated all my life. Did she honestly believe I'd surrender without a fight and runaway like David Cameron the morning after the Brexit Referendum? I was told in a letter from her mannish-looking solicitor, not joking I'm talking SS Officer in a dress, "Mrs Johnson will let you see the boys once a month for two hours".

My solicitor advised I accept saying "Two hours is better than nothing".

That expert opinion cost me £350 so I changed solicitors, and this time was advised to lie. "Mrs Johnson is saying some terrible things about you, so you must do the same, if not you're in grave danger of losing your children. Mrs Johnson is now saying you can only see the boys in private and only in public at somewhere like McDonalds". As you can see the odds were stacked against me. Social worker Peter Brown joined forces with my ex-wife because he wanted to be on the winning team. He told me: "You should stop fighting Mr Johnson. You're wasting your time because we never lose". Adding: "I have never lost a case. The Family Courts will always take the word of a mother over a father. Judges will always side with professionals and not the dad".

He boasted: "I can assure you Mr Johnson, you and your boys will soon learn you don't take on social services". I'm not being big-headed, maybe I am, but this was the first time he had met someone like me. He wasn't aware of my background and hadn't a clue about my personality. Mr Peter Brown was wet behind the ears and trying to impress a good-looking blonde by acting the 'big guy'. The truth is the pressure got to him and not me. Judge Roderick Newton was his ally and a big fish in a small pond, but as history proves I would eventually beat him in 2013.

Judge Moloney was not his ally and believed in fair play, it was he who first stripped Essex Social Services of their draconian powers.

Then along came The Right Honourable Lord Justice Munby at The High Court in London who put Mr Brown in his place. Lord Justice Munby was a true gent and man of the world who straightaway recognised my British Bulldog spirit and `never say die` attitude. His Lordship told Essex Social Services: "Mr Johnson won't just fade-away and disappear. He's like a dog with a bone and won't give up". Adding: "If I was you, I would try and work with him not against him".

When the barrister for Essex Social Services stood up he was quickly told to sit down and warned: "Whatever you've got to say I will not change my mind".

He then removed all the Gagging Orders and ordered Essex Social Services to handover all their documents. Peter Brown who'd bragged he never lost had just suffered a terrible defeat at the hands of a working-class Cockney rebel. And for him this was just the beginning of the end. I would now (and did) go for his jugular. The Judge unlike Peter Brown was neither gullible or a snob and didn't look down on my thick Cockney accent. He was highly intelligent and worldly-wise who understood having a `thick Cockney accent` didn't equate with being thick. Mr Brown and his high command at Essex Social Services would soon find this out. I didn't talk the way they all spoke but wasn't stupid. I was no ex-public schoolboy but `street smart` enough to hook up with two members of parliament. I told Mr Brown on day one that I would `fight to the death` to keep custody of my sons, and I kept my word. Before Lord Justice Munby stepped in I had spent three years ignoring Court orders and breaking injunctions but because of the Gagging Orders I had always been fighting with one hand tied behind my back. That was then this is now. In 2010 after five years of conflict I'd won the latest battle but not the war. There was no ceasefire. My case was no longer confined to the corrupt goings-on behind closed doors in secretive Family Courts. I'd already been to parliament, twice appeared at The High Court and illegally (without permission) spoken to various media organisations. I'd also been all over social media.

Essex Police knew all about me as did the Leader of Essex County Council. As with the police I discovered the higher you got up the `feed chain` of an organisation the better you are treated. Nicky O'Shaughnessy was the Head of Essex Social Services and a lady I must have driven nuts. Martha from Baby Reindeer had nothing on me. I bombarded her with phone calls, emails, letters and documents in Recorded Delivery packages on an almost daily basis. She knew all about the Johnson Family. I wasn't shocked when she became involved, I'd given her a blow by blow, day by day account of my complaint, but was 'bloody shocked' when she agreed to meet me in person. If nothing else it had to be curiosity. It also helped that she'd received a letter on my behalf from John Baron MP. When we met she wasn't cold or aloof and thought 'no way can this woman be a social worker'.

She was well-mannered, polite, respectful and human. This lady was nice and not a fascist robot. Nicky was more like a Record Company Press Officer than a social worker. As is my character I always speak as a find and told her "You are the first human being I've met". She smiled and then she laughed. We had the first of our many meetings at her plush office inside Chelmsford Town Hall. Now I had my 'foot in the door' I wasn't going away. The first time we met in person was a big shock to my system and almost caught me off-balance. She was not a stuck-up snob with a massive ego. Nicky was blonde, chatty and friendly with a warm personality. The polar opposite of Mr Brown and his motley mob of middle-class stormtroopers. She treated me like a paid-up member of the human race. It was all very civil with tea and biscuits instead of verbal abuse. We shared a joke and I made her laugh. To quote Margaret Thatcher after her first historic meeting with Russia's President Gorbachev: "I knew this was someone I could do business with". I handed over some letters and more documents which she promised to read. This was the start of our peace negotiations. We had a few more meetings where I turned on the charm and slaughtered Peter Brown. Nicky then did the unexpected and completely wrong footed me. I was lost for words. She asked if I would introduce her to Sam and Adam saying "I've read and heard so much about them I'd really like to meet them in person". Adding: "Can I come to yours and meet them?" I was genuinely stunned. People like her at the top of an organisation rarely leave the comfort and safety of their ivory towers. I would be even more shocked by what happened next. A few days later the high-flying Head of Essex Social Services was a guest in our home. Mr Brown was at her side and this time behaving more like a puppy dog than a Rottweiler.

Talk about "how the mighty fall". He was humble, silent, awkward and playing a weak second fiddle to his powerful boss. Brown was like the school bully who'd just been beaten up by a girl. The three of us were expecting a 'royal visit' but not a personal apology. It was the first time she'd met either Sam or Adam but instantly connected with them. Nicky O'Shaughnessy was unlike any member of her staff and everything Peter Brown was not. A kind and caring human being, I thought surely there's no way this woman was ever a member of the Essex Gestapo. Nicky shook hands with Sam and Adam and then gave both boys a friendly hug and almost a cuddle. She then did something that people in positions of power seldom do. She made a genuine and heartfelt apology saying: "I'm sorry boys, I really am sorry but we don't always get it right". The four of us chatted for about 45 minutes (Mr Brown was present but silent) and before leaving she said: "These boys are a credit to you Mr Johnson". I'm a pretty good judge of character and this was no act or face-saving exercise. We now had a verbal apology but just like Oliver Twist I wanted more (and unlike him I would get more). This wasn't the final curtain. The game hadn't ended. The war wasn't over. A moral victory maybe (and a slap in the face for Mr Brown), and it would take another three years before I was granted an official inquiry.

It was a 'heavy duty' investigation carried out by an investigator from a neighbouring county. It found in my favour, and I received what I wanted a written Apology. It was now on-the-record and 'written in stone' that Garry Johnson was innocent. Extract from the letter of apology written in December 2013 by Helen Lincoln who took over from Nicky O'Shaughnessy as Executive Director for Family Operations at Essex County Council. "Regarding the allegations about Mr Johnson the context is one of an acrimonious marital separation but it is clear that child protection procedures were not followed with sufficient rigour. I note that this episode occurred in 2006 but nonetheless this shortcoming needs to be recognised". They finally accepted that my ex-wife was a liar and that she and her boyfriend were guilty as charged. Now Social Services, The Police and the courts knew the truth. The only person who doesn't know the truth is my daughter who refuses to read any of the official and legal documents. When it comes to her mother, she's still in denial. I could go into graphic details about the behaviour of my former wife but have promised my children not to embarrass them by digging up the past. My ex-wife has had a 'lucky escape' because the facts I could legally reveal would not impress her work colleagues. One last word on the matter, if anyone doubts a word of my testimony they can make a FOI request to Essex Social Services, Essex County Council or Basildon Police. Or knock on my door and I'll show them 900 legal and official documents I handed over to my MP. He read and then he joined my campaign for Justice. I make the same offer to my daughter. Sam and Adam was mission accomplished I'd taken on and beaten Social Services but I still had to fight on to see my daughter. And as write today (August 2024), well let's just say that like Tyson Fury you can't win them all, but like the great Mike Tyson I'm still fighting. As is my character I've always preferred the funny side of life to the dark side of death and depression. When we separated one old mate betrayed me, I'm talking about Paul Wellings. A friend from 1979 who'd always fancied my ex-wife and thought he could take advantage of the situation. How did I react? Did I respond as me or as Harry Harris the fictional East End gangster 'loved' by Basildon Police?

In the early 1980s Wellings wanted a video of Scum the cult classic movie starring Ray Winston. At the time he was legendary for being a right tight bastard who never bought a round. Always wanting something for nothing and pestering to borrow my copy. He could have bought it for a £10 but, as always wanted something for nothing. With the help of my mate Si Spanner we hatched a plot to stitch him up. Spanner with a chain of Soho Sex shops had access to hardcore porn. I removed the Scum label from my video and stuck it to one of Spanner's sex tapes. The parcel was taken by Gal Bush to the Sounds post room and sent to Wellings home address. Jimmy Pursey was a plastic Cockney but at least he hailed from Outer London, whereas Wellings was from a sleepy little market town near Norwich. A world away from the East London he claimed to be his home. So, the story goes Wellings sat his parents down in front of the TV to watch the movie. Though God only knows why he wanted to watch Scum with his mum and dad.

Can you imagine the look on their faces when, instead of Ray Winstone punching a screw, there was some bloke banging a human Barbie Doll. Wellings was not amused. He blamed us but we swore "nothing to do with us". But he never forgave us. That's how I coped with his betrayal. It worked a treat and put a smile on my face and still makes me laugh today. Over the years I did various things to wind-up Wellings and looking back still amuses me. I wrote the review that 'killed off' his two-bob punk band The Anti-Social Workers, a great name, but nothing else. Tim wells the talented member of the band went on to become London's best comic poet, the Wit of Whitechapel. Whereas Paul Wellings became more sour and bitter than a lorry load of stale lemons, ranting and raving and stamping his feet like a spoilt brat and even shed a tear.

His childish reaction to my honest critique confirms that, as people, we really are chalk and cheese. Think about it, when Garry Bushell 'killed off' The Buzz Kids we became best mates. When I did the same to his band the country boy bore a grudge that lasted a lifetime. Thus proving there's a lot of difference between a genuine Cockney and a Mockney. It's worth noting that Tim Wels, a genuine London Boy and a genuine talent, took no offence to my write-up. We still talk and over the years have shared many a pint. Fact: When I made a comeback after my heart operation it was Tim who organised my comeback gig at The London Roundhouse. I've always been a wind-up merchant and loved a laugh. I can't handle people with no sense of humour and who flirt with depression.

I didn't just take 'fast drugs' to stay skinny but also to make sure I was never depressed. I played some great tricks on my old mate Frankie Flame but one night we crossed the line. That was me, Gal Bushell and Lol Prior, but it was me who made the prank phone call. Frankie always wanted a record contract so one night after a couple of drinks and a few lines in The Watt Tyler pub on the Ferrier Estate in South London I gave him a bell. It was just before closing time and I said "Frankie get here quick, there's a 'AandR' man in the pub looking for you. Frankie jumped out of bed but by the time he arrived in his leather jacket, flat cap and striped pyjamas tucked into Dr Marten boots, the 'AandR' guy had mysteriously vanished. All that remained was an empty beer glass. Frankie had great potential. He could have been the punk version of Chas and Dave had he gone down the Ian Dury route, but he couldn't be told. He was easy to wind up but the opposite when it came to taking genuine advice. After The Derby one year, the three of us took Frankie to Charlton Conservative Club. He got on the 'old Joanna' and all the old dears loved him doing Cockney Music Hall songs and 1950s rock and roll. He smashed it. So much so, a few weeks later they booked him to play a gig.

I told Frankie they wanted Glam Rock and he turned up with a synthesizer and dressed like Gary Glitter. They wanted 'Knees Up Muvva Brown' and 'Maybe I'm A Londoner' and 'Lambeth Walk' and he gave them Gary Numan, a moving tribute to Dick Barton and the Bowie-esque anthem 'If Looks Could Kill' (written by me).

The regulars were not amused by Frankie's first and last gig at the South London Tory HQ. It was also the night Garry Bushell almost got a lifetime ban, not for bringing Frankie along but because I wrote "Vote Labour" on the Darts blackboard. To smooth things over I bought the Chairman a pint and promised Frankie Flame would never again set foot on their stage. There were quite a few novelty acts knocking around at the time as Frankie and Paul Wellings. The worst of a bad bunch being punk poet Dave the Boil and legendary Bert and Col. I got to review them all, no, not as a punishment by my Editor, but because I've always had a soft spot for naff entertainment. As with TV shows like Bullseye, Supermarket Sweep, and Celebrity Juice, if it's really bad it's worth watching once in a while. I wrote as a joke, "Bert and Col are the best thing in pub entertainment since Chas and Dave went mainstream". In fact, they were dire, their songs like 'Why Pay to Go through the Dartford Tunnel when the Blackwall Tunnel Is Free', 'Mavis Davis Uses Avis' and the masterpiece 'I Could Have Been A Contender But My Face Didn't Fit'. All great titles but no tunes.

A funny thing happened to Colin the 6ft plus singer from Bert and Col a former swimmer almost selected to represent Great Britain at the

Olympics. Colin was exposed by The Sun as a 'love rat'. He was plastered all over the front page as a man who 'walked out' on his bride on the day of his wedding. They got married at 1pm and separated six hours later. Colin was last seen in a Bermondsey boozer knocking out old Cockney standards and telling everyone "This time next year I'll be on Top of The Pops". He wasn't. Have I told you people say I'm self-effacing, funny, friendly, loyal, mischievous and charming with no airs and graces. As down to earth as an East End Fish and Chip shop. I'm more than happy with those descriptions and live in hope that one day my estranged daughter will see the real me for herself. I'll always describe myself as old school working-class with middle-class manners with a dislike of champagne socialists.

Once an East End boy, always a East End boy. One of my old teachers said, "You're the worst behaved pupil I've ever taught" adding "but there's no malice in you". I was born naughty but had morals I'd steal from department stores but never from Corner shops. My DNA made sure I was always the joker in the pack and never a nasty bit of work. I took my sense of humour, talent for wind-ups and fabricating stories into Fleet Street. My love of a wind-up was responsible for a number of bizarre articles appearing in print. Bottles of David Bowie 'breathed air' being sold in Petticoat Lane, Jonathan Ross shaving his head to appear in Star Wars, Football star Gazza joining the cast of Eastenders and Paula Yates rubbing lettuce leaves on Sir Bob Geldof's private parts to get her pregnant. At times my imagination would run wild and had some crackers like Madonna to play Maggie Thatcher in Hollywood movie and Arab oil millionaire offers soap star Emily Simmons £250,000 for sex. A year later they printed a new version, this time a Russian Oligarch offering Emmerdale beauty Claire King a quarter of a million for a weekend of sex.

I would swap and change names, and no-one twigged because I only fabricated funny stories. I made readers laugh and never reduced 'victims' to tears.

I don't know how my rise through the ranks happened, but it did. There was no master plan, and to quote some old Tory politician "Events dear boy, events".

Things that happened in my head then appeared as facts in various publications.

You hear a lot of bad things about Piers Morgan but never by anyone who knows him. I knew him and haven't got a bad word to say about him. He was so sharp I never gave him one of my 'fabricated or enhanced' stories. Piers, was far too smart to be taken in. He was charismatic, and a charmer who got away with so much because of his charm. We spoke on an almost daily basis for more than a decade. Piers always looked after me at The Sun, News of The World and Daily Mirror. I was, without doubt one of his biggest fan and in awe of his ability. To quote Cockney great Michael Caine "not a lot of people know this", but I supplied a lot of the background material for his Jason Donovan biography. His chauffer came to my house in Essex and picked up all my old copies of Smash Hits, Record Mirror and Number One.

A lot of people don't like Piers because they are jealous of his many achievements. I speak as I find. He was always good to me and, unlike a lot of people, never late with the payments. I owe him a lot because he introduced me to Rebekah Wade. I love her to bits and would defend her with my life. She was the first person to phone on my release from Bellmarsh prison. Apart from my daughter and granddaughter, she is my number one female of the species. We met on her first day at News International and employed me for the next twenty years. As with Piers and because of the loyalty gene that flows through my DNA none of my `fabricated` or `enhanced` stories were never given to Rebekah.

This is a true story. One Christmas she was staying on Rupert Murdoch`s yacht in the West Indies and I was faxing her stories all over the festive period. Such is my admiration for the `redhead of the redtops`, my daughter`s middle-name is Rebekah. A wonderful woman who I always knew would get a "not guilty" verdict at The Old Bailey. There is no way she would have sanctioned the hacking of a young girl`s phone. I could write a true X-rated version of my marriage and give graphic details about my divorce but I won`t. Not because I`m scared of the truth but because I`ve promised my kids a Mills and Boon type version and don't want to embarrass them in any way. For those who want X-rated accounts of my teenage years I suggest you purchase a copy of my novel Serial Killer. Anyone wishing for graphic details about my marriage and divorce will have to look elsewhere. If that`s your thing go to Amazon and checkout Love Marriage Divorce.

My lips are sealed when it comes to revealing adult themes. Not because I`m `Mister Nice Guy` but can picture female friends, militant feminists and Mothers on Mumsnet calling me all the names under the sun for writing a X-rated kiss and tell. So I censor myself on the grounds of moral decency and not out of fear of retribution. Anyone desperate for the uncensored truth should make a Freedom of Information request to Basildon Police or Essex Social Services. One day maybe my daughter will follow in her dad`s footsteps and become a `seeker of truth and justice`. As previously admitted, I swindled my way into Journalism. I even blagged my way into the NUJ. And to this day, getting my NUJ membership is still one of my proudest achievements. Apart from being a rock star, a footballer or an actor it has got to be the best job in the world. That's why I impersonated one for so long. I realised I could never be a genuine member of Her Majesty's Press so I pretended. I became an actor in a reality drama. Should gangster novels carry a health warning for their authors? Garry Bushell wrote The Face and lost his job on The Sun. I wrote Till Death Us Do Part as Garry Jackson and as Garry Johnson got banged up in Bellmarsh Prison. Who was the last author in the United Kingdom to be jailed for writing a fictional book? The answer is Irish genius Oscar Wilde.

It was common practise in Nazi Germany of the 1930s and Communist Russia in the 1960s, but this was Great Britain 2007. I had a background of writing biographies about rock stars like David Bowie, Ozzy Osbourne and Paul Young.

'Till Death Us Do Part', was my debut novel with the main character based on Underworld legend Dave Courtney. It got write-ups in the national press, five-star reviews on Amazon and a splash in my local newspaper. As reported in The Sunday People, American producer Francis Fallon planned a movie version with pop superstar Robbie Williams in the lead role. Under the influence of my ex-wife, former in-laws and Sally Prevost the authorities were conned into believing 'Till Death Us Do Part' was a death threat rather than a crime novel. As is my character I 'borrowed' plots from classic British gangster films like 'Get Carter' and 'The Long Good Friday' but Basildon Police were convinced the Punk Poet was East End killer Harry Harris. They were either stupid or had never been to the movies. My ex-wife told them Harry Harris was my alter-ego and they believed I was an East End gangster. Her boyfriend was cautioned by Basildon Police after admitting his crimes, if you're curious you can read the graphic details in Love Marriage Divorce, still on Amazon and available in all good book shops, and I was banged-up in Bellmarsh maximum security prison for telling the truth.

Basildon Police arrested me on the 'non evidence' of my ex-wife and the medical notes of a psychiatrist who'd never met me. As I explained earlier within half-hour of meeting me Dr Best, the Harley Street shrink withdrew his allegations and asked to be discharged from the case. When we got to court the Judge ordered him to leave and told all those present to "ignore his evidence".

I completely understand my story is hard to believe, I still find it hard to believe and I was there, but to any doubters out there I have all the legal documents from The High Court, Chelmsford, Southend, Basildon, Colchester and Romford which confirm the factual content of my book. I did a tour of Essex Courts as I fought to clear my name and win my case. All these legal documents are supported by files from Essex County

Council and documents (which were very hard to obtain) from Basildon Police.

As with Essex Social Services and boss Nicky O' Shaughnessy my last dealings with Basildon Police ended with an apology.

Inspector Sage met me in his office and said "sorry". He said a lot more but promised family members not to say anything that could embarrass my ex-wife.

But for-the-record I've kept all the official paperwork in the hope that one day my daughter will be interested in truth rather than fantasy. She's almost twenty-four, a grown adult, and hopefully one day she'll grow up and do the decent thing.

I can honestly say fighting for my children and the fight to clear my name are the only things I've ever taken seriously in my life. Apart from taking 'fast drugs' and 'shagging', the only thing I've liked more is having a laugh. I believe there are many reasons Punk Rock fans took to me. They loved my poems but also liked my sense of humour and the fact that I was genuine. At times my comic side always wanting to get a laugh got me into trouble. On one occasion it cost me my friendship with song-writing partner Steve Kent. Together we wrote the classic punk anthem 'Suburban Rebels' which has just been re-recorded by Swedish rocker Soren Sulo Karlsson. We could have been the Lennon/McCartney of Streetpunk but he never forgave a joke I made in Sounds. To be honest, it was more than a one-liner, as I mocked his baldhead in a Live Review of his band The Bandits. So here is an extract and you decide if it's funny or did I overstep the mark.

"Were at Dingwalls in London and Beki's toy boy, Steve 'bald eagle' Kent, hairdresser by day and age-ing Bandit by night, took to the stage and dazzled the crowd by lowering his head. Much has been in fanzine circles of The Bandits resemblance to prime-time Chelsea, though in Kent's case his resemblance to Kojak is more worthy of note. Every eye was on his shinning pate, every brain considered the question, where's his wig? He really was beyond the fringe"

So what is your verdict? Was I 'out of order' or was Steve Kent a Diva? Even today I still think it's hilarious, but maybe I've got a weird sense of humour. It was years before he spoke to me, but there's more chance of his hair growing back then us ever becoming friends again. Just like my old song-writing partner I wanted to be a rock star but it wasn't going to happen because I can't sing. So I invented The Punk Poet and then the Tabloid Terrorist.

Unlike Harry Harris in Till Death Us Do Part an alter ego could be a good thing, it twice worked for me. I discovered through social media that I had worldwide popularity, I'm not talking mass popularity or being some kind of cult, for those who don't like me I did say "cult", it's not a misprint. But I do have a loyal following in the UK, Europe, Australia, South America and the USA. There's old punks and young kids all over the planet who like my poems. Since coming out of hospital it's been quite amazing and very humbling. Sometimes it's embarrassing, which is why I no longer answer my front door to strangers. One Saturday night, a bloke in full Army gear and his wife called at the door with a copy of `Boys of The Empire` and a pile of punk albums and asked me to sign them. His wife chips in, saying, "He's your biggest fan, he loves you, he recites `Deadend Yobs` non-stop which really gets me down because I think you're crap". The guy goes mad, calls her a silly cow and the two of them start arguing and fighting on my doorstep. I shut the door out of embarrassment. When I come back ten minutes later, they were still at it. Even more embarrassing, I got approached by a man once who said his wife was a fan and that she wanted to sleep with me. The wife wasn't blonde but pretty fit, but before I could even say "yes, thank you very much", he said he wanted to watch so that quickly became a no-no. I formed The Buzz Kids and although our first gig was also our last it launched me into Punk Rock which led to the wonderful world of Fleet Street. So although we never followed in the footsteps of The Jam or became as big as The Stone Roses, in its own way it was successful. I was proud to work in Fleet Street. It was one of my few ambitions that I actually achieved. I didn't find it anti-working-class, snobby or sexist. The truth is I would rather have a pint or share a line of Charlie with a tabloid journalist then a glass of wine with some champagne socialist. From personal experience, and my ears were always open, not once did I hear a showbiz hack sneer at the working-classor look down on poor people like Labour luvvie Lady Emily Thornberry. The multi-millionaire champagne socialist who mocked working-class football fans for flying flags. Snobs like her and posh boy PM Sir Kier Starmer look down on people who drive white vans and live in council houses. I was anti-authority, anti-establishment and anti-royal before I walked into Fleet Street and just the same when I left. Voting Labour is not Punk or even Mod it's a betrayal of your working-class roots.

 The art of politics and the blatant lying of all those involved has always interested me. I know by birth, background and moral decency that I should vote Labour, but I can't. New Labour is not the saviour of the Working-class, it's the enemy of the people. Name the last Labour MP who grew up on a council estate or lived in an inner-city tower block. Kinnock was a Welsh Windbag who became a Lord. Blair was a public schoolboy and posh Starmer the UK's worst Prime Minister. I still yearn for a Labour Party led by a loveable rogue with a Cockney accent. Both my working-class granddads would be turning in their graves they knew the Labour Party was now run by 'red Tories' and Oxbridge intellectuals. All the safe seats go to millionaire lawyers or the sons and daughters of former MPs. I love Paul Weller and felt let down when Lord Kinnock conned him into supporting Red Wedge. As a massive Oasis fan I was 'unhappy' when Noel Gallagher went to Tony Blair's party at Number Ten Downing Street. I was well impressed when Liam told him to "f*** off". Both the Modfather and Noel have since admitted they were conned by the champagne socialists.

## Chapter Eleven
## They Broke the Mould

I have no consistent political beliefs apart from always supporting the underdog whatever their race, colour or creed. Some White people hate blacks, some black people hate whites. I personally hate champagne socialists but love working-class footballers, rock stars, boxers and actors becoming super rich as long as they don't tell me how to vote. I have only ever looked-up to genuine working-class heroes like David Bowie, Paul Weller, Johnny Rotten, John Lennon, Georgie Best, Noel and Liam Gallagher and my two granddads. My Dad was on that list but the selfish bastard betrayed me, and with me it's not three strikes, it's "one strike and you're out". Right or wrong that's how my mind works. I grew up listening to my Cockney granddad talking about the War and his part in the Battle of Cable Street. He was proud talking about the time working-class Easterners stood shoulder to shoulder with Jewish boxers and gangsters to defeat posh boy Sir Oswald Mosley and his army of Blackshirts. It's a sad fact, but my 'Granddad Pop' would not be welcome in today's middle-class Labour Party. He didn't drink fine wine, speak French or live on a diet of Lentils and veggie burgers but he did throw a punch at Sir Oswald Mosley. He was old school and proud. I know he'd take the piss out of my Gluten Free veggie diet but he'd appreciate my love of the Crombie overcoat.

The best TV show highlighting the class divide was not a C4 doc it but BBC comedy Blackadder when Baldrick and his friends were involved in World War One. The moving final scene with the poppies said it all. Working-class boys were sent over the top to die so the then King could claim 'bragging rights' over his cousin. It was the biggest crime in history with arrogant aristocrats playing war games with the lives of poor people. Luckily, I grew up under the influence of my granddad Charles Alfred Johnson and read all about the adventures of Robin Hood, Jesses James and Dick Turpin. Maybe because of my Irish background I have always been attracted to scallywags and rebels. In a previous life I was either a pirate, or a highwayman or maybe Beau Brummell. I've also supported underdogs. The Jews in Nazi Germany, Blacks in apartheid South Africa and inner-city working-class communities being ethnically cleansed by yuppies. If you're being picked on or persecuted I'm on your side. I moved on from idolising infamous East End villains and cured my addiction to Georgie Best, but never lost my obsession with Ziggy Stardust or David Bowie. It's a life-long addiction I'll take to my grave. I met George Best in a Chelsea pub said "hello" and shook his hand. It got better when I followed him into the Beer Garden. There wasn't a ball, but we did kick a can around. There was no selfie as were talking early 80's, so all I have of this magic moment is a memory, but what a memory! I'm not a proper Patriot but at the same time don't like people attacking my country. I truly believe that nationality is just an accident of birth and doesn't make you superior or inferior to any other human being. A perfect world for me and if I had the powers of Harry Potter, I'd put East London 1973 in the middle of The Irish Republic and drop it near Bondi Beach in Australia. I was never a fan of Aussie soaps but often watched with the volume down to admire the scenery. If I won millions on the lottery I'd take all my family to Australia, which I consider heaven on earth.

My half-hearted support for Brexit had nothing to do with wanting to leave Europe. I never wanted to leave. I only wanted to leave (but never voted) because the champagne socialists wanted to stay. I only supported Scottish independence because the British Establishment were against it. Irish Independence is different I support that because of my Irish granddad. He was a life-long Irish Republican who like me despised the British Establishment. As a veggie if the The House of Lords wanted to ban meat I'd start eating it tomorrow. I'm such a class warrior I've never watched Strictly Come Dancing, Downtown Abbey or voted Labour.

I'm not sure why but I've always been anti-authority but as Johnny Rotten sung "Anger is a energy". Maybe the psychiatrist was correct when he suggested, "The emotional part of your brain could have frozen when you were fifteen". Was it the shock of my dad walking out?

I can relate to that or was it anything to do with twenty years of taking `fast drugs` or my Irish background and Cockney rebel DNA? I know reading about East End Gangsters and Robin Hood must have had an influence, but growing up I also read all the Enid Blyton Famous Five books and football magazines like Shoot and Striker. I left the world of Fleet Street as the same `Cockney Rebel` who walked through the door in 1984. In 2004 when my ill-health started with poor circulation and hardening of the arteries and slight chest pains I had no idea it would lead to five heart attacks, four heart operations, including two triple heart bypass operations, a minor stroke and 29 days in a coma. That medical history explains why I had blood flow `problems` below my belly button before my wife left.

I'll pass on elaborating about the original diagnosis for my illness because I've promised my children `no graphic details` to avoid embarrassing them. Let's just say it was a 'man problem' and led to my ex-wife leaving me for another man.

Was I really close to death? The answer is "yes". Twice I "died" and my children were told to prepare for the worst. But don't take my word for it. Below is an extract from my Discharge Letter from Basildon Hospital where my life was saved by world famous Heart surgeon Professor Khan, the former boyfriend of Diana, Princess of Wales.

BRIEF SUMMARY OF CASE:
Mr Johnson presented to Basildon A/E with acute inferior myocardial infarction and was taken to CTC for PPCI. He developed papillary muscle rupture and underwent CABG x 3 and mitral valve replacement. He had a VF arrest and returned to theatre for removal of clots and haemostasis. He developed septicaemia and multi-organ failure and spent a month in ITU.

So now you know why I am so grateful to be alive. Why I want to make hay why the Sun shines. I want to tell my story before my heart stops beating.

Since rising phoenix-like from what many called my death bed, I have rebuilt both my private and professional life. But before I returned to showbiz and the creative arts I had to deal with six years of harassment by Basildon Police, Essex Social Services and The Family Courts. The stress I suffered turned my circulation problem into a full-blown health scare that almost killed me. It took 30-plus court appearances and two spells in prison to 'clear my name' and get justice. My near-death experience awakened the freedom fighter in me and I decided to take on and eventually beat the system. I triumphed against all the odds after being told "you've got no chance in beating us because we never lose". I'm not religious but always believed that someone or something was looking out for me. What else happened after I survived my second triple heart bypass operation and came out of my 29-day coma? I went to a Nursing Home in Essex where day by day I got better. I learnt to walk again but my brain was fuzzy, and my memory was shot to pieces. I couldn't remember any of the lyrics of my favourite songs and it was so annoying, more frustrating than learning to walk. A doctor suggested I started writing lists to exercise my brain, my son brought in dozens of my favourite David Bowie and Punk CDs. Eventually my memory started to return, and such is my addictive personality I couldn't stop writing. I began work on my first novel since Till Death Us Do Part in 2006 and this time instead of Bellmarsh Prison I ended up in Hollywood. Three years after a coma following life-saving surgery at the world-famous hands of heart surgeon Dr Hasnat Khan (Princess Diana's ex-lover) I had more energy than a

Duracell battery. I'd recorded an album, returned to the stage, re-launched my poetry career and written a novel which was being made into a Hollywood movie. When this re-birth started, I thought I'd only been asleep overnight, when in fact I'd been unconscious for 29 days, during which time my organs collapsed and my young boys were twice told that their dad my not make it through the night, unknown to me I'd 'died' twice and was brought back to life.

I was born with a flair for football and the 'gift of the gab' which allowed me to infiltrate showbiz and journalism, but had no idea I could write a serious crime novel, not a East End gangster romp, but the story of a female serial killer.

I'd written a few short stories to get my brain ticking over, but the one featuring a beautiful blonde assassin stood-out. The main character was a female killer, and the story was told through the eyes of a woman. Somehow a copy found its way to Sandie West, a female film producer at Beach Dancer Films in Little Venice, Hollywood. She promised me the earth but I'm still waiting for her deliver. There is a two-minute trailer on YouTube but nothing on Netflix. The Walter Mitty character blames her lack of action on Covid. This time I made the killer female so there was no way Basildon Police could confuse me with a long-legged blonde described as looking like a glamour model. Like Till Death Us Do Part it was a revenge story and set in Essex. Sandie said, "This will make a great movie" which begs the question "Why hasn't she made it?"

Writing Serial Killer and recording my album 'Punk Rock Stories and Tabloid Tales' confirms I was right to fight for justice from 2006 to 2011, and to fight for life in 2013. After 27 court appearances, two spells in prison, five heart attacks and two heart operations The Punk Poet was back. My near-death experience re-awakened the freedom fighter inside me. It breathed new life into me, but I am not a born-again punk, because the punk rocker in me never died. The tabloid terrorist never went away, and still believed that facts should always be put into the public domain. It's a pity The Family Courts did so much and took so long to hide the truth. I don't know what a psychiatrist would make of this but something happened the night before I came out of my coma. I'm convinced I was visited by my dad, I recognised his voice and could smell his aftershave, I don't know anyone else who wears Brut, I don't think anyone does nowadays, but I could smell it. I could feel the pressure of his hand on my shoulder, and hear him urging me to get better, saying; "Come on Gal, you can do it". I was genuinely shocked when told he had died three years before. I soon had a PR, Emma Rule of Lip Up Media whose clients included punk rock legend Steve Diggle of The Buzcocks. I also appeared at a festival in Blackpool and did a mini tour of London where I shared a stage with TV star Phil Jupitus. I was also interviewed on various TV and Radio shows. I'm not bragging or being big-headed but I am living proof that you should never give up on your dreams. Paul the Mod Hallam re-published my old book of poems 'Boys of The Empire' and Teddie Dahlin published my new poetry book The Cockney Bard.

And there's more. I was much closer to becoming an OAP then I was a spotty teenager, but after so many years of trying I finally made my debut album. I was contacted by Swedish rocker Soren Sulo Karlsson and within weeks I was in the studio with Sulo, former Clash drummer Terry Chimes, top record producer Kevin Poree and Idde Schultz. The demo tracks were handed over to John Dryland of Cargo Records and we delivered a critically acclaimed album which got a five-star rating in Street sounds magazine. Did I mention Serial Killer got a five-star review in The Sun and unlike 'Till Death Us Do Part' there was no hatchet job in Private Eye or no knock on the door from Basildon Police. I don't sound like a man whose stared death in the face five times, I might not look like the 'bird bandit' of yesteryear but at least I look better and more alive than President Biden. Mentioning my dad just now has reminded me of the time I met one of his celebrity heroes. The Jewish crooner Max Bygraves was a superstar in the 1960s and I talked my way into one of his parties. A lavish launch party in Soho's Ketner's Restaurant for one of his awful sing-along albums. My dad was a huge fan and knew he'd be impressed by me meeting his hero so asked Max for a picture. As always Sounds snapper Tony Mottram was on hand to capture this historic moment. But Max refused saying: "I'm not having my picture taken with you," adding "You look like a dodgy South London second hand car dealer". I thought 'bloody cheek' I'm not from South London and how many second-hand car dealers have Rod Stewart haircuts with blonde highlights? I wasn't impressed by his attitude so gave his album a massive verbal kicking. The next day is another party and this time I had my picture taken with a glamorous drag queen who I mistake for a real woman. This time Mottram got a picture and recently posted it on social media. They do say too many drugs and burning the candle at both ends plays tricks with your mind but genuinely thought it was a real woman. Same thing happened the other day. I currently enjoy Podcasts everything from Terry Stone to James English and got it wrong again recently. I tuned in half way through and two women were having a conversation and mistook Transgender woman Chezza Blonde' for the interviewer. Either I need to visit Spec-savers or she has a great make-up artist.

My current favourite is Jonsey's Jukebox presented by former Sex Pistol Steve Jones. So why did I pose as a Tabloid Journalist? Well to start with it wasn't for the money. Honest Guv, I didn't do it as a means to obtaining money under false pretences. The truth is I've always been attracted to famous people, showbiz characters, pop stars and celebrities. As I couldn't sing or act pretending to be a tabloid journo seemed to be the perfect career choice. Sounds magazine got me a foot in the door but I know I wanted the key to a celebrity world.

As a teenager I watched every pop and magazine show and enjoyed watching great raconteurs on chat shows like Russell Harty and Michael Parkinson. I always appreciated characters like Kenneth Williams, Stephen Fry, Steven Berkoff and Peter Cook. All great talkers who could make subjects you knew nothing about interesting. Nowadays I can't get enough of MSM chat shows presented by Jonathan Ross, Piers Morgan, Graham Norton and Podcasts with UK presenters, like Dodge Woodhall, Terry Stone, Liam Tuffs, Shaun Attwood and James English. One of the reasons I love chat shows apart from the obvious is spotting the bullshit merchants. When it comes to spotting fakes and seeing through the lies I am like a human lie detector machine. That's why and how I beat Essex Social Services. Peter Brown looked like Principal Skinner in The Simpsons, dressed like Mr Bean and was more slippery than an ice rink. I am nothing like feckless fathers who appeared on the Jeremy Kyle Show and gave men a bad name, but Mr Brown treated me like shit, worse he treated my kids like shit. He was a bully with a badge and that's why I took him on and that's why I beat him. He'd never met anyone like me as he usually bullied housewives, but I became his worst nightmare. I so much got under his skin he had a 'breakdown' and was sent on 'gardening leave'. I fought him over everything, and the funny thing is he lost. He threatened to take my boys, it didn't happen. He accused me of being 'mad, bad and dangerous' and was over-ruled by medical experts. He hid behind 'secrecy' and ex-parte court hearings and then three judges removed the 'Gagging Orders' and said I could legally tell my story. I pretty sure that after the official investigation he didn't climb the greasy pole and become the Head of Essex County Council Social Services.

Case Number: CM14POO3OO. At Chelmsford County Court on December 13$^{th}$ 2013, my old foe Judge Roderick Newton followed in the illustrious footsteps of Lord Justice Munby at The High Court in London and Judge Moloney at Southend in Essex by ruling in my favour. He removed the 'Gagging Orders' on every aspect of my private and personal life. I could now legally tell my story but because of the adult content decided to wait. I did not want to expose my 13-year-old daughter to stories about sex, drugs and rock and roll. She was too young. I wanted to protect her from reading about the violence, harassment and intimidation.

I decided to wait until she entered the world but on reflection and a lot of thought I decided to tone done the content and protect all my children from the X-rated content. Judge Roderick Newton ate more humble pie than all the pies cooked on TV's Bake Off. Maybe through gritted teeth, but he was forced to obey the law of the land and confirm no subject 'was out of bounds'. At last, I could talk about anything and everything. I'd been smeared more times than a slice of toast. It was a great day for justice as well as being a great victory for the 'freedom of the press. As Judge Roderick Newton was making his historic ruling an army of Angels and heroic NHS staff were battling to keep me alive. One of the first things I hear after waking from my 29-day coma was my eldest son saying "Dad we won, we won, I opened your letter, and we won. Dad you did it". As well as bunches of grapes and bottles of Lucozade Sam would bring more good news. The next day "Dad I got a message from Sue to tell you we've won". Such was the state of my medical condition it was a few days before I took it all in, when the penny finally dropped, the magnitude of the decision sunk in. It had been a long time coming but now had the final piece of the jigsaw. I could legally write a hard-hitting and thought-provoking kiss and tell. I now had a smoking gun with more firepower than a KGB hit squad. I was transferred from Basildon to Billericay hospital for a month of rehab. My speech had returned but not yet my ability to walk. After 24 hours in a private room with a TV and my own shower another letter was delivered.

This time it was an apology from Helen Lincoln of Essex Social Services. It had taken almost eight years but now all my ducks were in a row. Basildon Police, Essex Social Services, The Family Courts had all admitted defeat and Judgement Day was getting closer. Basildon Police had acted on false information, Essex Social Services had ignored the facts and behind closed doors The Family Courts had denied justice. They had all turned a blind eye and a deaf ear to the truth.

They all underestimated me as I'm living proof that you shouldn't judge a book by its cover, unless your Basildon Police.

It wasn't a one-off. They mistook me for being Harry Harris a fictional character in a book, and recently arrested Essex Boy gangster Bernard O'Mahoney for something actor Sean Bean did portraying him in a movie. You couldn't make it up, and I'm not. I want my daughter to know the truth and everything there is to know about her dad. It would be so easy to drop a 'truth bomb'. I've personally got nothing to lose as she already hates me, so I could 'slaughter' her family, for the benefit of Basildon Police, I mean 'slaughter' her family in print, but luckily for her I've promised my sons (and extended family) not to write a X-rated version.

So what you are reading is a toned down family friendly version. As back-up in case one day my 'beloved daughter' does want to know the truth I have 900-plus court documents for her to read. What Peter Brown didn't understand the first time we met when he decided to take me on was that I wasn't a middle-class bloke who'd be impressed by his Mockney accent. Unlike Brown I was a genuine bonafide Cockney who would take him on. My anti-authority credentials were recognised by of all people the UK Communist Party. Don't take my word for it as proof can be found in official documents and confirmed by people who were there.

June 2015.

The Morning Star Poetry Festival at The British Library

Journalist Roxanne Escoboles wrote:

"An audio track by Garry Johnson, the heavily Cockneyed 'Young Conservatives' which opened the night, could easily have been written the day after the General Election". Peter Brown was supported by a combination of a fascist state, champagne socialist lawyers and secret courts. He held all the cards or so he thought but it was he and not me who would end up conceding defeat. Let me reveal the type of character he was taking on. I was no champagne socialist but a genuine Cockney Rebel. My first-ever interview took place in a Covent Garden pub and playing the part of Jonathan Ross was music journalist Garry Bushell.

He wrote in Sounds magazine: "The geezer in the shabby jacket with speed freak frame and impish smile knocks back his lager and pulls a bundle of tatty A4 exercise books out of the plastic bag at his feet. They're choc-a-bloc with poems, all neatly written out in longhand. "I've got about 300 of 'em," he laughs, "I reckon about 50 are good". Honest, self-effacing Garry Johnson. It's hard to picture this skinny herbart who lists his likes as 'Bowie, lager, football, rebels, gangster movies and the opposite sex', as a potential voice of a generation. Yet those who'd criticise New Punk as having nothing to say could do little better than check out his verses, proud prole manifestos that pull no punches, tolerate no hypocrisy and tell you no lies. And that's not just my opinion. Listen to Time Out's review of Garry's 'Boys of The Empire' collection: "A volume of ballads, streetwise, anti-militarism and fascism, anti-police and fiercely defensive of working-class pride. Very impressive." Born in Hackney, Johnson grew up in London's East End, getting a comprehensive non-education (six schools, one expulsion) and clocking-up DC and Borstal with convictions ranging from robber to burglary via such naughtiness as taking part in a riot and bunking fares, though he's not been nicked since he was 17. Despite a promising start as schoolboy footballer, he began working life as a builder's labourer and sort early retirement a month later. "I was originally inspired to start writing by The Sex Pistols, and a Janet Street-Porter TV show". Despite his hatred for the

Tories, police harassment et al, Johnson remains equally dismissive of the Labour Party, as illustrated by poems like `Labour MPs Ain`t Working Class`. "I think in some ways Labour are worse than the Tories," Gal opines, "Cos you expect Tories to be the enemy, they always have been, always will be, but I hate Labour more because they`ve let us down the most. They`re supposed to be for working-class people but in power they`re just as anti-working class as the Tories."

There`s little doubt in my mid that Garry Johnson will develop from the Linton Kwesi Johnson of punk into a much wider recognised figure, spraying words like machine gun bullets to tear through class injustice and establishment cant.

I think that interview gives a massive clue as to what Peter Brown, Essex Social Services and The Family Courts were up against. I wasn't some fake suburban rebel who was going to roll over. I fought the bastards every hour of every day.

The mention of legendary performance poet Linton Kwesi Johnson is interesting as thirty years into the future we`d share a stage at London`s The Roundhouse.

Extracts from another interview later in my career reveal that Mr Brown was also taking some-one on who did not lack confidence. POETRY IN MOTION was the headline and interviewer Johnny Waller was not impressed with my shambolic lifestyle and liberal use of drugs. "The way of life for celebrated Punk Poet Garry Johnson seems to be one of glorious chaos, rarely sleeping in the same place twice in a row and taking as much speed as possible. "Got any Wrigley`s, John?" he enquires as I question him about the beginnings on new Street Punk. Were all the bands friends before the `movement` came into being?

"Nah, not really, not to start with, like The Business are from the other side of the water, the posh side (he means South of the Thames) – Johnson himself hails from the East End. Garry became involved through his poems, the song lyrics which he`d been writing ever since he was in a group called The Buzz Kids, "I was the only one who wanted to take it seriously, he complains "At school, English was the only thing I was any good at besides football. Now when I write, I do two versions, one as a poem, the other as a song with a chorus. " It`s one of those song versions `Suburban Rebels` which is currently part of The Business set and under consideration as a future single. Johnson meanwhile has his own plans to go into the studio with a backing band to record a couple of songs for single release. So how does he see things developing? "Perhaps there`ll be a new Sex Pistols or Clash coming along, perhaps The Buzz Kids might be it". The Buzz Kids it should be explained, is Johnson`s own fledgling group! Describing himself as "an ex-skinhead and a Mod, waiting for something else now," He occasionally seems disenchanted with Street Punk already, reckoning 'Glam Rock' might return. "I hope so. If it was like Mott The Hoople, it would be great, Ian Hunter's lyrics are brilliant." His favourite album of all time is still 'Ziggy Stardust And The Spiders From Mars' and his infatuation becomes even more obvious "Just call me the Bowie of Street Punk" he says "I used to write dozens of different versions of 'Ziggy Stardust' but I'm holding them back until the revival." Are you a talented instrumentalist like Bowie? "No, he's a genius. I'd just like to be. I can mime to all his records though." It's doubly ironic that this immensely likeable unemployed 'Jack the Lad' has both talent and respect of others to become the focal point of the Street Punk Movement but fritters away his time and energy on drugs and daydreams. Having long ago given up hopes of a job, he's virtually retreated to his world of words and abdicated his right to any position of prominence he might have attained. His marvellous book of poems 'Boys Of The Empire' is full of biting sarcasm aimed at social injustices, and if they occasionally seem clichéd and riddled with a quaint class consciousness, that can be overlooked since, for him, ITS ALL TRUE. But, for all his rabble-rousing and brave intentions, it amounts to nothing more than empty words if Johnson doesn't back it up with action. With the comparative freedom of being an individual (one might say a celebrity even) rather than a member of a group, should be prepared to make a stand, organise benefits, speak out against violence and fascism. He should be attempting some of the wrongs which he so bitterly despises, instead of merely complaining.

Do you vote, Garry? "Good God, No, never. I suppose I'm a working-class liberal, I really like old TV programmes like 'When the Boat Comes In' when the working-class we're united. I don't like party politics or the Royal Family. If I was in charge of the country, I would break up the United Kingdom, give England its own parliament and legalise speed". It's a crying shame because punk poet Garry Johnson could have been a contender. He could have been a spokesman for a generation but prefers having a laugh to storming the barricades. My next interview with writer Jerry Harris was published in Punk Lives magazine and proves fast drugs' can make you a bit big-headed. Amphetamine Sulphate had been replaced by Cocaine and my ego was out of control.

Jerry wrote:

"Garry Johnson, the self-styled 'Cockney Dylan', is about to explode back onto the punk scene with the release of his debut EP 'The Empire Strikes Back', which finds the self-proclaimed 'working-class hero' backed by some of the biggest names in New Punk. Johnson's no stranger to Street Punk aficionados. He wrote the punk classic 'Boys of The Empire' and best-selling 'The View From The Deadend of The Street'.

For many people he seemed to disappear during '84 and early '85, but in reality, Johnson had been hard at work. He performed on stage as a poet and fronted his own band The Buzz Kids, at one-off gigs around the provinces, also finding time to write his first play 'The Clash', with the help of award-winning playwright Tony Marchant. He also auditioned for a part in Marchant's play, 'Thick As Thieves' but says "I turned it down because I didn't want to get a crop".

He left crops and spikes behind years ago, "Punk is a way of thought" he says, "not how you look". In recent months Johnson has been back writing witty reviews for Sounds, he's been screen-tested for a role in a US film along updated 'Bronco Bulfrog' lines after an American caught his "James Dean like performance" he grins in the Canadian TV punk documentary 'A Day In The Life'.

He's also written a new volume of protest poetry, a follow-up to his critically acclaimed 'Boys of The Empire', which will come out the same time as his EP.

A versatile character or what? To understand what makes him tick, let's start at the beginning. The only son of a Cockney song and dance man, Johnson's road to rock and roll was a rocky one, finally making it via Football, teenage delinquency (a string of DCs and Borstal) and boredom. "I went from Georgie Best to David Bowie," he grins, "Once I heard Ziggy Stardust, I hung up my football boots".

The interview took place in the heartland of Johnson's territory, barely half a mile from West Ham United Football Ground.

You've got two tracks on the 'Sun of Punk' album?

"Yeah, that's right, good aint they?"

I've heard the album and they rank amongst the best stuff. "Thanks Jerry, I'd been told you was a man of taste".

What do you think of the album? "I like it, Street Punk has found its feet again. Paranoid Pictures and Prole are the best new bands"

You actually appeared on stage with Paranoid Pictures recently. "Yeah that's right in Thurrock. They're very talented, a bit too much like The Banshees, but they'll go far. I blew 'em off stage". What about the other poets like Attila the Stockbroker, Seething Wells and Jimmy Mack? "If I was deaf I'd buy all their records". How did you come to write for Sounds?

"They needed me! Robbie Millar liked the cut of my trousers. No seriously I was headhunted by Garry Bushell, and he gave me a job". Bushell has featured heavily in your career? "Yeah, well there is a lot of him, but he has played a major role, yeah. He's pushed me all the way and really helped when I've gone off the rails".

Any future plans? "What, apart from the film?" Yes. "Well, I want The Buzz Kids to be a gigging band. I know we've got the songs to make a difference. The time is right for a new pop pin-up to appear on Top of The Pops. There's a vacuum to be filled and, in my modest opinion, the record buying public need me as much as I need them".

You sound a bit big-headed Gal.

"Yeah, but if you got it, flaunt it".

A few months after that interview, my life changed. I stopped believing my own publicity and writing punk anthems, reverted to being a Mod and blagged my way into Fleet Street. White lines didn't kill me but did harm my creative energies, I was full of physical energy, but my creative juices were running on empty.

I became lazy and more interested in partying than writing anthems or making music. It was the end of the Punk Poet and the birth of showbiz tipster and tabloid terrorist Garry Johnson. There I stood, staring at the carved stone wall sign on the wall outside the offices of The Sun, teeth shattering and body shaking. It wasn't cold. In fact, it was a beautiful and warm day in London, one of those days when the city shines and its inhabitants all seem to glow glamorously from within. Not me, though I was a wreck. It was of course, partially because of the nerves I felt I on this my first day.

However, I was trembling because of the amphetamine sulphate I'd snorted to boost my confidence. That's speed to the uninitiated among you when it comes to recreational drugs and it had far from boosted anything. I was a mess and felt too high to start a new position. I looked around with drug-induced hyper clarity, then glanced back up the gentle incline of the street I'd just done my best to confidently swagger down, back up to where it joined Fleet Street. The centre of all things press related. Should I run away back to the way I'd come? Just run and hide. I imagined it's how Southend's star player would feel after signing for West Ham on his first visit to the Training Ground. No longer a big fish in a small pool.

My heart hammered and my thoughts raced. My guilt weighed heavily as I stood under the chemically enhanced crystalline sky. All seemed keen and clean, yet I felt hurried and dirty from the speed. My gaze fell back upon the grey and imposing building in front of me. Inside these labyrinthine offices on Bouverie Street awaited an official job working for the paper that everyone in the country had heard of. I had been offered a proper job at The Sun. It was crazy. I had secured this enviable position based upon a string of 'massaged' stories that I'd been selling to them and other papers for years. I had no real right to be here. No qualifications apart from my phoney CV and was sure I'd be rumbled.

My fear of being found out was immense. I felt like the only kid stood amongst the adults. Popping in and out the office for ten minutes or ringing in tips was one thing but this was an 'interview situation. Imagine some bloke from the local Amateur Drama Club doing a West End audition and that's how I felt.

It was 1985: I was in London and about to start a dream career after being poached from Sounds magazine. I was wearing my best clobber for my first day and should have been feeling magnificent. The sharp single breasted blue suit with V-shaped white handkerchief in the top pocket. White Ben Sherman shirt with top button undone and loosely fastened tie. My trademark Crombie over the whole ensemble and black Saint Ferrier brogues on my feet. I wore my signature dark blue glasses, two gold bangles on each wrist, a stud in one ear and a hoop in the other. I looked like the Sting character in Quadrophenia. I was the 'dogs bollocks'. I didn't feel it though, quite the opposite in fact, as I looked down at my shiny brogues and realised I was shifting my weight apprehensively from foot to foot. What did I look like to those around me? I've always been a confident bloke but I was getting cold feet. Was I about to blow a once in a lifetime opportunity?

As bodies in other suits and fashions filtered past me, people with the right qualifications and careers that weren't forged on a web of lies. I reminded myself that I wasn't a villain. I was a decent bloke. I'd never hurt anyone. The stories I concocted could never be deemed as nasty. They were all tongue in cheek. The gigs I reviewed but never been to, had always contained positive feedback, especially the ones that resulted in book deals for me. David Bowie, Queen, Ozzy Osbourne, Paul Young. Unwittingly Gary Glitter. I hadn't lied to anyone within the magazines and papers about my background, but yes, I'd allowed them to assume that I had all the relevant qualifications. Was that in itself a lie, to just allow people around me, my peers, to never question me? It was like an angst dream, but real. I was a fish out of water. A pretender. An imposter. It was my biggest concern, that the grown-ups would discover my ruse. That, and being cut-off from the lifestyle I'd been accustomed to. The glitz, the glamour, the champagne lifestyle and mixing with the rich and famous. I couldn't bear the thought of losing that, not now. For years I'd been networking before the term had even been invented. It wasn't what you knew, it was who you knew. I was stood here as a living embodiment of that fact. I wasn't academically clever, but I was street smart. I knew now was not the time to push my luck. There was far too much at stake. To put it bluntly "I bottled it" and 'walked' before I was 'kicked out'.

I was pretty confident I'd get a second chance and didn't have to wait very long.

Garry Bushell who took me to Sounds magazine, the same bloke who `slaughtered` my band The Buzz Kids started working at The Sun and within months was Editor of the Bizarre pop column. This time the stars were aligned, and I would become a tabloid journalist. Garry Bushell was Editor of the Showbiz Column. News International had moved to Wapping and held no fear. This was East London and my manor. This time it was different as I'd been in and out of Fort Wapping many times, used their phones and sat at desks chatting to Piers Morgan, Peter Willis, Andy Coulson, Nick Ferrari. And Charlie Catchpole and Ray Levine at the News of the World. On one occasion I even sat with Garry Bushell at the same table as Kelvin Mackenzie. A fleet Street legend in the mould of Mike Bassett England Manager and a Mafia don. So I was looking forward to meeting Rebekah Wade who was herself the new girl on the block. It was Piers Morgan who set up the meeting and to this day I don't know why but we got on like a house on fire. In a plutonic way it was `love at first sight` and she'd acquired a life-long admirer. We went for lunch in Canary Wharf and within an hour I went from being Piers top tipster to her special contact, right-hand man and trusted confidante.

Rebekah showing faith in me boosted my confidence and against all odds I became a kosher Tabloid journalist. I ended up with a daily TV reviews column with a picture by-line and a weekly showbiz page. History proved I did the right thing by walking away from Bouverie Street because my `second chance` lasted 25 years. I ended up with the best of both worlds. I was still able to roam the pubs and clubs of London looking for tips and had a proper `grown-up` job writing columns with by-lines. I also wrote a TV column for the lads Magazine Front and Showbiz Column for Zit magazine. Although I went legit I still had my rebellious streak and continued to turn up for recordings of Bushell On The Box. It wasn't just the lure of various page 3 girls like Dee Ivens, Christine Peake and Zoe Anderson. Wait to you read the stories I did on them, and all with their permission. Another regular was impressionist Francine Lewis, who at the time was a regular on TV. Together we fabricated a sexy kiss-and-tell romp. One afternoon over a few drinks in a Kent Beer Garden we conjured up a fantastic collection of stories so entertaining that, 15 years apart, they made two `word for word` showbiz scoops. In 2013 Francine appeared on Britain's Got Talent. Simon Cowell loved her and so did the tabloid press, who once again published the `fabricated stories` about her love life. We invented a romp with Leonardo di Caprio and another that Francine loved having sex on the train at Southend's Peter Pan Playground. I loved hanging out with celebs and never stopped being star-struck. I also met comic Bobby Davro while appearing in panto at Southend.

He was a top bloke and invited my kids and eight of their friends backstage for pictures and autographs. The Eastenders star went out of his way to make all the kids feel special as they partied in his dressing room with fizzy drinks and chocolates. I really hit it off with Davro and weeks later spent the day at his luxury pad in Staines. I was more impressed more by the white piano and white carpets then I was by the swimming pool. He was much funnier in person than he ever was on TV. Years later I attended a showbiz garden party and in a different way hit it off with Eastenders legend Ross Kemp. He was with his wife and my boss Rebekah Wade. I was messing around with a champagne bottle and the cork shoot off and smacked him on the head. I froze on the spot. He looked like Grant Mitchell with the hump but luckily for me Rebekah laughed, so it didn't end in tears. He didn't lose a eye and I didn't lose my job. At another panto, this time Cinderella at Wimbledon, I got to meet TV star Bradley Walsh and Britt Ekland. Brad I'd met a few times, a nice and friendly bloke, but meeting Britt was like a Catholic meeting the Pope. Memories of her in 70s British gangster flick Get Carter rolling about topless on a bed and wearing black tights came flooding back. I was only about Thirteen and she was the sexiest thing I had ever seen in my life. Along with Susan George, she was my first pin-up. They both had everything most teenage boys wanted, blonde hair, cute bums, pert breasts and long legs. Many a man of my age had their first 'awakening' thinking of Britt Ekland and Susan George. Meeting Britt was another link to my childhood. I grew up fancying her and Susan George like mad, which explains my attraction to Lyn. We are talking massive crushes on all three. Two of them ended up on the arm of Rod Stewart, another life-long hero along with David Bowie and Georgie Best.

I've spent most of my life with some kind of Rod the Mod barnet wishing I'd also shagged Britt Ekland and Susan George. When she said "hello", I was tongue-tied.

She was no longer in her prime but still good-looking and would not have said "no" to a hotel room romp. Sadly, she didn't offer. Panto was good to me. One year I took my kids to see Gladiator star Falcon and she made a real fuss of them with pictures, sweets and backstage tour. I met lots of comedians on and off duty, all great storytellers but the best raconteur was Underworld legend Dave Courtney. Many times, I witnessed him holding court, swapping gags and anecdotes with various showbiz characters but few could deliver a punch line or a knockout punch like Dave. The more we met the more I liked him. He once gave me and my sons a guided tour of Camelot Castle and it was like being on a movie set.

Both boys sat on his throne, and I sunk a few shots on his famous pool table. The loveable rogue did my family a very special favour and I thought the world of him.

When they were young and spotted him on TV they would shout, "Dad, there's Dave". What was the favour? Behave yourself, I'm a genuine Cockney and even though Dave Courtney is sadly no longer with us I won't go 'public' unless his best mate Brendan gives me the green light. The Establishment had a real downer on Dave but if I revealed the favour, he did my family it would explain why he had so many supporters. He would have been brilliant on The Jonathan Chat Show or Desert Island Discs. I also met Page 3 legend Sam Fox before she came out as a lesbian. She wasn't one of my favourites as I've always been a leg man and preferred Suzanne Mitzi. But whenever we met, be it Stringfellows, The Hippodrome or a showbiz bash, we always had a chat. Why do I mention that? Well, one meeting in Hammersmith still stands out and this time Tony Mottram got a picture. It was an after-show party for chart-topper Bryan Adams. This time I was 'chatted up' and dare I say 'propositioned' by Ms Fox, though it wasn't Sam it was her mum. With the right handling, in the management sense I mean, Sam could have been the new Barbara Windsor. Talking of Carry On star Babs, I genuinely believe I helped to get her role as Peggy Mitchell in Eastenders. Over an 8-year period I would constantly invent stories that Barbara was moving to Walford. Eventually she did and became a soap opera legend. She was born to play landlady Peggy Mitchell and is, without doubt, the best character since Den and Angie. If and when they make Babs The Movie, the perfect choice would be Sheridan Smith. I would have chosen Daniella Westbrook before her nose 'problem', she was drop-dead gorgeous and the sexiest female to ever pull a pint in The Queen Vic. Of all the page 3 girls I met, I have to say Suzanne Mitzi was the most beautiful by a mile. She was a blonde natural beauty who could easily have been a massive Hollywood pin-up. I'm not blowing my own trumpet, but a lot of what I wrote in 'Boys of the Empire' is still relevant today. The funny thing is, the older I've gotten the more left-wing I've become. I've also matured and now respect all educated people and some posh people in the same way as a youngster I looked up to rock stars, footballers and East End gangsters.

# Chapter Twelve
## Poetic Justice

You will never take the Arthur Daley out of my character, but I have learnt to trust people who don't come from my background. I wouldn't vote for them but do feel comfortable in their company. The truth is I ain't anti-money. I'm not a whingeing working-class poet over-flowing with envy. I would love every council house resident reading this book to win the Lottery. I admire working-class entertainers from Jonathan Ross to Johnny Rotten for becoming multi-millionaires. I applaud working-class youngsters who go on Love Island or Big Brother to build a career, it's better than working. All my heroes from David Bowie to John Lennon to Mike Tyson rose from the slums to make personal fortunes. Good luck to them and, in all honesty who wouldn't love to join their ranks? The people I don't like are the 'silver spoon' brigade from King Charles to Lord Cameron. I object to champagne socialists like Sir Starmer, Lady Thornberry and Tony Blair telling working-class people what to do and how to think.

What this country needs is a leader with a social conscience, working-class DNA, a sense of humour and a warm heart. I would like to apply for the job. Looking back on my life it's funny that despite going to Borstal, a Top Security Prison, various schools and a Children's Homes I was only bullied once. Not behind bars, not in the playground.

Only once during a thirty-year career in magazines and tabloid newspapers was I treated like a second-class citizen. It happened at The Sun. It wasn't by a member of the elite squad made up of big beasts like Piers Morgan, Andy Coulson or Nick Ferrari. My verbal abuser was Tricia Martin. A posh bitch with an ego the size of Wembley Stadium. It started on day one of her brief reign as Features Editor on the TV magazine. It was a mutual dislike at first sight. She looked like a Conservative MP from the Shires and hated my Cockney accent. Toffee-nosed Tricia (as with Peter Brown) did her best to bully and intimidate me, but it didn't work. I had seen off much bigger and maybe even uglier snobs than her. When her cheap insults and bitchy remarks failed, she complained to the magazine's Editor Jonathan Worsnop about the poor quality of my stories. A wrong move on her part. A very wrong move.

My stories were always top of the range. Why would I waste my time making up boring stories? This had nothing to do with content, it was all about class. I was being persecuted because of my background and the way I spoke.

Like Social Services, Ms Martin made a big mistake in taking me on as she wasn't aware of my 'dog with a bone attitude'. If I thought something was unfair I'd fight for justice. This time I had 'friends in high places'. I put up with her constant snipping for months and not once did I react or complain about her bullying behaviour. That is not my style as I am not a fan of grasses. For me a grass is pond life and the same low-level scumbag as a rapist, child abuser and career politician. That changed when she went to Jonathan Worsnop and 'stabbed me in the back'.

That was an attempt at 'class assassination', it was personal rather than professional, so I retaliated. I had a word with my friend Marie Baylis. She was an unsung hero at News International and one of the nicest and most genuine people I have ever met. Marie had time for everyone, especially me. It was her who would chase my payments and, whatever the problem always came to my aide. A genuine Eastender who watched my back like an army sniper. She was a lovely kind-hearted lady who years later would arrange for my son Sam to do his work experience at The Sun. I had a word in the ear of Marie Baylis who in turn had a conversation with Rebekah. I wasn't 'grassing' it was more like self-defence.

I'm told that when Ms Martin was made aware of my 'special friendship' with the 'head honcho' that the blood drained from her face. The bully bird realised she'd over-stepped the mark and apologised for the error of her ways. Whatever was said, it certainly did the trick. I never heard another sarcastic quip from Ms Martin or her embarrassing attempt at a Cockney accent.

The Bolshie bully in high-heels and too much make-up was off my case and unlike me didn't last twenty-five years at The Sun. If only she'd kept her posh mouth shut as months later, I was promoted and left the Weekly TV magazine. I was given a Daily TV column with a picture bye-line. That was the one and only time I suffered any form of 'classism' or snobbery. I often wonder if she became a Social Worker or joined Essex Police. By contrast TV and Radio star Nick Ferrari was the polar opposite of Ms Martin who edited the Bizarre Showbiz Column. A very funny bloke and sharper than a surgeon's scalpel. I looked up to him because he was smart, educated, classy, but never a snob. A legendary ladies' man who could find a story on a desert island. My answer machine message would drive him nuts. It was:

"Hi there, fast-talking, good-looking Garry Dean Ronson Johnson here, star attraction, living legend, and superior sex symbol with the 'Just A Gigolo Escort Agency'. Please leave your name and number and I'll get back to you as soon as I can. But until we speak, or even meet, I leave you with these words 'Je t'aime, I love you all'. That was a heartfelt, sincere, joint living legend and heaven on earth production". I kept that message for years (cocaine does enhance your ego). Nick laughed the first time but as with everyone else (except me) the joke wore thin.

He was a proper newspaper man who now interviews Prime Ministers but whenever I see him on TV I'm reminded of the sexy secretary in the lift story.

But my lips are sealed as what happened in Wapping stays in Wapping.

The biggest beast in the history of The Sun is Kelvin MacKenzie. Only met him twice, but he was the Guvnor. I liken him in an affectionate way to a Mafia boss or old school football boss Brian Clough. Both times I was with Garry Bushell at a table in The Sun swanky cafeteria at Fort Wapping. He sat down and took control of the conversation. Garry hardly spoke and I never said a word. I just listened as he slaughtered various politicians, show business legends and half-jokingly told Gal Bushell he wanted more World Exclusives or else. Kelvin was a man who reduced grown men to tears. If you weren't any good at your job you didn't stay at The Sun simple as that. As luck would have it he completely ignored me on both occasions. I had a close encounter and lucky escape, as if anyone would have sussed me as an 'imposter' it would have been Kelvin MacKenzie.

He is a Fleet Street bruiser and tabloid talent spotter second to none. Look at those who graduated from the Kelvin School of Journalism. To name just a few Piers Morgan, Garry Bushell, Nick Ferarri, Peter Willis, Neil Wallis and Andy Coulson. There is no way I would have pulled the wool over any of their eyes.

Also worth a mention in dispatches from the Sounds days are heavy metal madman Stefan Chirvazi now based in Hollywood, and hard-drinking punk rocker Jerry Harris. Who I believe is now a pub owning, pornographic filmmaker in the North of England. I must mention two people from the opposite ends of tabloid journalism. One a party animal who could drink Oliver Reed under the table, and out snort Keith Moon at his worst and Liam Gallagher at his best. The man is the late and sadly missed Sun hack Sean Hoare, who looked like David Brent and partied like Ronnie Wood. He was a pleasure to know and spend time with.

The other is Sue Reid of the Daily Mail one of the poshest and most respected female journos in the business. She talks like a member of the Royal Family with the appearance of a Tory MP but this lady could survive on the toughest council estate in East London. Always one hundred per cent genuine with me and many times put her reputation on the line to protect me. I bet you are wondering if I was such a `nice bloke` why did my wife have two affairs (that I know of) and leave me?

The answer is `sex`. Or rather, the lack of it, and I hold my hands up I was to blame. Up until the Autumn of 2004 our relationship had always been `very sexual`, then all of a sudden it wasn't. I had money worries which I never shared, and the stress made me unfit for purpose in the bedroom department. I was also unbeknown to me, already suffering with the early stages of a serious health condition. It would get worse and end with me being in a coma and on a life support machine. Before discovering her affairs, I sought help from Basildon Hospital and most men will agree having your `manhood` examined by strangers is no fun. A `medical condition` which started with `circulation problems` would spread to hardened arteries and me `dying` twice in a 29-day coma.

Writing about this isn't a problem. I had to stand up in a crowded court and confess all in room of strangers but luckily I ain't a shy sort of bloke, so it didn't embarrass me. That's why I can write about it now. I was one per cent innocent of any wrongdoing, yet Social Services were trying to steal my children. My ex-wife had affairs, yet The Family Court were trying to take my children. It is believe me still as raw today as it was the first time I walked into those `secret` Family Courts where everything is carried out behind closed doors.

What is it they say about Karma? Maybe that old saying, "what goes round comes round around?" is true. I had two-timed most girlfriends and cheated on various partners but there was a big difference in my behaviour as at the time I didn't have three children. I also never went to Basildon Police or Essex Social Services and falsely accused anyone of being a `danger to my children`. A slur that took me 27 court appearances and two spells in prison to rebuke. It would also lead to five heart attacks and two triple heart bypass operations. The truth is apart from suffering with the early signs of a `medical condition` I hadn't done anything wrong. I could cope with losing my wife but not my children. There were weeks of cold turkey but I survived and came out the other end, but to be honest the first few days were hard. I was happy I had my sons but I'd lost my daughter whose never returned. I've read various books about Rod Stewart and Reggie Kray. The East End gangster was a childhood hero and Rod the Mod a life-long passion. Both admitted in print to being broken-hearted and destroyed after losing their wives.

Reggie Kray went to pieces when wife Frances walked out as did Rod when Rachel Hunter left. I can honestly say `hand on heart` that at the time I wouldn't have pissed on my ex-wife if she was on fire.

I still stand by that, the only thing that's changed is alongside the hate in my heart is a vitral metal valve. I took my medicine/bad luck like a man. I didn't cry but came close to breaking point as I was 'attacked' on all sides by my ex-wife, Basildon Police and Essex Social Services. I eventually got verbal and written apologies from Social Services and the Police but only after I took my case to the Houses of Parliament and The High Court. Has my ex-wife ever apologised?

No. She's spent Twenty years brainwashing my daughter against me and from a distance it seems she's created an Essex version of Megan Markle. If her father thinks he's been betrayed by his daughter then Mr Markle should read this book.

Without sounding like a wimp, which I'm not. Those who know me will confirm I'm a million miles away from being a wimp, but when it comes to kids I am a big softie. I willingly admit I thought about my daughter every day, and especially at times like Christmas. Even today I do miss my daughter and in a way sort of love her, though it's hard to have feelings for a person who hates you. It's almost impossible when you ain't got a clue why exactly you're hated, despised and ignored. When I came out of my coma I prayed to God my daughter would visit me and of course she never did.

I've no idea if my daughter ever got the letter written for me by one of the nurses or why she ignored the message from the Hospital Chaplin. I still have feelings for my daughter because however much she hates me I'll always be her dad.

I have various theories why she hates me. Number one will always be brainwashing' by my ex-wife, my former in-laws and Sally Prevost. Two: She was never given any of the Christmas or Birthday presents I sent and none of the cards and letters. Three: I wonder if she was bullied at school and blames me because her brothers were not around to protect her. I'm angry with her but not because she hates me, maybe it's the journalist in me, but can't understand why she doesn't want to read the official documents and discover the truth. Again, the journalist in me, but can't believe how a daughter isn't curious about her dad.

From the age of Twelve to Seventeen I did time in various lockups for teenage tearaways and mixed-up kids. Boyles Court Brentwood Essex (twice), Little Heath in East London (twice), Three months in Kidlington Detention Centre, Oxfordshire. It's now called Campsfield House and houses illegal immigrants awaiting deportation. It was a horrible and brutal place surrounded by barbed wire and eight-foot-high fences. I became best mates with a teenage Roy Heath, who went onto became a well-known South London bank robber. Three months at Redhill Special Unit in Surrey and a further eight months at Herts Borstal in Hertfordshire.

The adult Garry Johnson regrets this, but if it weren't for those days, I would not have written my punk anthem 'Ballad of the Young Offenders' or realised that crime is a mugs game. If you're not from a kosher crime family, or related by marriage to a top villain, one of the chaps, or a proper face, then crime doesn't pay. Another plus was that I got to mix with lots of black boys from all parts of London. Like me, they were natural born rebels. At school my best mate was black, and we shared a mutual love of Ska music (Trojan Reggae), girls, football and fashion. Together we took our first blue pill, and 'lost' our virginity to the same girl, on different nights. We were kindred spirits though he was more party animal than teenage tearaway. He was a lucky bastard; the day I got three months Detention Centre he was let off with probation. Was it because he was black or because I upset the Judge by shouting "you wouldn't talk to The Kray Twins like that".

In those days there was very little segregation between the races and the young black offenders were just like me. They broke all the rules on a daily basis and challenged the authority of the screws. They were my kind of allies.

When I wasn't being locked-up for things I hadn't done and getting away with things I had, my obsessions were changing. I was moving away from total dedication to football and getting more and more into music. Then I saw David Bowie on Top of The Pops. They say people never forget where they were when President Kennedy was shot, or John Lennon murdered. I'll never forget the first time I saw Ziggy Stardust on TV. It wasn't the Governments short sharp shock treatment that put me on the straight and narrow it was David Bowie and didn't want some prison barber cutting off my Ziggy Stardust haircut. Although I left my 'roots' and headed for the West End of London in search of fame and fortune I never lost touch with my best mate.

Years later he came with me to interview presenter James Whale at LBC Radio, visit the VIP bar at the Circus Tavern Lap Dancing Club and see The Stone Roses before they became famous. He was the first person I went to the pub with after my triple heart bypass operation. We were both in our fifties and reminiscing about our schooldays and teenage years as soul boys wondering if we ever met Sade at The Goldmine Night Club on Canvey Island. I of course repeated my many meetings with the UK's greatest ever female singer.

We spoke about our Hearing at the Guild Hall Courts when I got three months, and he got off with probation. An historic day as the last time I saw Lyn K my childhood crush and best-looking girl in Essex. I'm glad we've never been reunited as I still think of her as being 'drop dead gorgeous'. My mate mentioned he'd recently met the second best-looking girl from our teenage years, and said she now looked like "Coleen Nolan". He can say that because with his Bob Marley dreadlocks and ripped physique he could still pass for Thirty-five. I don't know what he's on (well I do), but he should bottle it and make a fortune. The Sun and the Mirror were, and still are, my favourite tabloids because they get great showbiz exclusives, and do brilliant football coverage. They also have controversial columnists like Tony Parsons and Rod Liddle. I don't always agree with what they write but they have the ability to make you smile and snarl in the same paragraph. The Mirror has Kevin Maguire who along with Olivia Uttley of GB News is my favourite political pundit. Both have the X Factor, I could listen to Kevin all day and look at Olivia all night. I just find educated women such a turn on. People knock GB News and I aint keen on their 'patriotic bollocks' and the playing of the National Anthem every morning but do like presenter Nana Akau and comedian Lewis Schaffer. I'm not really into party politics, have never voted and when it comes to national anthems, I prefer the American, French and German to our dirge. I don't always agree with Geordie Boy Maguire but love it when he puts the boot into corrupt politicians and members of the Establishment. He's one of the few media commentators who speaks out against the Royal Family. If only he'd turn his venom on the 'red Tories' who've transformed the working-class Labour Party into an elite club for champagne socialists. I literally lived on the street, been both homeless and penniless and never appreciated posh people with double-barrelled names telling me what to do and how to vote. Champagne socialists have a nasty habit of talking down to the masses with a snobby mantra of "do as I say and not what I do". As I wrote in one of my critically acclaimed poems "The sons and daughters of Labour MPs play on grass and our kids play on concrete".

    I started at Sounds with 'nothing in the bank' and after thirty-five years in Fleet Street and millions of words left with fuck all. Did I waste all my money on wine, women and song? No, I got divorced. The biggest mistake of my life was getting married. I wouldn't recommend it to my worst enemy, but as I always say "every cloud has a silver lining", I walked away with my two sons. When I met my ex-wife, I was scared the 'novelty' would wear off before I got her pregnant. I know my character better than anyone and knew how easily I got bored with things and always needed new highs. When Sam was born I was one hundred per cent obsessed with him. It was a warm feeling and an addiction I can't describe. He was, if you like, a gift from God and I worshipped him. I'm sure it's because I loved him to bits that my wandering eye never kicked in.

When I was younger it was always hard to have more than one special person in my life. As a kid it was my dad. Then various girlfriends filled the void. Becoming a dad gave me the ability to spread my feelings. I loved Sam, Adam and then my daughter. It was unconditional love both ways, bonds were made with my sons that have never been broken. Basildon Police, Essex Social Services, Judge Roderick Newton and social worker Peter Brown all tried and failed to tear us apart. Those who know me will confirm that as well as being a Mod, the Punk Poet, a Tabloid Terrorist, unorthodox and eccentric I'm also `ultra loyal`, and that `gene` was passed to my sons. Whatever corruption took place in the offices of Essex Social Services or behind the closed doors of the secretive Family Courts they would never `divide and conquer` the `Johnson Boys`.

## Chapter Thirteen
## Buzz Kid Adult Mod

In search of fame, I formed The Buzz Kids and although my rock and roll band never took off, it launched me into the media. I became a performance poet, then a music critic and a tabloid journalist. Some say The Punk Poet 'sold out' when he joined the current bun. I wasn't one of them. I genuinely believed The Sun was more in touch with the Working-class than the Morning Star. I wasn't betraying my background or class by entering the wonderful world of Fleet Street.

In my mind I was doing something University media graduates and journalists working on provincial newspapers would give their right arm for. I was going in one giant leap from Sunday morning football to the Premier League. I had the bottle without a single qualification to grab this once-in-a-lifetime opportunity with both hands. I followed my dream and then lived it in glorious technicolour. It was a 24-7 buzz enhanced by Columbian marching powder and German lager.

I'd rather share a line and a pint with a tabloid showbiz journalist than a British politician. The vast majority of MPs are liars, cheats, corrupt, self-serving and two-faced greedy bastards. They are only in politics for money, power, prostitutes and backhanders. I hope what you've read so far reveals the content of my character and explains why social worker Peter Brown, despite his threats and boasts, was never going to beat me. I fought the authorities, and I won. Not once did I stop protecting my children or fighting to see my daughter. Don't take my word for it. Here are the facts described to the Court by my barrister Peter Thomas-Pedder:

"It is clear Mr Johnson has fought with every fibre of his being on these matters and at times, he may well be judged to have acted unadvisedly. However, I truly believe that he has acted with good intentions and in good faith. Naturally, this is a matter for the judge to decide, but I would press this point in his favour. That is to say, that despite the amount of time that has elapsed since these proceedings began, Mr Johnson has fought for the right of his daughter to know her father".

Adding: "I am confident that my client has the capacity to tell his side of the story in a clear, coherent and honest manner when these matters are presented to the court". It took seven years and a massive toll on my health before I tasted victory but at the end of the day I won. That's all that mattered and, if need be, I'd do it all over again. I wouldn't change a thing, well maybe the two imprisonments (but they gave me a few anecdotes) apart from how long it took to get justice.

As the Great British public knows, Family Courts and biased judges are not interested in the truth or Fathers Rights. They only believe the lies of mean-spirited mothers and inept social workers. That's why it took seven years for Essex Social Services to admit they got it wrong. Lord Justice Thorpe sitting at The High Court in London ruled in my favour and ordered Essex Social Services to handover all the documents. They refused and appealed the verdict so representing myself I returned to the High Court. Lord Justice Munby ruled in my favour telling the barrister for Essex Social Services "I don't care what you say I will not change my mind". Judge Moloney said: "Mr Johnson will not go away. He is not that type of character and will keep on coming. He is like a dog with a bone".

Essex County Council had no choice but to carry out the orders of the court and seven folders containing 900-plus documents were personally delivered to my front door. The documents were dynamite and confirmed everything I'd been saying for seven years. That's one of the reasons I'm writing this book as, unlike The Family Courts and Essex Social Services, I believe in the truth, the whole truth and nothing but the truth". To any doubters out there including the Megan Markle of Essex copies of all documents can be obtained by using the Freedom of Information Act. My daughter has two options make a FOI request to Essex County Council or have the decency to read my copies. If my daughter can't be bothered to meet me or spare the time to look through 900 pages of official and legal documents there is one letter I beg her to read as it confirms she's been 'brainwashed' to hate me and brought up on a 'tissue of lies'. Let me quote 'word for word' from the letter my criminal lawyers Nelson Guest and Partners sent to my Family Law Solicitors HKH and Cox Solicitors: "We understand that you act on behalf of Garry Johnson in connection with a matter of Family Law.

We are asked to write in respect of a contact application made by our mutual client in respect of his daughter Lucy, who he has not seen for some considerable time. We understand the basis of this are allegations made by his ex-wife about various matters relating to Mr Johnson and things that he is supposed to have done. We can tell you that our involvement in this matter is to act on his behalf when he was arrested in relation to allegations made by his ex-wife,

that he had posted on the internet. We can tell you that following a police investigation this was found not to be the case and that all the allegations were for want of a better way of putting it malicious on the part of her. He has not been subject to any prosecution, and it is quite clear that the matter was for want of a better expression manipulated by her to reflect upon him. But he had not done anything which could or should be regarded as wrongdoing".

The police agreed. All charges were dropped, my computers and laptops returned. Essex Police found no evidence because there was none to find.

My solicitors were not happy with the conduct of the police and advised I made a complaint. A `clear the air` meeting was arranged with Inspector Sage of Essex Police. We met and he made the following promise "If your ex-wife makes any more allegations, I promise we won't turn up on your doorstep mob handed.

We will ring first and ask when would be a convenient time to call".

I never heard from the police again, but it wasn't the end of the harassment.

My ex-wife reported me to the RSPCA for cruelty to a cat even though I never owned a cat. One morning I was visited unannounced and cleared.

She then reported me to Environmental Health Department claiming my home was a health hazard. Again, I was visited without warning and cleared.

Next, I was visited by the DHSS and investigated for fraud. I was interviewed under caution and accused of falsely claiming Child Benefit.

She told them my sons were not living with me but the content of their bedrooms and a phone call from the school confirmed they did. It was all a load of bollocks, extremely annoying, time consuming and petty. I wonder if my daughter is aware of any of the above. Does she know I was falsely accused of being `mentally ill` and planning to carry out seven murders and that I was threatened with life imprisonment? Does she find that amusing? I would love to know her views and discover what facts she`s actually aware of. I began as a Punk Poet and ended up as tabloid terrorist, but I was never sued or asked to retract a single fabricated story. Although I had no qualifications, I was very street smart when it came to creating world exclusives. I wrote about everyone from David Bowie to Madonna to Maggie Thatcher to George Michael and all A-Listers protected by an army of managers and press officers. So how did I get away with it for so long?

I only created flattering stories and massaged ego`s. Never wrote a hatchet job or harmful kiss and tell. Example: I made up a story about Michael Jackson getting married, this was years before Lisa Presley. I wrote the Prince of Pop was planning to marry Matt Bianco singer Basia, and the Daily Star published it as a front-page World Exclusive. Well, they got it half-right. It was an `exclusive`, as I made it up in the pub. Why did I choose Basia? I was good friends with her Press Officer, and it was great publicity for a young band on the verge of a hit record. My first Sun front page and World Exclusive was that old rubber lips Mick Jagger was spending £60,000 on new lips. That was a lot of money in 1986. I followed that with `Maggie The Movie`, decade before the Hollywood film starring Meryl Streep. My version would have been much better with Madonna playing the Iron Lady and Miami Vice star Don Johnson cast as Dennis Thatcher. I also invented `Blair the Movie` starring Tom Hanks, years before Welsh actor Michael Sheen played the war criminal. During my time as Stone Roses manager, I linked Ian Brown with Angie Bowie, wrote George Michael was joining the cast of Eastenders, and that Morrissey had been signed-up as a scriptwriter by Coronation Street.

Revealed rock star Rod Stewart was buying Leyton Orient Football Club and Robbie Williams to guest star in an episode of Only Fools and Horses.

Another story I made up also came true a few years after it was created. This one was written in anger rather than humour. Erica had mentioned me to her friend Martin Dunn, who at the time was the Number One showbiz hack.

We arranged to meet at Stringfellows Night Club for a drink. Martin had been Editor of The Sun Showbiz Column for about six months and in 1985 Martin was `the man to know` if you wanted to get on. We ended up being joined by the legendary Peter Stringfellow who ordered a bottle of champagne. As we talked, something was said to me that was almost certainly innocuous in its intentions. However, my working-class background and lack of schooling had me continually on high alert and my antennae was always up and sent signals if I suspected someone talking down to me. Martin Dunn, in the middle of a conversation, asked me a simple yet seriously misguided question. "You`re from the East End, Garry. I bet you knew The Kray Twins". In the film of my life the camera would zoom in on my face at that exact moment. The club around us would go silent and darken as you watched my frown deepen and mouth open to respond.

Nearly all people in my shoes at that moment would just knock the question aside and say they did or didn't know Reg or Ronnie Kray. Not me.

Was he taking the piss out of my Cockney background? Probably not.

The camera would then pull back and zoom in for a close up of my mouth, as in slow motion I utter a few words that were about to change things forever. Innocent, thoughtless, unplanned, yet, with massive ramifications, I replied:

"Yeah, I do actually. And I know people who know the Krays very well".

"Do you?" now they were both sat forward in their seats.

"Yeah, in fact, I've got a great story about them. You know the Spandau brothers Gary and Martin?" Of course, they both nodded in agreement. "They're gonna play the Kray twins in a movie!" I still don't know to this day where that came from. I just made it up on the spot and it came to me in a split second.

It gave me the confidence to earn a living as a 'tabloid terrorist' for the next twenty-five years. And all because I thought I was possibly being belittled for my Cockney accent, which to be honest makes both Ray Winstone and Danny Dyer sound posh. My 'exclusive' earned me a few quid and the Kemp Brothers did play the Kray Twins, but not until five years after I said they would in 1990.

It turned out to be the first of many made-up stories that were self-fulfilling prophecies. I was like the Mystic Meg of Tabloid Journalism. Martin Dunn's eyes lit-up, he was even further in his chair saying: "Now that's a story". That was the first time I had spun a completely made-up yarn that ended up as a world exclusive in a national newspaper.

Martin was convinced I had solid contacts feeding me information, and from then on, everything I said was greedily gobbled up and printed without question, and so began a rampage of selling stories to every tabloid newspaper in the UK.

Yes, the entire United Kingdom, as my net spread all the way to Scotland and exclusives in The Daily Record. Other journalists would see me around at various events and automatically assume I was 'one of them'. Informal conversations would be littered with me name-dropping and them offering phone numbers.

Before being endorsed and given credibility by Martin Dunn I was just another young gun from the music press, the latest 'new kid on the block' with his finger on the pulse. But as they say "you shouldn't judge a book by its cover".

I wasn't a bona fide journalist like Tony Parsons or Danny Baker and I wasn't a youngster. I was in fact 25-years-old and only looked much younger because of my use of 'fast drugs', veggie diet and Rod Stewart haircut. I'd spent five years infiltrating the music press, networking with Fleet Street and now decided the time was right to go full on tabloid terrorist.

I'd now seen close up how a throwaway remark could instantly and easily be fabricated into a story. That moment gave me the green light to come up with more gossip and turn rumours into exclusives. People started ringing me for stories and instead of having to blag my way into swanky parties I was now receiving VIP invites. I would ring people up and say, "Garry Johnson from The Sun" and not one single person ever doubted me. It was such a buzz walking into places like The Playboy Club surrounded by all these beautiful women in bunny outfits and black tights. I was like a kid in a Candy Shop, or because of my frozen brain a randy teenager in a lap dancing club. I filled my pockets with souvenirs, as they say you can take the boy out of the East End, but not the East End out of the boy. I don't know what a shrink would make of this confession but there I was surrounded by beautiful scantily clad women drinking free champagne and I'm thinking about my dad. I knew (hoped) he would be proud and thought `if only he could see me now` as this was his idea of heaven. I had to get him some souvenirs, but me being me I went over the top. I don't smoke but with so many ash trays in my pockets I rattled when I walked. Tell me Doctor. "Why was it so important for me to impress my dad? The first thing I thought of when attending that showbiz bash at Chelsea Football Stadium was getting a souvenir for my football fanatic dad. I sneaked out of the party and found myself on the centre-circle of the pitch and then in the First Team Dressing Room.

I took a shirt off one of the pegs, I'm a West Ham so didn't want it. I stole it for my dad. Why? This is the bloke who destroyed my chance of a football career but here I was trying to impress him. I knew he'd be impressed when I met East End Legend Barbara Windsor, Georgie Best, gangster Charlie Kray, Great Train Robber Buster Edwards, West Ham Manager Harry Redknapp and singer Max Bygraves.

I always thought of him first when meeting `golden oldies`. He was never impressed by the likes of David Bowie, Johnny Rotten, Paul Weller or Underworld legend Dave Courtney. It was `old school` celebs who won me his approval. I also enjoyed ringing up and passing on my gossip because I knew it would wind up his wife. After he died I was told by relatives, "he was proud of you Gal and of what you achieved, but would only say so when she was out of the room". That still makes me angry so I'll move on before I get `upset` but one question that can't be answered, "How can a dad betray his own child?" Charles Alfred Johnson was a great person to have as a friend, a very funny bloke and always the life and soul of a party` but a rubbish dad. He was great in the role of a granddad, adored both my boys and they in turn `loved him to bits`. But they were never aware of his lousy track record as a dad. All I ever wanted was an explanation of why he walked out and why he felt so little of me. I wanted to ask one question "how could you look yourself in the mirror?" And all I wanted to hear from him was an apology, but such is my character I would never have accepted it and probably have thrown it straight back in his face. It was great fun `hanging out` for `free` in trendy happening places like Stringfellows, The Hippodrome, The Limelight and Camden Palace. Getting backstage passes for concerts at Wembley and the Hammersmith Odeon. Travelling First Class for free all over England and being paid to stay in luxury hotels. At first, I kept waiting for a 'tap on the shoulder' but like most things in life the more you do something the easier it gets. The fantasy had become reality. I was never rude or vindictive and always gave good reviews. Even when I hadn't been to the gig, not because I was a saint, I didn't want to risk getting caught. That's why I got away with it for so long. No one complains about a good review. Although I'm living the dream it's not just memories of my dad I can't forget, and again, not sure what a psychiatrist would say, but why am I still 'turned on' by images from my teenage years. There was an incident when I was 12 years old that I'm sure triggered my life-long addiction to blondes. A friends parents were away for the weekend, so we went to his house to watch TV and raid the drinks cabinet. We walked into the lounge and his older brother had beaten us to it. He was only seventeen, but when you're 12 that seems like a proper adult. He wasn't alone as underneath him on the sofa was his half-naked girlfriend. The startled pair both jumped up and she was topless, but it wasn't her naked breasts that aroused me. The blushing blonde was wearing black tights, revealing a hairy bush and pert bum. I don't know why and didn't ask, but she wasn't wearing any knickers. It was all over in few seconds as they both fled the room, but I'd seen enough to be hooked for life. Thank God the girl wasn't ginger as it could have put me off women for life. From that moment I had a thing about black tights and no knickers. That's why I loved the Britt Ekland scene in UK gangster movie Get Carter. I never tired of watching her rolling about on a bed wearing black tights and nothing else. Now you know why I was so excited about the first time I went to The Playboy Club. I loved it when Debbie Harry wore mini-skirts and black tights on Top of The Pops, but not as much as future girlfriends in the bedroom. In her heyday the Blondie star was without doubt the sexiest singer of all-time, but she was out of reach. A fantasy figure on a TV screen, whereas girlfriends are flesh and blood. As you've realised by now, I have an addictive personality, be it Bowie, fast drugs, or blondes. So posing as a tabloid journalist was another obsession I couldn't give up. At 15-years-of-age I gave up a promising football career and wouldn't repeat that mistake. There was no way I'd walk away from the wonderful world of showbiz. Despite massive provocation from my ex-wife and her boyfriend I did nothing to risk losing my children. An old friend and East End tough guy who appears alongside me in the Private Eye expose said: "Gal, do nothing. Do you really want to spend twenty years behind bars for 20 seconds of violence?" Adding: "I've got too many mates inside regretting their moments of madness."

I took on board what he said but the desire for Old Testament justice and, if you like, revenge would not go away. A phone call was made and two heavies from East London arrived on my doorstep. They turned up five minutes before Adam got home from school. The driver waited in the car, the other walked in. I couldn't believe that a 6ft 7in giant was standing in my lounge, so tall he had to bend down to get into the conservatory. He was like a body-building version of Mark Labbett, better known as TV`s chaser The Beast. Adam was so impressed that he dashed out and brought some of his mates in to have a look.

I was waiting for Sam to get home and look after Adam, but the guy was in a hurry, so left Adam watching TV. Where were we going? I bet you`ve guessed.

We were visiting the home of Shrek, the child-abusing boyfriend of my ex-wife.

Our car pulled up on his drive and we knocked on his front door and luckily for me he was out.

As we hung around on his drive we were spotted by nosey neighbours and curtains were twitching. I mean a 6ft 7in giant in a leather jacket is going to draw attention. We waited fifteen minutes then left before Neighbourhood Watch called the police. Why was I lucky he was out? It`s because the giant from London had not been sent to say "hello". He was there to do some serious damage.

It was the one and only time I dropped my guard and lost control. I wasn't worried about losing my liberty, but that would mean losing my kids.

Then my friend in London suggested another plan which I couldn't resist.

He was great mates with a South London A-List gangster who offered to help.

I visited the legendary home of the `friend of a friend` in his famous castle and told him all about the situation. The Underworld legend was both `angry` and `disgusted`.

He patted my youngest son on the head saying: "don't worry son I`ll sort it out".

I gave him a name, description and an address.

He phoned the next morning with an update and again that evening saying "We`re outside his house". Twenty minutes later I got another call saying "He squealed like a pig". Adding

"Tell your boys they won`t be hearing from him again".

Working in Fleet Street never turned me into a Tory or a champagne socialist, I dislike Lord David Cameron and Sir Kier Starmer equally as much.

The Punk Poet never changed, the OAP and teenage version still hold the same beliefs and want both the House of Lords and Royal Family abolished.

Life like entertainment is meant to be fun. The titles of the publications changed but I never did. Social Worker Peter Brown sneered at me "Mrs Johnson says you're a tabloid journalist". The tone of his voice was so confrontational it was if I was the Editor of The Daily Mail or the Political Editor of The Sun. He added "I was on the picket line at Wapping". Was I meant to be impressed or scared? He hadn't a clue who he was dealing with. I wasn't some wimpy middle-class house husband I was `The Punk Poet` a genuine Cockney Rebel who would not respect his so-called authority or abide by his petty rules and regulations. He threatened "don't fight me Mr Johnson because we never lose". Well, that didn't go to plan.

He ended up calling me "Garry" and begging me to co-operate. I won the `war` and Peter Brown was sent on `gardening leave`, according to the Judge "Mr Brown was emotionally drained". I took that as code for `having a mental breakdown`. As I said earlier five years of fighting a guerrilla war against a cockney rebel transformed Mr Brown from a Rottweiler attack dog into a pet poodle.

The bully boy with the university degree wasn't just beaten by me. He was also defeated by the truth. I was determined from day one to take him on and convinced I would beat him. He was supported by Basildon Police, Essex Social Services and The Family Courts but I had one thing on my side that he didn't.

The truth, the whole truth, and nothing but the truth. When it all kicked off Mr Brown thought it was just another case and probably last a few weeks rather than seven years. As with Basildon Police he had been duped by the lies and `false allegations` of my ex-wife. Mr Brown had all his certificates and a degree but when it came to understanding the truth he was dunce. He was also a `figure of fun` for my kids who described him as looking like Principal Skinner from The Simpsons and dressing like Mr Bean. The allegations against me diminished at every Court Hearing, what started with `false allegations` of `death threats` declined in severity to being accused of writing "Happy Birthday" on Facebook.

My ex-wife reported me to Basildon Police, Social Services and The Family Court, but as I always say "every cloud".

She complained I'd breached a Court Order by wishing my son Sam a, "Happy 21$^{st}$ Birthday" on Facebook. The so-called criminal act being I signed it from Dad, Adam, and your sister Lucy". It was hardly the 'crime of the century' but I got 28 days in Chelmsford Prison. I hear you asking what about your claim "every cloud has a silver lining?" The show trial held in Basildon Crown Court was more like a 'Kangaroo Court' and unlawful. A classic example of the corrupt British Justice system. The media were banned, and no recording was made of the Hearing.

I was sentenced in secret and behind closed doors, and here comes the 'silver lining'. A few days later my story was on the front page of the Daily Mail and reported in mainstream media. Everything from breakfast TV shows to Sky News. The pictures of my sons in their West Ham football kits featured in every paper review. It was corrupt on many levels. I didn't have a solicitor, and a person cannot be imprisoned without legal representation. Also, the 'Gagging Orders ' had expired, the High Court in London and courts in Southend and Chelmsford had removed them twelve months earlier. The secret Hearing in Basildon Crown Court was more like a political show trial in Soviet Russia or Nazi Germany, then a family dispute in Essex. I can hear you shouting, "what about the bloody silver lining?"

Well, not only did my story make the front page of The Daily mail, it attracted the attention of two MPs and on my release from prison I was invited to The Houses of Parliament. To anyone out there doubting the authenticity of this story I say get a copy of the Daily Mail dated 1$^{st}$ June 2013.

The front-page headline is 'Secret Court Jails Father for Sending Son Birthday Greetings on Facebook'.

It became a worldwide story, and I was contacted by people from all over the English-speaking world. I will now repeat 'word for word' what the Daily Mail published on the front cover and page 5. "A father has been jailed at a secret court hearing for sending a Facebook message to his grown-up son on his 21$^{st}$ birthday. Garry Johnson breached a draconian gagging order which stops him publicly naming his son, Sam, whom he has brought up and who still lives with him. In a case which is certain to fuel concerns about Britain's shadowy network of secret courts, a judge sent the former music executive to prison for contempt at a closed-doors family court hearing in Essex at the beginning of last month.

He was not arrested by the police or even represented by a lawyer. The order silencing Mr Johnson, which follows an acrimonious divorce eight years ago, means he cannot mention either of his boys, 21-year-old Sam and Adam, 18 in public, even by congratulating them in a local newspaper announcement when they get engaged, married or have children in the future. The extraordinary gag is set to last until the end of his life, although his boys are now adults. Last night they condemned their father's jailing as 'cruel and ludicrous'. After their parents' divorce, the two boys chose to live with their father, following a series of rows with their mother over her new boyfriend. But within a year of the divorce, Mr Johnson's ex-wife made allegations to Essex social workers that he was neglecting the children and not feeding them properly at his smart family home.

An investigation by Social Workers cleared him of any wrongdoing and said the boys were fine. A year later in 2006, she made further allegations to social workers that he was unfit to care for the boys. Medical documents shown to the Mail by Sam and Adam reveal that Mr Johnson was examined three times by a local psychiatrist hired by social workers. The doctor wrote to social workers saying "There is no evidence of mental illness. I cannot understand why there are concerns about Mr Johnson's mental health". In 2007, the ex-wife started private care proceedings to remove the boys from their father. A judge put the boys under a "living at home with parent care order". It meant they would continue to live with their father, but under supervision by social services. The care order was accompanied by the gagging order to stop an increasingly anguished Mr Johnson talking about the case publicly. Even naming his sons in the most innocuous circumstances, such as on Facebook, became a contempt of court. The care order on Sam expired on his 18$^{th}$ birthday three years ago, the one on Adam in October last year when he reached 18. Normally a gagging order imposed by a family court judge on a parent expires at the same time as a care order. This one did not.

Mr Johnson was imprisoned at the height of the Mail's campaign against jailing's by this country's network of secret courts. The secretive family court system, which jailed Mr Johnson, deals with custody wrangle, children's care orders and adoption. Mr Johnson received a letter in late April from Chelmsford County Court ordering him to go to Basildon Magistrates Court building on May 2 for a hearing regarding his children. He was not warned he might face imprisonment or that the hearing was about his Facebook message, posted on Sam's birthday a few days earlier on April 23. On arrival, he was escorted by court security guards to a private room in the building for a half hour hearing under family court rules before His Honour Judge Damien Lochrane. He was not warned that he might need a lawyer. At the private hearing, Mr Johnson learned he had breached a gagging order imposed by the family courts in 2007, by sending the Facebook message. He informed the judge that he had had four heart attacks and was awaiting a triple by-pass operation. But he was sentenced to 28 days' jail and sent down to a court cell to await transport to Chelmsford prison. In the court cell, he had a heart attack caused by the shock. Rushed to a local hospital by ambulance, he was then shackled and handcuffed to a bed while on oxygen and receiving morphine.

A team of prison officers were put on 24-hour shifts beside the bed to make sure he did not escape. He recovered and was sent to prison two days later, serving two weeks of the sentence before being released.

Details of the horrifying case were made public to the Mail by his sons, who are not subjected to any gagging order according to their Essex-based lawyer, Alan Foskett. The jailing provoked a horrified response from MPs last night. John Hemming, the Lib Dem MP who has campaigned against the secret courts, said "This is yet another example of how the secret courts are stopping freedom of speech. I have never heard of a gagging order of this kind in adulthood.

This is a surreal case". Mr Johnson's local MP, John Baron said: "I have helped Mr Johnson and his sons, who always wanted to live with him, over several years. To find he has been imprisoned for sending a birthday message to one of them is troubling. Whilst I appreciate the need to protect children, the family court system often ignores the legitimate wishes of families. This needs to change, and quickly." Sam said last night; "My dad is a good father and has never been in trouble with the police. He was treated like a criminal. This ludicrous gagging order should not exist and must now be lifted.

Both Adam and I are adults. This cruel ruling is now hanging over my father to silence him about the sons he loves for the rest of his life. This is a terrible thing in what is meant to be a free country". Mr Johnson was imprisoned a day before senior judges, on May 3, reacted to the Mail campaign by saying they planned to stop courts jailing defendants in secret for contempt. Every cloud has a silver lining and shortly after my release, The High Court lifted the draconian gagging order on me naming my children in public or in print. They also lifted the ban on me writing my autobiography. My ex-wife was running out of corrupt 'friends' in high places, even Peter Brown 'saw the light' and washed his hands of her.

First she lied to the police, followed by Social Services and then The Family Court he Family Court ruled in my favour. Eventually they all saw through her 'tissues of lies'. There would be one more twist in this roller-coaster ride of a story and this time Basildon Police would be on the right side, my side. I'll save this revelation till the end as it really was the final act in a long-running drama. After The High Court removed the draconian gagging orders and The Daily Mail restored my reputation life got darker, as I battled with far bigger enemies than Essex Social Services, Basildon Police, The Family Courts and my ex-wife. I took on The Grim Reaper and Dr Death. I'd been smeared by the legal system at the time headed by Sir Kier Starmer, persecuted by Essex Police and twice been sent to prison, but this was far more unpleasant. I'd won a seven year 'fight to the death' but was now facing actual death. It really was a life-or-death situation. As always, the odds were stacked against me but I refused to give in. I'd taken on and beaten the system but this was by far the biggest battle of my life. Once again, I was victorious, but only because of Professor Khan and the wonderful staff at Basildon Hospital. The six-year battle with the authorities not only messed up my head it literally broke my heart. I was told by medical experts that the 'stress of fighting' combined with hardening of the arteries that brought on my heart problems.

    I had five heart attacks, two triple heart bypass operations, a minor stroke and two pacemakers fitted but don't regret taking on the authorities and fighting for my kids. I would do it all again, though maybe I wouldn't 'shoot from the hip'.

## Chapter Fourteen
## Happy Ending

I willingly admit I've got no filter and say what I mean, without considering the consequences. My way of life wasn't planned, it just happened. In the months leading up to meeting Garry Bushell I formed The Buzz Kids. We were a mixture of Punk and Glam Rock, a Cockney version of Welsh band The Alarm.

We had great haircuts, attitude, big ideas and little, if any, musical ability.

Our debut gig was also our last and some of the details might amuse. I was so 'out of it' I couldn't hear the laughter and mistook 'boos' for cheers. I thought we'd cracked it and that I'd be crowned the future of rock and roll.

I approached Garry Bushell at the bar full of confidence and amphetamine "What do you reckon Gal?"

There was no immediate response.

"Good, weren't we?" Bushell's reply was blunt and to the point: "you were rubbish". The Punk Poet not deterred and under the influence replied, "Yeah but I did look the part". Bushell "You didn't". As you know I ain't the sort of bloke to give up without a fight and will always fight my corner. I suggested "maybe you want to sleep on it Gal". He laughed at my bravado. Then, just as I thought all was lost, he threw me a lifeline. I was thrown a scrap which I gobbled up and have lived off ever since. Garry Bushell liked my lyrics but said I couldn't write.

Actual quote: "The band can't play and you can't sing, but I like the lyrics".

Adding: "take my advice, give up singing and concentrate on writing".

That night I broke up the band and days later got a writer's job at Sounds music magazine. I was living the dream twenty years before Jade Goody on Big Brother and Gareth Gates on The X Factor. Here is the Garry Bushell review that 'killed off' my band. "I wonder if that peerless pop pioneer David Bowie knew what he was inflicting on us when he recorded Diamond Dogs. A classic concept album for sure, but ever since then, doom-laden youths with acne have been recycling his ideas and boring the rest of us to death. This East London five-piece make the sort of music that ought to accompany a three-hour long TV documentary on the life and times of East Berlin gravediggers during a major plague.

They're dull, grey, grim, shallow, worthless and pointless. The Buzz Kids sound like Gary Numan in a tumble-dryer, look like a drugged drag act and just listen to their song titles 'Big Brother', 'Beat Of The Street', 'No Land Of Hope And Glory' ...do us a favour. Just reading the set list is enough to bring on depression in a clown school. All these fifth-rate David Bowie impersonators are first-rate bores. What makes Bowie great is his ability to change and challenge. He's never been stuck in a rut, he's a pioneer. Buzz Kids singer Garry Johnson is a piss-poor pub performer who is never likely to break out of that cul-de-sac. Garry will appear on Top of the Pops around the same time life is found on Mars". The dream was over. Was that the end of Garry Johnson the pop performer? Not everyone agreed with Garry Bushell and some guy who'd had a number one record with Max Splodge wanted to be my manager. Dave Long and his partner John Doolan were a dodgy duo, a worse double act then the Chuckle Brothers or Brown and Blair. A couple of conmen who dined out on getting 'Two Pints Of Lager and A Packet of Crisps' to the top of the charts. Long was a Pound-land version of Malcolm McClaren and Doolan the image of the piano player in Sparks. If you remember he looked like Adolf Hitler. They promised to make me the next Max Splodge! Was that a good or bad thing?

I'm not joking about their Arthur Daley management style, which included getting me to take a fridge from outside a shop in Lewisham High Street to see, according to them if I had confidence.

They never signed me, but Dave Long did get a nice new fridge for his kitchen.

So why did I pose as a tabloid journalist? Well, apart from the money it had a lot to do with being star struck. I didn't do it as a means to obtaining money under false pretences, honest Guv.

The truth is I've always been attracted to famous people from footballers to pop stars and everything in between. As a kid I loved watching chat shows and seeing footballers interviewed on Match of The Day.

I grew up loving football and without sounding like one of those boring old guys who go on about "things were better in my day" I think many things were. In my day football was better there I've said it. I prefer the old Division One to the Premier League when most teams had a long-haired rebel who I wanted to be.

'Bad boys' like Georgie Best Man Utd, Charlie George Arsenal, Stan Bowles QPR Alan Hudson Chelsea and Rodney Marsh Man City.

In my opinion Pele of Brazil and Eusabio of Portugal were as good as Christiano Ronaldo and Lionel Messi.

All four probably better then George Best but my loyalty gene forces me to tell my kids "George Best is the greatest player of all-time".

But when it comes to comedy the golden age was not the 1970s. Apart from Fawlty Towers and The Likely Lads it was pretty crap. Nothing from that era compares to The Office, The Inbetweeners, Gavin and Stacey, Extras, Alan Partridge or Only Fools and Horses.

I like Tyson Fury but unlike iron Mike Tyson he'll never be the greatest boxer of all-time. As much as I like Sade, Adele and Amy Winehouse they will never be as good as Diana Ross. I loved Line of Duty but for me no TV drama will ever come close to replacing Minder or The Sweeney. Apart from Billy Connolly very few stand-up comedians made me laugh before the year 2000.

Ricky Gervais, Jimmy Carr, Lee Mack, Mickey Flannagan, Steve Coogan and Katherine Ryan are my comedy giants and Lewis Schaffer makes me laugh.

What I'm trying to say is although I'm a Mod I still cling loyally to selective things from the past. I'm probably showing my age by saying Oasis were the last great band and the last great English band.

I know all about The Beatles and The Rolling Stones but for me music started with

The Small Faces.

I then grew up with David Bowie, Roxy Music, Mott The Hoople and Cockney Rebel.

I was inspired to perform by The Sex Pistols, The Clash and The Jam then became a massive fan of The Stone Roses and Oasis.

For me music died when Liam and Noel went their separate ways.

I screwed up at football, flopped as a singer and through personal choice never made it in the world of crime. But I was and am a 'top dad', the Don of Dons and Al Capone of Fatherhood.

I came into my own as a single parent. Sleeping alone is strange, as is watching what used to be 'our' favourite TV show alone and not being able to discuss it afterwards. Listening to the radio is no fun as they play records that used to be 'our song'.

But all that mattered was making sure both my boys knew they were loved and remained happy. And I did both with flying colours

I could not have done it without the help of mates and a close group of platonic female friends. They all broke the law and put their necks on the line for us with two ending up in court and charged with contempt.

One was even accused of planning to smuggle them out of the country.

There were many funny incidents like doing passenger swaps in railway car parks and hiding them both in safe houses. This includes driving both boys to safe houses all over Essex and South London.

At one time Adam was taken to Hertfordshire and put up in a house next door to the Eastenders studios and Sam had his own flat in Billericay.

The funny thing was the lady looking after Adam was the ex-wife of a mate and a former copper.

The boys were on the run for eight months before Basildon Police wrote a letter to Essex Social Services saying 'we will no longer waste our time chasing Sam and Adam Johnson all over Essex'.

Though in truth they'd given up weeks before and stopped being a private army for my ex-wife and acting as 'bounty hunters' for Essex Social Services.

When Sam turned up for his school prom not only did they not arrest him, they escorted him into the building and said "Have a nice time Sam".

When the custody battle started, I had my ex-wife, the police, the Family Courts and Essex Social Services all lined up against me, but I refused to be bullied or destroyed by lies.

I fought them every day of the week and bit by bit and little by little the tide turned in my favour and I beat the lot of them.

It was so funny when, after my heart bypass operation and awakening from my 29-day coma, reading a letter from Essex Social Services admitting I'd been right all along.

Even sweeter was being informed about a court Hearing in Chelmsford which because of circumstances beyond my control I couldn't attend, (I was attached to a life-support machine).

Judge Roderick Newton had revoked all 'Gagging Orders'. If only I could have been there to witness my final victory.

But on reflection, maybe not, as my cheers and wild celebrations would have taken the roof off.

Looking back on my life I'd forgotten my previous brush with death. Aged seventeen I was standing at the bar of The Castle pub in Plaistow when two masked guys burst in and shot some bloke standing next me.

The bullets missed me but his blood went all over my Harrington Jacket.

I also survived an IRA bomb. I was drinking in a Covent Garden pub around the corner from Stringfellows about half-hour before it was blown-up.

So how does my story end?

Well, I won all the legal battles, cleared my name and twice came back from the dead so there was a happy ending. The final act was far more exciting than an episode of Eastenders or a slushy sentimental Mills and Boon novel.

After leaving hospital I recorded a concept album `Punk Rock Stories and Tabloid Tales` wrote a crime novel and signed a movie contract with Sandie West of Beachdancer Films.

But me being me there's always a drama and due to a worldwide pandemic filming is three years behind schedule. There is a two-minute trailer on YouTube, but nothing to show on Netflix.

Garry the Mod also returned to the stage as a punk poet performing timeless rebel anthems from the re-released `Boys of The Empire` and showcasing new poems from `The Cockney Bard`. And saving the best till last I became a Granddad.

I didn't make it on to Match of The Day or Top of The Pops but lived long enough to become a granddad and hear my grandchildren call me "Mod Pop". It gives me the biggest buzz of my life.

I went back to court in 2022 and this time the police **were** in my corner and not treating me like a criminal. The Judge ruled in my favour and for the first time since 2007 I was a free man.

Ever the optimist I always knew there'd be a happy ending. I had a new pacemaker fitted in June so confident life will continue to get better for many years to come.

The last word must go to my dad, there was no love lost but he's always with me and somehow connected to the good and bad things in my life.

Like me both my sons were football mad, we were all good players but none of us were left-footed.

My grandson who sleeps in his West Ham kit is left-footed just like his great grandfather. How spooky is that?

www.ingramcontent.com/pod-product-compliance
Lightning Source LLC
Chambersburg PA
CBHW071713160426
43195CB00012B/1664